THE ULTIMATE BINGE GUIDE

Rotten Tomatoes

THE ULTIMATE BINGE GUIDE

296 MUST-SEE SHOWS THAT CHANGED THE WAY WE WATCH TV

Running Press

PHILADELPHIA

Running Press
Hachette Book Group
1290 Avenue of the Americas, New York, NY 10104
www.runningpress.com
@Running_Press

Printed in Thailand

First Edition: October 2021

Published by Running Press, an imprint of Perseus Books, LLC, a subsidiary of Hachette Book Group, Inc. The Running Press name and logo is a trademark of the Hachette Book Group.

The Hachette Speakers Bureau provides a wide range of authors for speaking events.
To find out more, go to www.hachettespeakersbureau.com or call (866) 376-6591.

The publisher is not responsible for websites (or their content) that are not owned by the publisher.

Cover design by Yerania Sanchez. Interior design by Alex Camlin.
Infographics pages by Yerania Sanchez (pages 16-17, 90–91, 166–167), Yasmin Tayag (pages 82-83), Courtney Kawata (pages 112-113, 122-123, 148-149), and Alex Camlin (pages 50–53, 129-133, 182-183).

Library of Congress Control Number: 2021935013

ISBNs: 978-0-7624-7366-3 (hardcover), 978-0-7624-7365-6 (ebook)

RRD-S

10 9 8 7 6 5 4 3 2 1

Contents

COMMERCIAL BREAK

❚❚ Five Ways Netflix Changed TV Forever...*103*

GENRE GROWS UP: NEXT-LEVEL HORROR,
HEROES, SCI-FI, AND FANTASY

COMMERCIAL BREAK

❚❚ Know Your TV Superproducers...*129*

REAL(ISH) WORLDS: COMPETITIONS AND
DOCUSERIES THAT CAPTURED THE ZEITGEIST
(AND, YES, STILL HOLD UP)

COMMERCIAL BREAK

‖ Mini Milestones...148

COMMERCIAL BREAK

‖ From Playing Cards to #Hashtags...166

COMMERCIAL BREAK

**‖ Thoughts on the Future of TV (From Those
Who Make It)**...182

Introduction

It's hard to pinpoint the exact moment our era of the "binge-watch" officially dawned. Was it with the advent of the DVR, a once magical-seeming technology that suddenly allowed us to gorge several saved-up episodes in a single endorphin-saturated viewing? Or was it with the arrival of the DVD box set, which shrank the time between cliff-hangers from a week to however long it took you to put in the next disc? Perhaps it began even earlier than that, flickering to life in the form of special double episodes and Saturday morning series marathons.

The very dawn of the binge era may be hard to pin down, but we *can* point to the precise moment we were officially living in it. Or, at the very least, the precise year.

In 2013, Netflix's chief content officer, Ted Sarandos, told *GQ* magazine that the goal of his company was "to become HBO faster than HBO can become us." It was a bold statement, especially considering that Netflix had only just the year before launched its first original series, *Lillyhammer*, largely to a collective shrug, and faced huge skepticism about its move from DVD-mailer to online streaming service. But then came *House of Cards* in February, followed by *Orange Is the New Black* and the rebooted *Arrested Development*. Like *Lillyhammer*, all episodes of those series were available at once. Unlike *Lillyhammer*, the series were huge hits.

People seemed to take to this idea of "binge-ing." By October of that year, Netflix hit 40 million subscribers, surpassing HBO; today, it has more than 200 million subscribers worldwide.

Another little bit of history was being made in 2013, if we may be so bold. That September, after 15 years of focusing only on movies, we at Rotten Tomatoes began to publish Tomatometer and Audience Scores for TV shows. That meant welcoming some of the best TV journalists in the world into our pool of Tomatometer-approved critics, collecting their Fresh and Rotten reviews, and generating scores for series, seasons, and episodes of television.

In addition to sourcing reviews for every new scripted show released—a huge task, considering that the number of original scripted series on US TV soared past 500 in 2019 alone—our team of review "curators" worked to find reviews for series from as early as the 1940s and '50s. Today we're proud to offer the most comprehensive collection of TV criticism available anywhere, one where you can see just how much critics loved the very first season of *I Love Lucy*—well, *liked*: Desi and Lucy failed to amuse the *The Washington Star*—and just how much they hated the very last season of *Game of Thrones*, Rotten at 55% on the Tomatometer as we go to print.

The move into TV was core to our central mission as a brand, which we've worked toward since we first came online back in 1998: to help you discover the best things to watch, period. And with TV and streaming proving with every grizzled antihero and epic space saga to be just as good as anything on the big screen—arguably better—and *so much* of it now to choose from, we wanted to help potentially overwhelmed viewers sort the amazing from the merely *meh*, the Fresh from the Rotten.

Which is where this book, *The Ultimate Binge Guide*, comes in. Think of it as eight years' work, covering seven decades of television, so you can choose something to watch in minutes. Of course, we'd encourage you to stick with it a little longer than that, and to return when the credits roll on the final episode of the latest great binge you discovered within. Because we haven't just assembled what we consider the 296 most binge-worthy shows of all time, we've dug into what makes them so compulsively watchable, widely beloved, and, in some cases, criminally underrated.

In these pages you'll learn about the shows that shaped TV as we know it today: series that established formulas and series that bent them brilliantly to their will; showrunners who brought a cinematic quality and new ways of telling stories to the small screen; formidable fresh talents who turned genres on their heads; and shows whose cultural impact was so mammoth they changed the way we think and talk. (For the record, I'm a Miranda . . . and I think I know a *tad* more than Jon Snow.)

Each had to clear a high bar for entry: they had to be not just *good*, they had to be *Can't stop watching, Screw it I'm calling it an all-nighter, Where did my weekend just go?* binges.

We organized the book into 10 chapters that focus both on specific genres and eras of TV and streaming. You will find an epic section on comedy—seriously, it's *huge*—and a chapter devoted to sophisticated sci-fi, fantasy, horror, and superhero TV. There's a collection of the antihero-driven series, developed as cable networks and streamers chased HBO's *Sopranos* success, and a tribute to animated shows that respected—and challenged—their audiences, no matter how old they were.

We write *a lot* about some shows. Want to know why *It's Always Sunny in Philadelphia* is the longest-running sitcom on American TV? We've got a couple of pages on that. And we write much less about others, because, well, hasn't *everything* already been said about the show about nothing? (OK, we find a teensy bit more to say.) And we feature several "binge battles" along the way, settling the score on some heated, not-quite-settled TV debates, like which version of *The Office* is better—the UK's or America's?—by Tomatometer, Audience Score, and other categories.

While this guide is no academic history of TV as technology or art form—we're fans at Rotten Tomatoes, not professors—our chapters do trace evolutions in small-screen storytelling and tap into many of the defining moments that led us to the binge era. Crucially, they also chart the change in the diversity of the faces we see on our TV screens, and the backgrounds of those in the writers' rooms and sitting in the directors' chairs. That change has not been dramatic enough, but it has enriched the quality and range of stories being told on TV more than any technological development.

To help you follow the path from some of the earliest network classics of chapter 1 to our final chapter on foreign-language series now accessible across the planet, we've peppered the book with infographics, essays, and even a comic strip, all of which illustrate the evolution of TV technology, fandom, and our viewing habits. We even have a few pages on how Netflix did exactly what Mr. Sarandos said it would back in 2013—and then some—changing TV forever.

Just as there are a few boxes to check before you start a good binge—got your snacks ready and a good excuse for coming in late tomorrow?—there are a few things to note before diving into our *Ultimate Binge Guide*. The first is that at Rotten Tomatoes, we have Tomatometer and Audience Scores for TV shows at the series, season, and episode level. The Tomatometer score you see with each entry in this book is the overall *series* Tomatometer score—which averages out a show's season scores—unless otherwise noted. Ditto for the Audience Scores. If there isn't a score for a show, it just means not enough Tomatometer-approved critics have reviewed the title to generate one, or not enough users have left a rating for the Audience Score. (Confused? Or just want more details on how our scores work and definitions of some of the Rotten Tomatoes and TV industry terms used in this book? Check out our glossary on page 198.)

The second thing to note is that things change. That applies to our scores, which shift as new reviews and ratings are added. So if you notice that a score in this book is different from what you see on our site, it's because more reviews were added to that title since we went to print. And it also applies to where you can watch certain shows. Each entry in this book includes the original network, cable station, or streaming service on which the series first aired—with the original overseas network noted if applicable. But with rights issues and streamers scrambling to buy up popular series, be sure to check out rottentomatoes.com for the most current info on where to access something you want to watch.

You might want to go to the website anyway. Or follow us on our social channels. Or, *hey*, check us out on your TV—we have our own streaming channel, too, and we think you'll find it pretty Fresh. Our dedication to covering television and streaming has only expanded since 2013. Along with guides to the best-rated shows on every streaming service out there—as well as hidden gems to discover on them—we produce handy, bite-sized video binge guides and oral histories of some of your favorite series, and go deep on the creative process of the showrunners behind some of the most groundbreaking new shows being produced.

Also, the website is where you'll find my favorite thing to read—and the thing that, frankly, Rotten Tomatoes wouldn't exist without: reviews. Behind every score you read in this book is a battalion of written and spoken reviews from professional critics and fans alike, all packed with thoughtful insights to help you choose what to watch and add meaningful context to the thing you are watching.

The story told in these pages brings us to 2021, but the evolution is ongoing. Technology is constantly changing, new voices are telling new types of stories, and the line between TV and cinema is blurrier than ever.

These are exciting times and we're glad to be bingeing through them with you.

—Joel Meares
Editor-in-Chief, Rotten Tomatoes

Classics That Made the Molds

(AND THOSE THAT BROKE THEM)

It's hard to believe that not too long before a series as sophisticated and modern-feeling as _The Twilight Zone_ first aired in 1959, television was still a primitive technology. Until then, it was a passion for tech lovers and hobbyists who were mostly limited to sporadic lo-fi broadcasts only viewable within a short range of a broadcast tower. For most others, it was a futuristic curiosity to read about in magazines. By the 1950s, though, the technology had come a long way, and Americans embraced it — many bought their first set to watch the first-ever televised World Series, between the Yankees and Dodgers, in 1947. The strange new box in the living room was on its way to replacing the wireless as America's primary form of entertainment.

The rush of scientific experimentation that led to that point would only be matched by the creative experimentation that came in the decades that followed. The world now had moving pictures in its homes, but what stories would they tell? Minds like Rod Serling, Joe Connelly, and Alfred Hitchcock went to work on their answers to that question early, producing some of the first examples of genre TV, the sitcom, and more. In the decades that followed, the likes of James L. Brooks, Gene Roddenberry, and Norman Lear would build upon their efforts, creating long-cherished favorites, and establishing and expanding upon a new art form.

In this chapter, we're honoring the classics that laid the foundations for the stories and storytelling formats that dominate TV and streaming today. (And we're stretching that term _classics_ a little to include series that graze decades as late as the 1990s, like _The Golden Girls_ and _Dallas._) These shows established the formulas that networks still use (like America's first hour-long drama and the granddaddy of the courtroom procedural, _Perry Mason_); ambitiously pushed the envelope of what was even possible to show in the new medium (_The Twilight Zone_); seized upon TV's place in the heart of so many homes to challenge prejudice and push for national introspection (like Lear's pioneering work); and introduced the tropes today's writers still utilize and audiences still love.

Best of all: They're still just as binge-worthy as the current TV greats for which they paved the way.

I Love Lucy

CBS / 1951–1957
6 SEASONS / 180 EPISODES

🍅 -- 🗑 **98%**

Just how influential was *I Love Lucy*? Well, without this sitcom, starring real-life husband and wife Lucille Ball and Desi Arnaz as the oft-quarreling and always-loving New York couple Lucy and Ricky Ricardo, TV as we know it might look a lot different. Consider that the show introduced the concept of shooting in front of a live studio audience, its star-producers renovating two Hollywood studios in compliance with stringent fire safety regulations to make it happen. Or that it pioneered the now-standard three-camera setup, utilized so that Ball, Arnaz, and costars Vivian Vance and William Frawley (so beloved as the Ricardos' friends and landlords, Ethel and Fred) could perform full sequences for their live audience in single takes, just as they would for a play. And then there was the time *Lucy* accidentally invented the rerun when, with Ball pregnant while shooting the second season, the production couldn't meet its 39-episode order, forcing CBS to air past favorites. Of course, those innovations aren't what made *Lucy* a smash back then—number 1 for five of its seasons—and a perennial, still totally bingeable favorite now. We continue to love *Lucy*, along with the 13 hour-long episodes of *The Lucy-Desi Comedy Hour* that followed it, because of its two stars—the always-game Ball, still the greatest slapstick comic to tumble across our screens, and Arnaz, her patient and quick-witted foil—and the rom-com chemistry they shared.

Alfred Hitchcock Presents / The Alfred Hitchcock Hour

CBS, NBC / 1955–1965
10 SEASONS / 361 EPISODES

🍅 -- 🗑 --

The silhouette, the music, the wry introductions—even the opening sequence of *Alfred Hitchcock Presents* is itself the stuff of legend, mimicked and parodied countless times since it first aired in 1955. Thankfully, the anthology series was more than just a proto-meme, offering home viewers a taste of the mystery and intrigue that had become Hitchcock's trademark on the big screen. Of course, he was rather busy at the time, churning out cinematic treasures like *Vertigo* and *Psycho*, so he left the lion's share of directorial duties on *Presents*—and on *The Alfred Hitchcock Hour*, as the show was rebranded when it outgrew its half-hour runtime—to others.

> *Episodes that "Hitch" helmed himself are among the show's best, like "One More Mile to Go," which feels like a spiritual precursor to* Psycho.

But the episodes that "Hitch" helmed himself are among the show's best, like "One More Mile to Go," which feels like a spiritual precursor to *Psycho*, or "Breakdown," an inventively shot piece of psychological horror, starring Joseph Cotten. It wasn't the first anthology series of its kind, but it was among the best, establishing the Master of Suspense's famous persona and paving the way for series like *The Twilight Zone* and *Black Mirror*.

Perry Mason

CBS / 1957–1966
9 SEASONS / 271 EPISODES

 -- 🗑 --

Characters don't get much more iconic than Perry Mason. Percolating through pop culture even before every living room had a television, he first came to vivid life in 1933 with Erle Stanley Gardner's series of novels and was then adapted to radio 10 years later. But it was the 1957 screen adaptation for CBS that solidified the character's staying power. Unlike anything before it, *Perry Mason* became the small screen's first-ever weekly, hour-long drama, and helped lay the groundwork for courtroom procedurals for decades to come. Embodied by the formidable Raymond Burr (who took home two Emmy Awards for his performance), Perry Mason was etched in stone as a titan of the genre: a brilliant and relentless defense attorney of wrongfully accused murderers and more. Everyone from Christine Baranski's Diane Lockhart (*The Good Wife*) to James Spader's Alan Shore (*Boston Legal*) owe a little something to the original legal noir great.

The Twilight Zone

CBS / 1959–1964
5 SEASONS / 156 EPISODES

🍅 82% 🗑 95%

There are shows that are ahead of their time; then there's *The Twilight Zone*. Rod Serling's thought-provoking and unnerving sci-fi fables feel as fresh today as they did when they were first spooking audiences 60 years ago. (Don't believe us? Press PLAY on "Nightmare at 20,000 Feet.") Serling, who worked himself to exhaustion as creator and a writer on the bulk of *Zone*'s episodes, came to the genre out of frustration. On projects like his acclaimed TV play *Patterns* (broadcast as part of NBC's Kraft Television Theatre) and *Noon on Doomsday* (which had attempted to skewer the lack of national outrage at the murder of Emmett Till), his work had been compromised. He wagered that sci-fi and fantasy stories might be just the stealth vehicles he needed to *say something* without network and sponsor interference. It was a solid bet—critics loved it so much that season 1 is Certified Fresh at 100%—and still is: Jordan Peele's reboot proved a hit recently for CBS All Access (now Paramount+). Welcoming us into the place that "lies between the pit of man's fears and the summit of his knowledge," Serling challenged and terrified us, changing TV forever in the process.

Bewitched

ABC / 1964–1972
8 SEASONS / 254 EPISODES

 -- 🗑 --

Few series evolved quite so much as this relentlessly syndicated favorite about powerful witch Samantha Stephens (Elizabeth Montgomery), mortal husband and ad man Darrin (Dick York), and spell-happy mother Endora (Agnes Moorehead), who can't believe her pride and joy has abandoned a life of hedonistic sorcery to play housewife in the suburbs. The series's biggest evolutions were born of necessity. To keep up *(Continued on page 6.)*

Police Squad!

ABC / 1982
1 SEASON / 6 EPISODES

🍅 90% 🍿 76%

▶ **CRITICS CONSENSUS** Wacky, inventive, and endlessly quotable, *Police Squad!* is a hysterically funny leap forward for TV comedy that was tragically ahead of its time.

▶ **WHAT IT'S ABOUT** Lieutenant Frank Drebin (Leslie Nielsen); his superior, Captain Ed (Alan North); and other members of the task force known as Police Squad tackle crimes plaguing their fair city in the most illogical ways possible.

After creating the funniest spoof movie ever, surely the guys behind *Airplane!*—David Zucker, Jim Abrahams, and Jerry Zucker, or "ZAZ" as they're collectively known—would have no problem crash-landing their next anarchic comedy into theaters. Studios were receptive to whatever the trio could come up with, but the trouble came from the project they were developing itself. They had their star: the dramatic thespian turned comedy god, Leslie Nielsen. They had the concept: a parody of 1950s and 1960s cop movies, replete with deadly dames and overwrought, hard-boiled narration. But ZAZ couldn't fit all the pieces together in the shape of a clean, theatrical-length film.

A pre-Disney Michael Eisner, then CEO at Paramount, offered them a TV contract instead. Soon, *Police Squad!* was on ABC as a spring addition to their 1981–1982 lineup, ready to start building a small but dedicated legion of comedy fans, but otherwise confounding viewers as they clicked their way past to get to *Magnum, P.I.*, which aired during the same time slot on CBS.

Each episode of *Police Squad!* is like a violently shaken comedy snow globe, a flurry of choreographed slapstick, wordplay, visual puns, and non sequiturs, all swirling around the unflappable police officer Frank Drebin (Nielsen). There are so many jokes in each 25-minute slice of *Police Squad!* that they even spill over into the opening credits: First, when the title of the episode appears, the narrator reads something completely different; then, the opening sequence over which the credits are announced reveals a guest star (the likes of William Shatner and Robert Goulet), only for that actor to be immediately killed off just as they're announced (by firing squad, or getting crushed by a safe, or . . .) never to actually appear during the episode itself.

Even during scenes of exposition, ZAZ can't help but insert hilariously distracting jokes in the background; if you're not concentrating, it's easy to lose the narrative thread. Not to say the plot is all that important in a show like this. But, like *Arrested Development* or *The Simpsons* after it, it's a comedy that only improves on rewinds and repeat viewings, an impossibility in the early 1980s when audiences watched as it aired or expected never to see it again.

So it was that ZAZ, who had captured the movie comedy zeitgeist with *Airplane!*, got slapped with a new label on TV, one that's catnip to critics but a kind of death knell when it came to actually keeping your job: They had become "ahead of their time." The then-president of ABC famously criticized the show as something that forced people to pay attention—God forbid!—and canceled it after four episodes in March 1981, airing the remaining two that July.

ZAZ would return to the movie space, releasing *Top Secret* in 1984, and *Ruthless People* two years later. Meanwhile, ABC released *Police Squad!* on home video in 1985, taking advantage of the exploding VHS market. Suddenly, people could watch episodes on repeat and hit that REWIND button. A fan base grew, clamoring for more, and *Police Squad!* emerged as one of the earliest properties to be saved by the home aftermarket. When David Zucker returned to Paramount with the idea to bring back the series as the movie *The Naked Gun*, it was a no-brainer.

▶ **BEST EPISODE** Season 1, Episode 1—"A Substantial Gift (The Broken Promise)." The show comes roaring out of the lineup—complete with a prolonged pun-based conversation worthy of Abbott and Costello's "Who's on First?"—plus a ridiculous close-quarters gunfight and a decent mystery behind it all.

▶ **CHARACTER WE LOVE** Johnny the Snitch (William Duell), who appears in each episode as a parody of the shoeshine guy who seems to know everything. And we mean *everything*, from the whereabouts of the kidnapped girl to how the Dodgers can fix their pitching game.

DEEP ▼ ▼ DIVE

with the times, *Bewitched* began filming in color in its third season. Dick Sargent famously took over the role of Darrin in the fifth season after Dick York left due to recurring back problems. Other off-screen events also influenced on-screen happenings, including Montgomery's pregnancy, which led to the season 5 episode "Samantha's Good News" and ultimately a baby brother for the Stephenses' daughter Tabitha. But as much as the real-world lives of its cast and crew prompted the resourceful *Bewitched* to change things up plotwise, the show also thoughtfully embraced and reflected on changes in television and America more broadly.

Bewitched thoughtfully embraced and reflected on changes in television and America.

Samantha was someone exceptional for the airwaves at the time, a woman stronger and smarter than her husband, and Endora's disappointment in the marriage had a sharply feminist edge: Why *wouldn't* she turn Darrin—or "Derwood" as she derisively refers to him—into a goat when he was asking her daughter to hide her true self? That theme of repression resonates, and many have wondered if *Bewitched* was an allegory for the struggles of the closet for gay men and women. (Notably, the show featured many LGBTQ+ people in its cast and crew—including Sargent, who would come out in 1991, and a fabulous Paul Lynde as warlock Uncle Arthur.) Asked about this by *The Advocate* in the early '90s, Montgomery said: "Don't think that didn't enter our minds at the time . . . If you think about it, *Bewitched* is about repression in general and all the frustration and trouble it can cause."

Get Smart

NBC, CBS / 1965–1970
5 SEASONS / 138 EPISODES

When he was thinking about developing a TV show in the 1960s, comedy legend Mel Brooks observed that "No one had ever done a show about an idiot before." With *Get Smart*, he says, "I decided to be the first." While Maxwell Smart (Don Adams), agent 86 for the US counterintelligence agency CONTROL, is hilariously slow on the uptake, there's nothing stupid about the show around him, a shrewd satire of the espionage genre. The pratfalls and sight gags hold up—the hilariously impractical shoe phone was once displayed in the corridors of CIA headquarters—but *Get Smart* remains vital because, like covert agents of KAOS, Brooks and co-creator Buck Henry stealthily pushed the genre of TV comedy into the future, even as they tickled out big guffaws. There are digs at government bureaucracy that feel fresh even today; blink-and-you'll-miss-them *30 Rock*–style inside jokes about the TV industry; and a single-camera look that distinguished *Get Smart* from the blander sitcom fare that kept it out of the nation's top 10–rated TV programs throughout its run. The show also featured one of small-screen comedy's first working women, Barbara Feldon's iconic—and not-at-all idiotic—Agent 99.

Batman

ABC / 1966–1968
3 SEASONS / 120 EPISODES

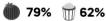 79% 62%

Before moviegoing audiences knew him as a brooding vigilante, ABC took a chance at turning the exploits of the Caped Crusader into a colorful, campy adventure show, largely aimed at teens. It was a gamble that paid off, providing a much-needed dose of upbeat escapism during the tumultuous mid-1960s, and it remains a beloved part of the character's legacy. Adam West's Bruce Wayne and Burt Ward's Dick Grayson are responsible for some of the most memorable superhero tropes—think Robin's "Holy [insert object here], Batman!" or the brightly animated "BAMs" and "POWs"—and their earnest heroism amid all the Pop Art chaos has endeared them to even the most die-hard fans of Wayne's darker incarnations. Full of silly, self-aware performances by heavyweights like Cesar Romero, Burgess Meredith, Eartha Kitt, and Julie Newmar, it's difficult to imagine what the Dark Knight's canon would look like without this goofy splash of pure joy.

Columbo

ABC, NBC / 1968–1978, 1989–1990,
SPECIALS ON AND OFF UNTIL 2003
9 SEASONS / 69 EPISODES

Columbo is the comfiest, coziest show about murder ever made. Every episode, a guest celebrity (ranging from Leonard Nimoy to Ruth Gordon) offs another member of high society out of passion or premeditated personal gain. And every episode, the murderer comes up against LA Police Lieutenant Columbo, played to bumbling perfection by Peter Falk, whose insistently circuitous speech and drab appearance lull crooks into a haughty sense of false superiority. The show reverse-engineers the whodunnit structure by revealing the murderer and motive in the opening of each episode, with most of what follows framed

from their point of view. The joy is in watching how they'll get caught. The other joy is, of course, Columbo himself. The brilliant conceit of his titular detective is that he is always in "character"—how much of Columbo's lack of social graces and apparent incompetence are real, and how much of that is a front to lure suspects out? You never see any of Columbo's personal life (though he frequently mentions a never-seen wife); he exists only within the context of the crime. The series's break from the whodunnit format and Columbo's offbeat, unorthodox approach expanded the field for comedic detectives, paving the way for shows like *The Rockford Files* and *Monk*. Each episode of *Columbo* is movie-length and since they can be watched in any order, why not start with the best? We recommend "Murder by the Book" (directed by a 24-year-old Steven Spielberg), "Suitable for Framing," and "Try and Catch Me."

The Mary Tyler Moore Show

▶ GAME-CHANGER

CBS / 1970–1977
7 SEASONS / 168 EPISODES

The character of Mary Richards, actress Mary Tyler Moore's sweet-natured Minneapolis-based TV news producer, makes quite an entrance in the first episode of James L. Brooks and Allan Burns's CBS sitcom. We first meet her when she's newly single (having dumped the doctor who happily took her support but would never set a wedding date) and touring an empty apartment in a brand-new city, ready to start anew. The understated, deliberate intro established two things: It succinctly separated Moore from her other *(Continued on page 10.)*

BINGE BATTLE

DALLAS ◀ VS ▶ DYNASTY

It's the ultimate knock-down, drag-out, catfight: Ewings versus Carringtons, Alexis versus J. R., outrageous cliff-hanger versus even more outrageous cliff-hanger.

Dallas	Dynasty
Dallas	**Dynasty**
CBS / 1978–1991	ABC / 1981–1989
14 SEASONS / 357 EPISODES	9 SEASONS / 220 EPISODES

 ◀ RATINGS PEAK ▶

 **1980–1982 / 1983–1984**

1984–1985

▶ **WHAT IT'S ABOUT** Big state, big hair, and big drama proved a very successful formula for this Shakespeare-via-the-ranch story of a Texas oil family, the Ewings, and their feud with the Barnes clan—a feud that heats up when idealistic youngest brother Bobby Ewing (Patrick Duffy) marries Pamela Barnes (Victoria Principal). Famous for its high-rated cliff-hangers and daring stunts—it's revealed that one season was entirely a dream—*Dallas* redefined primetime soaps.

▶ **WHAT IT'S ABOUT** ABC set up *Dynasty* as a direct rival to the ratings-dominant *Dallas*, and it didn't tinker much with the formula. Enter the Carringtons, headed by John Forsythe as patriarch Blake (yes, you guessed it, an oil tycoon) of a super-rich Denver family, whose secrets, rivalries, and tensions come to the fore when Blake's young new wife Krystle (Linda Evans) enters the picture. After a moderately successful first season, *Dynasty* hit its stride when Blake's ex-wife Alexis (Joan Crawford) arrived at the start of season 2.

 ◀ AWARDS ▶

4 Emmys

(including for Lead Actress in a Drama for Barbara Bel Geddes)

1 Emmy

(for Costume Design in 1984)

BINGE BATTLE

◀ RESIDENT VILLAIN ▶

J. R. Ewing. How good was Larry Hagman as J. R., the always-scheming, Barnes-hating, money-hungry, marriage-undermining eldest brother of the Ewing fam? So good that though he began as something of a side character, he would eventually become the series's driving force, the only character to appear in every single episode, and get top billing in the first *Dallas* reunion TV movie, *J. R. Returns*. Sorry, Bobby, nice guys do finish last.

Alexis Carrington Colby. Joan Crawford is credited with almost single-handedly driving *Dynasty* from the 28th-ranked show on US TV when it launched—*without* her deliciously evil Alexis—to number 1. The series's writers have lamented that her introduction changed the tenor of the show, but audiences were too busy soaking up those nasty zingers, giant hats, and infamous catfights to notice. She was the very definition of the character we "love to hate."

WHO SHOT J.R.?

WILDEST
CLIFF-HANGER

THE MOLDAVIAN MASSACRE

Being the resident bad guy does have it downsides: like being so hated that everyone is a suspect in your attempted murder. This definitional TV cliff-hanger began in the season 4 finale, "A House Divided," at the end of which J. R. is shot by a mystery assailant in his office, and was resolved in "Who Done It," the fourth episode of the next season, which drew an estimated 90 million viewers.

ABC pinched Dallas writer Camille Marchetta—who'd come up with the "Who Shot J. R.?" story line—and installed her as head writer and producer in season 5. No surprises then that the season would end with a bang. Well, *bangs*, actually: The wedding of Amanda (Catherine Oxenberg) and Prince Michael of Moldavia (Michael Praed) is thrown into chaos when a terrorist group peppers the chapel with bullets. Who lived? Who died? Let's just say the season 6 payoff was not quite as thrilling as the setup.

▶ OUR PICK   We know *Dallas* was the original, the longest-running, and the (slightly) more grounded, but we're a sucker for **Dynasty**'s wild story lines, outrageous fights—remember the lily pond?—and the glamorous schemer at the center of it all. Sometimes the print just pops a little brighter than the original.

well-known TV part—Laura Petrie, devoted wife and mother on *The Dick Van Dyke Show*—and it spoke to legions of single women who were wondering if they, too, could make it after all. The series's run coincided with, and reflected, the second-wave feminist movement in the United States and grappled with subjects that may seem tame now but were then taboo. In the third-season premiere, "The Good-Time News," Mary (tactfully) tackled wage inequality; "Just Around the Corner" and "You've Got a Friend" dealt directly with the idea of premarital sex (in the latter, the show famously made a sly reference to contraception when Mary's mother told her father, "Don't forget to take your pill!," and Mary reflexively responds, "*I won't!*"). A pioneer for female representation, *TMTMS* is equally remembered for how it upended and established so many of TV's well-known tropes. Standout "Chuckles Bites the Dust," the Emmy-winning sixth-season episode in which Mary can't keep a straight face while reporting on a dead clown, relaxed the way television depicted and discussed death. The will-they/won't-they shtick present in so many series also has some roots in the relationship between Mary and her boss, Ed Asner's spunk-hating Lou Grant.

lives defending our country can also be bored pranksters—see Alan Alda's functioning alcoholic, cut-up Captain Benjamin Franklin "Hawkeye" Pierce—or folks who just don't want to be there at all. It was also rare for being one of the earliest TV examples of what we now know as a "dark comedy," laying the groundwork for *Orange Is the New Black*, *Scrubs*, and other shows that threw ice-cold humor onto deadly serious situations and locales.

One episode features a character death so shocking even the show's actors didn't know it was coming.

Important episodes like season 7's "Point of View," shot from the vantage of a wounded soldier, or season 5's "The Nurses," where Loretta Swit's head nurse Major Margaret "Hot Lips" Houlihan gets to speak for underappreciated bosses everywhere, remain noteworthy. As does season 3's "Abyssinia, Henry," which features a character death so shocking even the show's actors didn't know it was coming when the cameras were rolling.

M*A*S*H

▶ GAME-CHANGER

CBS / 1972–1983
11 SEASONS / 256 EPISODES

🍅 -- 🗑 **93%**

Lasting nearly four times as long as the Korean War during which it's set, creators Larry Gelbart and Gene Reynolds's story about the medical staff at the United States' 4077th Mobile Army Surgical Hospital was a rarity of its time. It showed that the heroic military doctors and nurses risking their

Happy Days

ABC / 1974–1984
11 SEASONS / 255 EPISODES

TV has always trafficked in nostalgia. Case in point: This classic 1974 sitcom created by Garry Marshall, which showcased an idyllic slice of 1950s Midwestern life. While the show revolved around Ron Howard's innocent Milwaukee teen Richie Cunningham at first, it was his leather jacket–wearing, motorcycle-riding bad boy pal Arthur "Fonzie"

Fonzarelli (Henry Winkler) who really caught the audience's attention, joining the cast full-time in season 2 and anchoring the series long after Howard left to pursue his burgeoning directorial career. *Happy Days* inspired five spin-offs, including two important sitcoms in their own right: *Laverne & Shirley* and *Mork & Mindy*. And Howard and Winkler aren't the show's only major contributions to the industry: The sitcom is responsible for the term "jumping the shark," coined following a special episode that featured Winkler literally jumping over a shark while waterskiing—a tonal shift now synonymous with the moment the quality of a series shifts for the worse.

Cheers

NBC / 1982–1993
11 SEASONS / 275 EPISODES

 92%

Co-created by the legendary director James Burrows, this NBC favorite is beloved for its titular Boston bar setting, stable of Emmy-winning stars, all-time-great theme song, and an array of scene-stealing supporting actors that would go onto staff several series of their own. (Kelsey Grammer's *Frasier* became one of the rare spin-offs that equals the excellence of its origin series.) The romance between arrogant bar owner Sam (Ted Danson) and snooty waitress Diane (Shelley Long)—the standard for the enduring will-they/won't-they trope—took center stage in the beginning, but superb writing and those standout performances from the rest of the gang at Cheers helped turn a workplace comedy into a deeper story about a de facto dysfunctional family that is never more at home than when sitting together on saloon stools.

Murder, She Wrote

▶ HIGHLY ADDICTIVE

CBS / 1984–1996
12 SEASONS / 264 EPISODES (PLUS 4 TV MOVIES)

This Sunday night CBS favorite, like *Columbo* before it, mixed murder and mayhem with warm and fuzzies. Nix that: *murders*, plural, because there were a ton of dead bodies showing up in Cabot Cove, the fictional Maine enclave in which the series was set, in the '80s and '90s. In fact, a 2012 study claimed that with 274 killings across the course of the series and a population of just 3,500, this idyllic hamlet would have been "murder capital of the world" if it actually existed.

A study claimed that this idyllic hamlet would have been "murder capital of the world" if it actually existed.

Thank God, then, for local widow Jessica Fletcher (Angela Lansbury), the former English teacher turned successful mystery novelist who may not be able to prevent the bloodshed but is awfully good at deducing who did the spilling. Warm, disarming, and packing a stockpile of GIF-able expressions, Fletcher became the career-defining role for Lansbury, who had dabbled in "charming sleuth" before—she played Agatha Christie's Miss Marple in 1980's *The Mirror Crack'd*, the first of four planned Lansbury-Marple movies. The decision to kill those subsequent projects, freeing up the Broadway and screen legend to step into Fletcher's sensible pumps, is frankly a murder we cheer.

Those Were the Days

THE GROUNDBREAKING 1970s COMEDY OF NORMAN LEAR

If every generation gets the TV it deserves, audiences in the 1970s must have been doing something right to earn the work of producer Norman Lear.

Lear had long been a supporter of liberal political and social causes in his personal life, and he thought America deserved to see those topics presented in a realistic, humorous way on television. Enter one of the medium's most transformative series, *All in the Family*. The Lear-created CBS sitcom pits conservative working-class bigot Archie Bunker (Carroll O'Connor) against his son-in-law Mike (Rob Reiner), a liberal hippie whose ideas Archie finds so repulsive he refers to Mike as "Meathead." Women's rights, race, Richard Nixon, abortion, anti-Semitism, and homosexuality are but a few of the subjects the two men tussle over, with Mike appearing more morally and logically sound—though just as loud and stubborn as Archie. After a slow start, the show spent five seasons as the number 1 series on TV.

All in the Family directly begat a pair of similarly influential, pioneering Lear classics with the premieres of spin-offs *The Jeffersons* and *Maude*. The Jeffersons—George (Sherman Hemsley) and Louise (Isabel Sanford)—are, as their infectious theme song (a hallmark of all of Lear's '70s hits) says, "movin' on up," out of Queens (where they were the Bunkers' neighbors) and into Manhattan, thanks to the success of their chain of dry cleaning stores. African American George, the Archie of his household, is unafraid to share his often offensive POV, especially when it comes to his neighbors, Tom and Helen Willis, the first interracial couple prominently featured on TV. George's main foil: wisecracking live-in maid Florence (Marla Gibbs), one of the best representatives of another Lear comedy trademark—the scene-stealing supporting character.

Meanwhile, in her pre–*Golden Girls* days, Bea Arthur stars in another *All in the Family* spin-off as wickedly sharp-tongued Bunker cousin Maude Findlay, "that uncompromisin', enterprisin', anything but tranquilizin'" feminist (as Donny Hathaway sings in the theme song), who rules her home as iron-fistedly as Archie and George do theirs. Maude is a frequent drinker and pill taker, the victim of domestic abuse, and in the series's most controversial episode, gets an abortion. *Maude* just as importantly gave us Lear's *Good Times*, the spin-off series about the Evans family, led by mom Florida (Esther Rolle), who had been Maude's housekeeper. In *Good Times*, the family lives in a poor, Black housing project in Chicago, with three kids and a constant struggle to find work and pay their bills.

Lear's reign of influential '70s sitcoms continued with *Sanford and Son*, the Redd Foxx vehicle about a Black father and son who live together and run a Watts junkyard. Fred is the narrow-minded, scheming father, while Lamont is the calmer, hardworking son who tries to keep Fred out of trouble and out of fights with (scene-stealer alert) Lamont's feisty, Bible-quoting aunt Esther (LaWanda Page).

And then there's *One Day at a Time*, with Bonnie Franklin as the newly divorced Ann Romano, who moves to Indianapolis with two teen daughters (Valerie Bertinelli and Mackenzie Phillips) to start her life as an independent woman. That's the signature Lear premise, and it has an infectious theme song and breakout supporting character, too, in Emmy-winning Pat Harrington as Schneider the superintendent. All elements were intact in the critically acclaimed 2017 remake of the series that ran on Netflix and then for a season on Pop TV.

Many of those same core Learisms appear, too, in dozens of series that followed, many of which don't bear his name. Some are still on the air today. The Lear DNA lives in just about every TV family we meet (in *black-ish*, *Modern Family*, and even in *The Simpsons* and *Family Guy*, albeit with sharpened edges). Below are some of Lear's finest and most envelope-pushing moments.

SIX ESSENTIAL LEAR EPISODES

All in the Family
CBS / 1971–1979
9 SEASONS, 205 EPISODES

Season 2's "Sammy's Visit," in which Sammy Davis Jr. retrieves a misplaced briefcase from Archie and thanks him with a big kiss.

The Jeffersons
CBS / 1975–1985
11 SEASONS, 253 EPISODES

Season 7's "Sorry, Wrong Meeting," in which George is called upon to save the life of a white supremacist who used an ugly racial epithet.

Maude
CBS / 1972–1978
6 SEASONS, 141 EPISODES

Season 1's two-part "Maude's Dilemma," in which she gets an abortion two months before the landmark US Supreme Court decision *Roe v. Wade*.

Good Times
CBS / 1974–1979
6 SEASONS, 133 EPISODES

Season 1's "Too Old Blues," in which the family prematurely plans a celebration when James is sure he's getting a high-paying new job.

Sanford and Son
NBC / 1972–1977
6 SEASONS, 136 EPISODES

Season 1's "We Were Robbed," in which Fred claims he was robbed to cover up accidentally breaking Lamont's figurine collection.

One Day at a Time
CBS / 1975–1984
9 SEASONS, 209 EPISODES

Season 1's "Ann's Decision," in which her rebellious teen helps frightened Ann find the courage to deal with being a single mom for the first time.

The Golden Girls

 ▶ HIGHLY ADDICTIVE

NBC / 1985–1992
7 SEASONS / 180 EPISODES

🍅 – – 🍿 **94%**

▶ **CRITICS CONSENSUS** Worth its weight in laughs, *The Golden Girls* brings together an outrageously talented cast of television veterans and a raunchy sensibility that proves that youth needn't be wasted on the young. (Season 1)

▶ **WHAT IT'S ABOUT** Four women in southern Florida end up living together after homeowner Blanche Devereaux (Rue McClanahan) posts an ad on a bulletin board at a local grocery store: sarcastic substitute teacher Dorothy (Bea Arthur); her sharp-tongued mother, Sophia (Estelle Getty); dotty but endlessly kind Rose (Betty White); and Southern belle with an eye for men, Blanche.

By any measure, *The Golden Girls* had a dream sitcom run—and is still having it. The series premiered as the number 1 show on TV in its first week—on a Saturday night at 9 p.m., no less—and continued to be a smash through seven seasons, its finale drawing 27 million viewers to Dorothy's wedding. The show racked up 11 Emmys, drew high-profile fans (Princess Diana and Freddie Mercury among them), and eventually spawned two spin-offs, *Empty Nest* and *The Golden Palace*, which featured Blanche, Rose, and Sophia running a Miami hotel, sans Dorothy, the newly minted Mrs. Hollingsworth.

The original series has, over four decades, become a syndication staple, a streaming favorite, and a genuine "pop-culture phenomenon." Don't

believe us? Type GOLDEN GIRLS into Etsy and enter a wild, pastel-licked world of homemade Blanche bodega candles and "Zbornak/Petrillo 2020" mugs. Still don't believe us? Visit your town's next Gay Pride parade.

But in the lead-up to its debut, *The Golden Girls* was anything but a sure bet. TV had not really had a hit show that rested on the shoulders of four women, and it definitely had not produced a hit show about four *older* women. It was a risk, but that was part of what appealed to creator Susan Harris, whose résumé included *Soap* and who had written "Maude's Dilemma," the groundbreaking episode of *Maude* in which Bea Arthur's title character gets an abortion. Harris told *Entertainment Weekly* that she was drawn to *Golden Girls* because it spoke to a "demographic that had never been addressed." (She also told Yahoo that NBC's idea of "older" had initially meant women in their forties, and the show she wrote shifted that out by about 20 years—though the characters' ages aren't mentioned.)

The Golden Girls established a new mold and showed how successful that mold could be. Marc Cherry, who worked on the series and would go on to create *Desperate Housewives*, has described it as "the model for any female ensemble show," and said, "You can trace Gabrielle [Eva Longoria's *Housewives* character] right back to Blanche." You might also trace *Sex and the City*'s Carrie Bradshaw back to Dorothy, or *Girls*' Shoshanna Shapiro back to Rose.

None of it would have worked without genuinely sharp scripts by the likes of Cherry and the writing team, which also included *Arrested Development* creator Mitchell Hurwitz. *Golden Girls*'s best episodes weren't just rich with zingers about Blanche's boudoir and running jokes about Sophia's possible Mafia connections in Sicily; they thoughtfully grappled with issues dominating the late-1980s national conversation. And wisdom often came from the unlikeliest places: It's Rose who gets surprisingly deep on the issue of nuclear disarmament in the fantastical season 3 episode, "Letter to Gorbachev," and it's fiercely Christian Southern belle Blanche who, in season 5, tells Rose that "AIDS is not a bad person's disease . . . It is not God punishing people for their sins" as the latter awaits test results after a mishap with a blood transfusion.

It wouldn't have worked without the women bringing those scripts to life, either. The actors' characterizations mix played-for-laughs (and to the rafters) exaggeration—Blanche's Southern accent is delivered as if in competition with every other Deep South drawl ever committed to screen—and emotional complexity. And the chemistry between the women, despite gossip of behind-the-scenes frostiness between White and Arthur, is singularly warm. It's why that finale, in which the foursome split, is so heartbreaking, and why more than 10 million people a month still tune in on Hulu to catch up with Blanche, Dorothy, Rose, and Sophia to this day: *The Golden Girls* is both a history-making groundbreaker and—like a late-night slice of cheesecake in your nightie with friends—the ultimate TV comfort food.

▶ **BEST EPISODE** Season 2, Episode 5—"Isn't It Romantic?" Dorothy's friend Jean (Lois Nettleton) visits the girls after the death of her partner and develops feelings for Rose—who has no idea of Jean's sexual orientation. Daring for the time, funny—yes, Blanche gets hilariously jealous—and sensitively handled, the episode won director Terry Hughes an Emmy.

▶ **CHARACTER WE LOVE** Sophia, who was never meant to be a series regular but tested so well with audiences that the creators quickly changed that. Which meant Getty—younger than two of her costars—would spend seven seasons in three-hour hair and makeup sessions and battle a reportedly crippling case of stage fright to deliver one of the all-time sitcom standouts.

DEEP ▼ ▼ DIVE

BINGEING
BEFORE THE BINGE

Think marathon viewing is an invention of the streaming age? Think again.

Entertainment lovers have been parking their keisters for a good binge for almost a century. Here's how.

THE DOUBLE FEATURE BINGE

2 for 1*

The movie double feature may not be a strict "binge"—different stories, different characters—but it did train our attention spans and introduced the behavior of pressing PLAY on "just . . . one . . . more."

The idea dates back to 19th-century opera, when houses would put on two shows in one night to save on the cost of staging separate extravaganzas, and economics would drive its popularity in film, too: The double bill caught on during the Depression as movie houses offered two flicks for the price of one to keep business up.

* Usually, the first movie to play was a low-budget B-movie (thus the term), followed by a bigger-budget A-movie.

The '70s and '80s
Convention Binge

Streaming has torn down TV borders— see chapter 10—but adventurous and clued-in fans of foreign shows found ways to binge their faves well before broadband; heck, anime fans were getting their fix decades before dial-up. In the 1970s and 1980s, as VHS tapes became more widely available, fans of Japanese animation would gather together for marathons in living rooms to watch series on imported VHSs—or copies of copies of copies of imported tapes—and sometimes take their VCRs and tapes to pop culture conventions for mega-screenings.

Bay-Con 1986, a sci-fi and fantasy convention in the San Francisco Bay Area, held an 80-hour anime marathon for the more extreme early bingers.

The Saturday Morning Cartoon Binge

If a big part of binge watching is simply staring at the TV zombie-like and slack-jawed for hours on end, many of us surely got our earliest training via Saturday-morning cartoons.

From the 1960s to the 1990s, NBC, CBS, and ABC dedicated the 8 a.m.–noon Saturday slot to kids' animated series in an effort to create a concentrated block for advertisers hawking toys, candy, and the like.

Of course, we were too caught up in the *Adventures of Superman*, *The Brady Kids*, and *The Smurfs* to think of ourselves as a "demo." (Though, come to think of it, we did always have a curious hankering for Rice Krispies by about 9:30 a.m. . . .)

THE NICK AT NIGHT BINGE

The "binge" as we recognize it today is sometimes said to have started with Nickelodeon's introduction of the Nick at Nite block in 1985.

It was then that the channel began adding beloved "oldies" to its roster—*The Donna Reed Show* and *Route 66* were among the first—and often promoting them with multi-episode marathons. These marathons would go on for hours, and for part of the '90s you could expect a different binge watch every night of the week (*Bewitched* Be-Wednesdays! *Jeannie* Thursdays!).

The marathons also got very creative. Consider Halloween week, 1990, when **Nick at Nite** aired an *Alfred Hitchcock Presents* marathon and asked viewers to count the number of deaths in the show; those who got the number correct entered a drawing to win a prize.

THE BOX SET BINGE

The rise of VHS allowed fans to buy or rent collections of their favorite shows and watch them in multi-ep sittings.

But while VHS sets were popular enough—we guarantee you'll see a set of *Andy Griffith Show* tapes on at least one garage sale table in your life—the box-set binge really took off with the arrival of the digital versatile disc (DVD) in 1996. Individual discs could hold multiple episodes; they came with fun extras like outtakes, deleted scenes, and commentaries; and they were easy to mail (something a little company called Netflix took note of).

Box sets could also be elaborate. Just how elaborate? The 21-disc 25th anniversary collection of the *Golden Girls* came in a golden replica of Sophia's purse. Today, it will set you back a cool $700 on Amazon.

THE DVR BINGE

DVR, or digital video recording, was a game-changer when it became widely available through services like TiVo and was integrated into cable TV offerings.

Suddenly, fans could record and save multiple episodes of their favorite shows across weeks, to be gobbled up all in a row at their leisure. In fact, one study, conducted as recently as 2014, found that the primary method for Americans watching three or more episodes of a series in one day was DVR and not subscription video-on-demand services like Hulu and Netflix.

Of course, cord-cutting and the streaming wars have changed all that, but we do fondly remember this magical tool that allowed us to zip past the commercials. We less fondly remember the stress of seeing our DVR library edging toward 100% full. Time to clear out some of those saved-up eps of *Grey's Anatomy* . . .

▌▌ COMMERCIAL BREAK

Primetime Profes- sionals

PROCEDURALS THAT BROUGHT A LITTLE SOMETHING EXTRA TO WORK

After a hard day at work, sometimes you just want to sink into the La-Z-Boy and watch other people have a hard day at work. (Or, more accurately: a hard 42 minutes.)

As TV flourished in the second half of the 20th century, procedural dramas about professional workplaces began to dominate Nielsen ratings and Emmy nominations. The idea of a "case"—an unsolved crime, an injury our beloved surgical team has never come across—paired perfectly with a medium that demanded weekly dilemmas with neat resolutions. Throw in a handful of compelling personalities, and the procedural gave viewers plenty of reason to tune in week after week.

So it was that with each new TV season, the big networks threw open the doors to fictional hospitals and cop shops and courtrooms all across the country. In the 1980s, we met the vice team of Miami and the officers of *Hill Street Blues*—which would anchor NBC's first-ever Must-See TV Thursday night lineup—along with the fashionable litigators of *L.A. Law* and the doctors of *St. Elsewhere*. Such shows built on the foundations of classics that came before—*Perry Mason* and *Dragnet*, *Doctor Kildare* and *Medical Center*—leaning into grit, or high style, or, in some cases, soap and sex, and building out formulas for the next decades' mega-hits: *ER*, *CSI*, and beyond.

Also being established as the procedural took hold: A new generation of mega-producers putting their stamps on the genre. No name is more famously associated with the procedural than *Law & Order* creator Dick Wolf, whose ingenious structural twist—one half of the episode would focus on the chase, the other on the trial—struck a chord (*dun-DUN*), and ignited a multi-series franchise. He's rivaled only, perhaps, by the late writer and producer Steven Bochco, whose mastery of procedural formula—and determination to mess with it—gave viewers some of the biggest evolutions in TV drama in the late 20th century. In *Hill Street Blues*, Bochco set the blueprint for a complex look at the workings of inner-city law enforcement that would lead to *NYPD Blue*, which he also created, and, ultimately, *The Wire*. In his early '90s legal drama *Murder One*, we saw some of the earliest stirrings of cable-style prestige serials.

This is a chapter full of TV titans and innovators; look closely at their work and you'll see clues to the golden age of Peak TV that was just around the corner.

Hill Street Blues

▶ GAME-CHANGER

NBC / 1981–1987
7 SEASONS / 146 EPISODES

Every new golden age drama that came after *Hill Street Blues* owes a debt to the Steven Bochco–created police procedural for giving viewers a realistic peek at life in an inner-city neighborhood rife with drugs, prostitution, and murder. Captain Frank Furillo (Daniel J. Travanti) is the calm leader his precinct—located in an unnamed city—needs, delicately balancing keeping his officers safe and allowing them to do their jobs, while also dealing with the local criminals whose power he must acknowledge to keep violence at a minimum. Moments of levity—like wild man undercover Detective Mick Belker (Bruce Weitz) biting perps—are a welcome break from the more intense action, often shot with handheld cameras, a rarity on TV at the time. Writer David Milch, in his first TV job—he would go on to co-create *NYPD Blue* with Bochco, and *Deadwood* solo—is responsible for much of the NBC series's poetry, which illuminates the unrelenting pain with which characters on both sides of the streets live.

Miami Vice

NBC / 1984–1990
5 SEASONS / 112 EPISODES

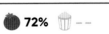 72%

Before serialized cop dramas, *Miami Vice* kept its audience coming back every week with a style cribbed from music videos of the day and executive producer Michael Mann's own distinctive eye. And that's to say nothing of its reliance on the era's popular artists, like Phil Collins and Duran Duran, to provide musical accompaniment in key scenes. That stylishness still resonates today—even when it brushes up against dated (and sometimes cheesy) fashion choices. Centering on a Miami vice squad, tasked with policing illicit drugs and prostitution, the series was propelled by the smoldering good looks of star Don Johnson and the pressure-cooker energy of co-lead Philip Michael Thomas. Cases varied from deadly undercover assignments to a search for stolen bull semen. (Really.) The tone was often cynical, but refreshingly so, with the cops themselves often questioning their own effectiveness.

L.A. Law

NBC / 1986–1994
8 SEASONS / 172 EPISODES

This 15-time Emmy-winning series from Bochco and former lawyer Terry Louise Fisher helped shape public perception of lawyers during its eight-year run. The attractive, well-dressed litigators of a luxe Los Angeles law firm—played by the likes of Corbin Bernsen, Harry Hamlin, Jimmy Smits, and Susan Dey—introduced sexy concepts like "torts" and "ethics" to the audience while outfitted in a reported $40,000 per-episode wardrobe. *L.A. Law*'s topical episodes—about abortion, sexism, gun control—even affected the outcomes of real-life court cases. Rather than stick to the cut-and-dried procedural case-of-the-week formula, the serialized story lines focused on the lawyers' personal *and* professional lives. Occasional zaniness—death-by-elevator shaft, gorilla suits, and a made-up sex position called the Venus Butterfly—made it a perfect fit for

NBC's dominant Thursday night lineup—just before Must-See TV was introduced in 1993—which also included *The Cosby Show* and *Cheers*.

NYPD Blue

ABC / 1993–2005
12 SEASONS / 261 EPISODES

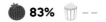 **83%** 🗑 --

Bochco and Milch brought their *Hill Street Blues* vibes to this similar cop drama, with the action moved to ABC and Manhattan's 15th precinct. The mix of focus on the cops' professional and personal lives was still there, though, along with the realistic portrayal of crimes and the toll the characters' jobs take on them, most notably the alcoholism that gruff Detective Andy Sipowicz (Dennis Franz) battles. Bochco and Milch wanted viewers to know this was a randier bunch of men and women in blue, however: There was nudity aplenty, something so shocking in network TV shows at the time (and still a rarity) that ABC would eventually be fined $1.4 million by the FCC for a shot of actress Charlotte Ross's naked tuchus. *NYPD Blue* is also remembered for its rotating lineup of leading men, which began when David Caruso notoriously left early in season 2. He was followed by Jimmy Smits, who won a Golden Globe for his portrayal of Sipowicz's beloved partner Bobby Simone, then a pair of former teen idols, Ricky Schroder and Mark-Paul Gosselaar, who also portrayed new partners for Sipowicz (who, obviously, deals with a lot of loss).

Bochco and Milch wanted viewers to know this was a randier bunch of men and women in blue.

ER

▶ HIGHLY ADDICTIVE

NBC / 1994–2009
15 SEASONS / 331 EPISODES

🍅 -- 🗑 **80%**

Michael Crichton, best-selling author and man behind pop-culture phenomena *Jurassic Park* and *Westworld*, added "TV revolutionary" to his résumé when the pilot based on his emergency room residency hit the airwaves in 1994. Over 23 million viewers tuned in for *ER*'s two-hour series premiere—one of the first of its kind—where they were introduced to a group of character actors that would soon become household names, including George Clooney as womanizing pediatrician Doug Ross. With its dedication to high-stakes emergencies, authentic-seeming medicine, and soapy intrigue, *ER* took up the mantle of *St. Elsewhere*, which had ended six years earlier, and would soon become the standard for the genre. Though later seasons never captured the magic of the landmark early run—Clooney left in 1999, and similarly popular Julianna Margulies left her role as nurse Carol Hathaway shortly after that—*ER* still pumped out captivating and award-winning story lines into its twilight years.

Murder One

▶ GONE TOO SOON

NBC / 1995–1997
2 SEASONS / 41 EPISODES

 **91%** 🗑 --

For the late Steven Bochco, *Murder One* was a flex; for network TV as a whole, it *(Continued on page 24.)*

LAW & ORDER

ORDER

CASE FILES

"IN THE CRIMINAL JUSTICE SYSTEM…" Well, you know the drill—at least you do if you've been anywhere near a TV since 1990, the year Dick Wolf launched the original *Law & Order* series on NBC. In doing so, he kicked off what would become, over three decades and counting, a game-changing cops-and-lawyers franchise with seven spin-offs, a TV movie, and thousands of hours of murder, assault, and mayhem. A few of those spin-offs were quickly dismissed by the TV-watching jurors at home — *Trial by Jury*, which focused on both sides of a jury trial, lasted just 13 episodes after debuting in 2005 — but others went the distance, none more so than the still-running *Special Victims Unit*. Below we're opening the case files on the best eps of the series in the *Law & Order* franchise.

LAW & ORDER

THE SERIES: Wolf's original *Law & Order* reinvented the traditional one-hour police procedural, following a single, often ripped-from-the-headlines case all the way through each episode. Those eps were divided into two halves—investigation and capture before the court case component—and covered all major stops of the justice system along the way.

THE ESSENTIAL EPISODE:
Season 6, Episode 21–"Pro Se,"
May 8, 1996.

THE VICTIM(S): Violence breaks out in a vintage clothing shop while one sales clerk is out to lunch, leaving the owner, his cashier, and a customer dead by stabbing.

THE VERDICT: Central schizophrenic attorney, James Smith, who decides to defend himself against the multiple murder charges, is one of the franchise's most irresistibly devilish—and memorable—foes. Watching consummate character actor Denis O'Hare as Smith go toe-to-toe with our favorite series regulars is enrapturing fun.

LAW & ORDER:
SPECIAL VICTIMS UNIT

THE SERIES: The first and most successful *Law & Order* spin-off series, *SVU* centers on a specially trained sector of the NYPD that handles all sexually related crimes.

THE ESSENTIAL EPISODE:
Season 7, Episode 3—"911,"
October 4, 2005.

THE VICTIM(S): A young girl is being held captive by a tech-savvy child abuser, and the police are unable to trace her calls.

THE VERDICT: *SVU* demands a strong stomach from its viewers with the real-world atrocities of rape and molestation it often examines on-screen. As detective-turned-captain Olivia Benson, Mariska Hargitay gives the series heart. "911" sees the actor at the height of her powers: fearless, dogged, compassionate, and brilliant. Her performance in this hour of cat-and-mouse with a kidnapping child pornographer earned Hargitay a well-deserved Emmy in 2006.

1999–

LAW & ORDER:
CRIMINAL INTENT

THE SERIES: The second of the *Law & Order* spin-offs, *Criminal Intent* changed the game in part by showing the crime from the perpetrator's point of view while following members of the NYPD's Major Case Squad, which is tasked with the city's highest-profile cases.

THE ESSENTIAL EPISODE:
Season 2, Episode 23—"A Person of Interest," May 18, 2003.

THE VICTIM(S): The suicide of an anthrax scheme suspect sets this episode in motion, as disgraced Detective Robert Goren (Vincent D'Onofrio) is blamed for pushing him over the edge.

THE VERDICT: No one is safe when Nicole Wallace (Olivia d'Abo) is around, and that certainly proves true in delicious, plot-twisting fashion in this season 2 finale. While Goren had been barking up the wrong tree investigating the anthrax scheme of the season's penultimate episode, the sociopathic serial killer from his past, Wallace (now going by the name Elizabeth Hitchens), is the real culprit. With stellar performances from D'Onofrio and d'Abo, and one jaw-dropping revelation after the next, this is an all-time best.

was a detonation—even if its impact was muted at the time. In several of the shows in this category Bochco had perfected the formula for legal procedurals, and in the first of *Murder One*'s two seasons he upended it, ditching the case-of-the-week approach and focusing on a single murder and trial that ran for 23 episodes. Week by week, viewers followed the story of actor and accused murderer Neil Avedon (Jason Gedrick), his lawyer Ted Hoffman (a grizzled Daniel Benzali), and a coterie of colorful side characters, including philanthropist Richard Cross, played memorably in an Emmy-winning turn by Stanley Tucci. It was twisty, complex stuff. Without the option to binge the next episode immediately, though, viewership fell off during the first season's run. The drop-off led to tweaks for season 2: Benzali was out as the central lawyer, replaced by Anthony LaPaglia as new Hoffman and Associates boss Jimmy Wyler, and the season followed *three* cases, rather than one. It was a quality comedown, but didn't do enough damage to tarnish *Murder One*'s rep as a must-watch, ahead-of-its-time groundbreaker.

The West Wing

▶ **HIGHLY ADDICTIVE**

NBC / 1999–2006
7 SEASONS / 156 EPISODES

 75%   94%

In the wake of shows like *House of Cards* and *Scandal*, it's difficult to imagine that the White House was, once upon a time, not considered a great place to set a TV show. There had been a few tries—among them, *Hail to the Chief*, starring Patty Duke as the first female president, which lasted just seven episodes—but few successes. Then along came playwright-turned-screenwriter Aaron Sorkin, with a

stirring, optimistic, and very wordy vision. Sorkin had enjoyed success with his first show, *Sports Night*, a dramatic look at the behind-the-scenes goings-on among the crew of a fictional sports news program, and wrote political romance *The American President*; but it would be his detailed, serialized insider's take on the workings of the presidency and Washington that would become his career-defining work. The bulk of *The West Wing* centers on the presidency of Jed Bartlett, played by Martin Sheen, and the staffers who keep his White House running amid national crises, assassination attempts, burgeoning and failing romances, and an election or two.

The show became known for its almost Shakespearean soliloquies, and now-iconic "walk-and-talks."

The impeccable cast included veterans—John Spencer (Chief of Staff Leo McGarry), Bradley Whitford (Deputy CoS, Josh Lyman), Allison Janney (who steals the series as Press Secretary C. J. Cregg), Richard Schiff (Communications Director Toby Ziegler), and Rob Lowe (Deputy Communications Director Sam Seaborn)—in addition to talented newcomers, like Dulé Hill, *Sports Night* transplant Joshua Malina, and a young Elisabeth Moss as Bartlett's daughter. The show became known for its almost Shakespearean soliloquies, alongwith the now-iconic "walk-and-talks"—rapid-fire dialogue exchanged as characters plow through the West Wing's narrow corridors of power. When Sorkin departed the show after season 4, there was a distinct drop in quality—season 6 would even earn a Rotten score on the Tomatometer—but the series still enjoyed excellent ratings and remains the perfect comfort food for those who can't bear to binge-watch the real-life happenings in the capital.

The Wire

▶ GAME-CHANGER
▶ PERFECT CERTIFIED FRESH STREAK

HBO / 2002–2008
5 SEASONS / 60 EPISODES

🍅 94% 🗑 97%

They say to "write what you know," and for former journalist David Simon and former detective and teacher Ed Burns, that meant crafting a rich, complex crime drama set in Baltimore, Maryland. The duo had already found success doing exactly that with the Emmy-winning HBO miniseries *The Corner*, based on their coauthored nonfiction book, but with *The Wire* they sought to further develop its themes and incorporate more elements of inner-city life. The result was an expansive look not just at the drug trade in Baltimore, but also at the ways in which it intersects with and influences the city's local politics, port industry, education system, and print media.

> *The Wire struggled to maintain an audience during its run . . . but it's clear now the series was simply ahead of its time.*

The ensemble cast is so strong and so vast that it's difficult to single out individual performers—Michael K. Williams's Omar Little, the outlaw with a code, and Idris Elba's Stringer Bell, the business-minded right-hand man, are fan favorites—and each of them is given such authentic, lived-in material to work with that there are no wasted roles. Despite these strengths and critical acclaim, *The Wire* struggled to maintain an audience during its run, with some citing the series's complexity as the cause of its declining ratings. But it's clear now that the series was simply ahead of its time. It premiered just as what we now call "Peak TV" began its ascent, and, as viewers grew accustomed to increasingly sprawling, ambitious storytelling, *The Wire* quickly became a must-see recommendation. Over a decade later, it's hailed as one of the most engrossing and sophisticated portrayals of urban life in America and one of television's greatest achievements.

House

FOX / 2004–2012
8 SEASONS / 177 EPISODES

 90% 🗑 96%

Before Fox picked up the show that would eventually become *House* (its pedantic, original title was "Chasing Zebras, Circling the Drain"), the network had one stipulation: no white coats going down the hallway. Setting his drama apart from the likes of *ER* and *Chicago Hope*, creator David Shore developed his medical procedural as a cross between Sherlock Holmes and *CSI*. Centered on the cantankerous Dr. Gregory House (a caustic but charming Hugh Laurie), *House* rarely strayed from the patient-of-the-week formula wherein a medical mystery forced the Vicodin-addicted know-it-all to think outside the box to save his patients. Diagnosing everything from lupus to leprosy triggered by anthrax, House anchored a hit broadcast drama that, in its eight-season run, offered as many boldly inventive episodes (the ingenious use of flashbacks in "Three Stories") as it did clunkers (that third season Detective Tritter story line, for starters).

Justified

 PERFECT CERTIFIED FRESH STREAK

FX / 2010–2015
6 SEASONS / 78 EPISODES

🍅 **97%** 🍿 **95%**

CRITICS CONSENSUS ▶ A coolly violent drama, *Justified* benefits from a seductive look and a note-perfect Timothy Olyphant performance. (Season 1)

WHAT IT'S ABOUT ▶ Based on Elmore Leonard's Raylan Givens stories, the series follows Deputy US Marshal Raylan Givens (Olyphant), who is reassigned to his Kentucky hometown as censure for a deadly shooting. Raylan employs an unconventional style of law enforcement, one encapsulated by his quote, "You make me pull, I'll put you down."

You'd be forgiven for thinking that actor Timothy Olyphant summoned the spirit of his sheriff, Seth Bullock, from HBO's *Deadwood* out of the 1870s to help forge *Justified*'s Old West–style modern gunslinger Raylan Givens. In both roles, Olyphant wears a gun at his hip and packs a swagger so assured it's elevated to an art form. It can't be an accident, then, that Olyphant appears as yet another gunslinger—portraying actor James Stacy on the set of the 1960s TV Western *Lancer*—in Quentin Tarantino's Oscar-nominated feature film *Once Upon a Time . . . in Hollywood*. Or that he was plucked by *The Mandalorian* to play a lawman in Tatooine. Like Givens himself, he's very good at what he does.

Olyphant shares the screen in *Justified* with a wealth of talent, including Margo Martindale, Jeremy Davies, and guest stars Sam Elliott, Mary Steenburgen, and Neal McDonough. Most notable,

though, is the underappreciated Walton Goggins as the series's main antagonist, Raylan's slippery old pal Boyd Crowder (they used to work the coal mines together as young men). The rivalry between the two men drives the drama and is told through crisp dialogue and violent encounters, both of which are credited to the influence of Leonard, who was an executive producer on the series up to his death in 2013 and whose novels—like *Get Shorty* and *Out of Sight*—were frequently adapted for screen.

Justified quickly takes root with the pilot "Fire in the Hole," which finds the deputy US marshal exiled home to Harlan County, Kentucky, where he must now chase down the dirty deeds of eccentric locals—some of whom he's related to—and prevent incursions from outside criminal enterprises. Based on Leonard's short story of the same name, the episode immediately nails down the series's architecture, characters, and relationships, while also promising a deep well of backwoods sin and intrigue upon which a, say, six-season series might thrive.

With three 100% Certified Fresh seasons and three more Certified Fresh at 93% and above, *Justified* had no problem garnering critical acclaim, but when the awards seasons came around, the series and its star were largely bypassed; somehow, Olyphant managed only one nomination for an Emmy as Lead Actor in a Drama Series in the series's six seasons, and the dynamic Goggins only one nod for Supporting Actor in a Drama Series. Martindale did secure an Emmy for Outstanding Supporting Actress in a Drama Series for her role as "Mags Bennett," the matriarch of a criminal clan, and Davies won Outstanding Guest Actor in a Drama Series the following year for playing "Dickie Bennett," one of Mags's three sons, who has a long-standing beef with Raylan that dates back to their youth.

The general lack of industry recognition for Graham Yost's remarkable creation and its stars' performances, however, beggars belief. And it did not go unnoticed. "There must be an alternate universe where *Justified* is fully recognized for what it is: one of the greatest shows in television history," Mark Dawidziak of the *Cleveland Plain Dealer* wrote about the final season of the series, an opinion that we think—just like Raylan—is perfectly on target.

BEST EPISODE ▶ Season 1, Episode 1—"Fire in the Hole." The series's first episode introduces Deputy US Marshal Raylan Givens at a trendy hotel reminding a slick Miami mobster (Peter Greene) of the ultimatum previously placed before him: 24 hours to get out of town or be shot dead—and the clock is ticking down. Quick-draw Raylan shoots the guy as he reaches for his gun, which immediately rankles brass at the Marshals Service and earns Raylan a ticket out of town.

CHARACTER WE LOVE ▶ Olyphant's balance of laconic restraint, bemusement, and an undercurrent of barely contained rage made Raylan a character for the ages, but Goggins's charismatic villain Boyd deserves credit for being so perfect a foil for the show's antihero that the premiere episode broke from Leonard's story and didn't kill off the character.

DEEP ▼ ▼ DIVE

BINGE BATTLE

CSI ◄ VS ► NCIS

How do you like your mega-hit TV procedurals: With blood, guts, and brooding aplenty? Or with a side of sailors and quirk? We're solving the case of which ratings-smash procedural is greater in this forensic look at their scores, best moments, and franchise-building powers.

CSI	NCIS
CBS / 2005–2015	**CBS / 2003–2017**
15 SEASONS / 337 EPISODES	17 SEASONS / 409 EPISODES
🍅 **92%*** 🍿 **95%***	🍅 **61%*** 🍿 **80%***
*SEASON 1	*SEASON 1

WHAT IT'S ABOUT ► In this high-octane, gory, forensics-obsessed procedural, a crack team of crime-scene investigators working for the Las Vegas PD go deep on physical evidence to solve weekly murder cases. They're led for most of *CSI*'s run by criminalist Gil Grissom (William Petersen) and his 2IC, Catherine Willows (Marg Helgenberger); later seasons see Laurence Fishburne, Ted Danson, and Elisabeth Shue join the cast. Their efforts spawned "the CSI effect": the development among victims and jurors of unrealistic expectations surrounding the capabilities of forensic science.

WHAT IT'S ABOUT ► This *JAG* spin-off traces the exploits of the Navy Criminal Investigative Service's Major Case Response Team—basically, another crack team of crime solvers, this time within the titular branch of the armed forces. They're led by former Marine sniper Major Leroy Jethro Gibbs (Mark Harmon) and include in their ranks former secret service agent Caitlin Todd (Sasha Alexander) and forensic scientist and choker-wearing goth Abby Sciuto (Pauley Perrette), who stole the show—and much of the world's hearts—until she left in 2015.

CSI: Miami
(2003–2012)
🍅 -- 🍿 **66%**

NCIS: New Orleans
(2014–)
🍅 -- 🍿 **60%**

CSI: NY
(2004–2012)
🍅 -- 🍿 **84%**

◀ **SPIN-OFFS** ▶

CSI: Cyber
(2015–2016)
✳ **34%** 🗑 **36%**

NCIS: Los Angeles
(2009–)
🍅 -- 🍿 **70%**

◀ **MOST MEMORABLE CASE** ▶

"GRAVE DANGER"

Season 5, Episodes 24–25—This high-stakes, two-part season finale had everything: gore (hello, coiled intestines); great guest stars (including *Batman*'s Riddler himself, Frank Gorshin, who died two days before the episode aired); and the kidnapping of one of the team's own. Most of all, it had Quentin Tarantino, a huge *CSI* fan, who conjured the story and directed both parts himself.

"BLOODBATH"

Season 3, Episode 21—The bloodbath of the episode title is a gory shock, but soon discovered to be staged in an episode that is all about finding out who is stalking Abby. *NCIS* is full of episodes that showcase audience favorite Perrette's comedic chops, but "Bloodbath"—one of the actress's personal favorites and one she admits was hard to shoot—allows us to see her full and impressive range.

▶ **OUR PICK** The Navy show may be the longer-running effort, and we'll be damned if that Mark Harmon isn't as handsome as hell, but we're with Tarantino on this one. Despite being the product of serious money and a mega-producer in Jerry Bruckheimer, there was something almost punk rock about *CSI*'s graphic violence and visual dynamism, and, of course, we have to give props to the iconic use of The Who's "Who Are You?" for its opening theme.

The Good Wife

CBS / 2009–2016
7 SEASONS / 156 EPISODES

 93% 92%

The Good Fight

CBS ALL ACCESS (NOW PARAMOUNT+) / 2017–
4 SEASONS / 40 EPISODES

 96% 78%

▶ **CRITICS CONSENSUS** *The Good Wife:* Along with Julianna Margulies and a fine cast, the gripping drama *The Good Wife* boasts hook-heavy plotlines torn from the headlines. (Season 1)

The Good Fight: Solidly follows its predecessor while allowing for new storytelling styles, a wider narrative scope, and a chance for its lead to explore new territory with a relatable human struggle. (Season 1)

▶ **WHAT IT'S ABOUT** *The Good Wife:* When her husband, the Cook County State's Attorney, is jailed in the wake of a high-profile corruption and sex scandal, Alicia Florrick (Julianna Margulies) returns to law after 13 years out of the workforce. Taking a job as a junior litigator at Stern, Lockhart, and Gardner, she must prove herself from under the shadow of public disgrace—and work out her feelings for old flame and senior partner Will (Josh Charles).

The Good Fight: After losing her savings in the aftermath of a Bernie Madoff–like financial scam, *The Good Wife's* Diane Lockhart (Christine Baranski) joins a Black-owned firm notorious for taking on cases involving police brutality. Also at the firm: Maia Rindell (Rose Leslie), a young associate whose father was the Madoff-like scammer, and Lucca Quinn (Cush Jumbo), who worked for Diane in the final season of *The Good Wife.*

Michelle and Robert King might be the most exciting thing to happen to network TV this century. Over and over, these writing partners, co-showrunners, and husband and wife have been proving there's room at the Peak TV table for broadcast networks, right alongside the cool-kid cable channels and streamers. Consider *BrainDead*, their short-lived slice of experimental bizarreness about alien bugs crawling into DC politicians' heads, or *Evil*, their religious twist on the *X-Files'* skeptic-plus-believer formula, which features a priest who communes with angels via 'shrooms.

Both aired on CBS, where they stood out next to the likes of *The Big Bang Theory* and the network's traditional procedurals.

Their masterpiece, though, was *The Good Wife*, which for seven seasons managed to be just as smart, dark, and daring as any of HBO's Emmy darlings—and managed to do it over 22 episodes each season. With ad breaks.

The opening scene of *The Good Wife* recreates the real-life scenes that inspired it: A shell-shocked woman stands by her politician husband before flashing cameras and jabbing mics, silent as he apologizes for his failings. Moments later, we are hit with something we *haven't* seen countless times: In a corridor away from the press, the woman stops and—in what plays out like satisfying fanfic for anyone who followed the stories of Hillary Clinton, Elizabeth Edwards, Silda Wall Spitzer, and others—slaps him in the face.

The woman is Alicia Florrick, the man is power-hungry Peter (Chris Noth), and their complex relationship undergirds the acclaimed legal drama but never constrains it. Punctuating the action with compelling cases of the week—always with a smart approach to technology and politics—the Kings unfurl a multifaceted world of characters and seasons-arching subplots that weave between law firms, courtrooms, and campaign trails. Never just the sympathetic victim, Alicia will evolve into a political animal herself, reel in and out of love and lust with her ex, Will, and duke it out with a colorful set of supporting characters. (No wonder she so often turns to those deep glasses of red at the end of a long day.)

Among those standout supporting players is Christine Baranski's Diane Lockhart, the fabulously bejeweled senior partner, women's rights advocate, voice of reason, and series scene-stealer. Little surprise, then, that she would get a spin-off when *Wife*'s run came to an end.

For many, *The Good Fight* was an evolution and even an improvement. *Fight* gets political, too, even kicking off with a scene in which Lockhart watches the inauguration of President Donald Trump. As with Florrick's press conference in *Wife*'s pilot, the moment lays out the themes of the show that will unfold after it and the woman driving its drama: Lockhart is a creature of the women's rights movement, a Hillary Clinton acolyte who has been—in her rise to the top of the legal profession—the living embodiment of what she wants women to know is possible. When we catch up with her in the first season, an unscrupulous man has wiped out her fortune with his Ponzi scheme, and a man she believes to be corrupt is in the White House, laying waste to the country and her life's work.

Her journey from that moment is every bit as complicated and thrilling as Florrick's, mixing intra-firm intrigue with challenging cases and real-world events. And she is surrounded by a rich cast of new characters—Delroy Lindo is all charm and calculation as oft-embattled name partner Adrian Boseman, fighting to balance books and maintain his firm's Black identity—as well as some old favorites.

If Florrick's story is one ripped from the headlines, Lockhart's is one oppressed by them. Both series show the Kings' acute ability to take the events of our world and wring rich characters and stories from them—stories that shock and surprise, stimulate and challenge, and prompt us to reflect and rail. The world's getting crazier—thank the TV gods we have the Kings to help us process it.

▶ **BEST EPISODE** *The Good Wife*, Season 5, Episode 15—"Dramatics, Your Honor." It's a tough call between this and the high-octane "Hits the Fan"—in which Will fires Alicia after discovering her plans to strike out on her own. But "Dramatics," now notorious among fans, features, arguably, the most shocking TV death outside of that show about the dragons.

▶ **CHARACTER WE LOVE** Elsbeth Tascioni. Played by the great Carrie Preston, the seemingly scatter-brained Elsbeth—one in the roster of great lawyers who pop up regularly as foes or allies of our central players in both series—is hilariously inappropriate one moment, and disarmingly shrewd the next. Underestimate her at your peril.

Veronica Mars

UPN/THE CW, HULU / 2004–2007, 2019

4 SEASONS / 72 EPISODES (AND A MOVIE)

 92% 78%

Plenty of series wind up in the "canceled too soon" hall of fame, but not nearly as many are as lucky as *Veronica Mars*, whose devoted fan base of "marshmallows" inspired both a follow-up movie (funded via one of the most successful Kickstarter campaigns ever) and a streaming service revival. The teen detective noir from creator Rob Thomas—no, not the singer—followed the fast-talking, pop-culture-loving titular character (Kristen Bell) as she turned her after-school job assisting her PI dad (Enrico Colantoni) into a side business solving cases for her classmates—and trying to solve the murder of her best friend, the event that turned her whole family's life upside down. While the original three-season series premiered the year after *The O.C.*, this was a very different look at high school in southern California: The sunny skies and palm trees were a backdrop for difficult topics like sexual abuse, childhood trauma, and abandonment, but viewed through the eyes of the sarcastic, funny, and ultimately lovable Veronica. She might have a tough exterior, but deep down she's soft and sweet, like a marshmallow.

Grey's Anatomy

▶ HIGHLY ADDICTIVE

ABC / 2005–

17 SEASONS / 370+ EPISODES

 84% 77%

We could fill this whole book just listing *Grey's Anatomy*'s stats and records. The hospital drama, created by Shonda Rhimes, is ABC's longest-running, scripted, primetime show and, in 2019, became the longest-running, scripted, medical drama ever, overtaking *ER*. The series reaches more than 230 territories and is dubbed in more than 65 languages. While ratings have declined over its run, they're nowhere near critical condition: *Grey's* remained even recently ABC's best-rated series "in the demo." So, it's a "phenomenon," "juggernaut," "game-changer"—pick your word or phrase, no one's going to argue. But why? Rhimes tapped into something deep when she introduced the world to the surgical interns of Seattle Grace Hospital (now Grey-Sloan Memorial Hospital after multiple name changes), led by Meredith Grey (Ellen Pompeo).

The nation was torn between McDreamy and McSteamy.

While the series featured the intense medical procedures and novel cases viewers of this genre demand, the writers were more interested in the personal lives of the residents, conveyed with rare empathy, humor, and, when it came to love, *heat*. So it was that the nation was torn between McDreamy and McSteamy (nicknames for Patrick Dempsey's and Eric Dane's characters and love interests for Meredith), and the lexicon swallowed up new words like "vajayjay," first shrieked by Chandra Wilson's Dr. Bailey while giving birth. The show has never matched its early seasons' emotional highs—season 2's finale, in which Snow Patrol's "Chasing Cars" is used to devastating effect in one of the series's signature "songtages," might be its absolute peak—but compelling new characters, frequent twists, "must-watch" event episodes, and Pompeo's masterful work as Meredith, now chief of general surgery, have kept *Grey's* in top TV health.

Rake

ABC1 / 2010–2018

5 SEASONS / 40 EPISODES

 100% 84%

Australia's socially conscious crime drama *Rake* is so well written, acted, and executed that it's little wonder Hollywood tried to adapt it for an American audience. That Fox outing with Greg Kinnear was canceled after season 1, but thanks to streaming, you can now watch creators Peter Duncan, Richard Roxburgh, and Charles Waterstreet's original celebration of men behaving badly. Roxburgh stars as Cleaver Greene, a criminal defense attorney who's known for taking on unwinnable cases with the slimiest and guiltiest of clients—bigamists, terrorists, and cannibals, oh my!—and for self-destructive behavior. He fits the titular bill (a "rake" is colloquial slang for an immoral man), sleeping with any woman with a pulse and indulging in a cocaine and gambling addiction. At the end of the day, though, Cleaver is a man on the right side of justice, holding the powerful to account—he's just allowing himself some fun along the way.

Sherlock

▶ CERTIFIED FRESH STREAK

BBC ONE, PBS / 2010–2017

4 SEASONS / 13 EPISODES
(INCLUDING A CHRISTMAS SPECIAL)

 78% 83%

Benedict Cumberbatch and Martin Freeman starred in this modern reimagining of Sir Arthur Conan Doyle's legendary detective from *Doctor Who* creator Steven Moffat and writer Mark Gatiss. Before their turns as Doctor Strange and Bilbo Baggins, Cumberbatch and Freeman were perfectly cast as the original odd couple, Sherlock Holmes and Dr. John Watson, delighting critics and fans for three straight Certified Fresh seasons until a fourth—and *final*?—season that many felt had lost its way in the long hiatus between 2013's season 3 and season 4's 2017 airing. Cumberbatch's Holmes is written as a "high-functioning sociopath," stalking the streets of modern London, while Watson is a medical doctor and Afghanistan War vet. Each season played out in three movie-length episodes that are praised for their masterful storytelling and sharp dialogue. In the series, Holmes's wry observations and obsessive behavior bump up against Watson's righteous nurturer, resulting in congenial bickering that, under Gatiss and Moffat's care, feels thoroughly contemporary and classic at the same time.

Suits

▶ HIGHLY ADDICTIVE

USA NETWORK / 2011–2019

9 SEASONS / 134 EPISODES

 90% 86%

When *Suits* premiered in 2011, it was a change of pace from USA Network's "blue sky" shows—the quirky, breezy procedurals for which the network was known from the mid-2000s to the mid-2010s. While still determinedly shiny and full of cast members with impeccable bone structure, *Suits* took a slightly more serious tone, paving the way for the network's pivot to darker content like *Mr. Robot*. The series starred Gabriel Macht as high-powered lawyer Harvey Specter and Patrick J. Adams as his protégé Mike Ross, a talented slacker dropout who becomes Harvey's law associate despite never attending law school.

Naturally, there's only so long the duo can keep that secret, and the show suffers after the ruse is revealed. But the well-rounded cast—including Gina Torres and Rick Hoffman as fellow lawyers, and future Duchess of Sussex Meghan Markle as a paralegal turned lawyer and Mike's paramour—sells both the legal intrigue and the soapy personal plots equally well. (And, yes: They did wear a lot of really well-tailored suits.)

American Crime

▶ **PERFECT CERTIFIED FRESH STREAK**

ABC / 2015–2017
3 SEASONS / 29 EPISODES

 96% 88%

Following an Academy Award win for his *12 Years a Slave* screenplay, John Ridley set his eyes on television. What emerged was the anthology series *American Crime*, a probing examination of the broken US justice system. A critical darling—all seasons Certified Fresh, its final season at 100%—the show nevertheless struggled to find a sizable audience. With a stable roster of actors across its seasons, which included Regina King, Felicity Huffman, Timothy Hutton, and Richard Cabral, Ridley's drama was a rarity on 21st-century broadcast TV: Here was a raw, powerful limited series, focusing on the fraught intersections of race, class, religion, and sexuality in encounters that are often seen as much too cut-and-dried in the eyes of the law. In Ridley's hands, the death of a war vet, a same-sex sexual assault accusation, and the search for a missing son across the US-Mexico border each set up intentionally thorny season-long plots that were as gripping as they were eye-opening.

American Crime Story

FX / 2016–
2 SEASONS / 19 EPISODES

 93% 93%

The People v. O. J. Simpson, the first season of anthology series *American Crime Story*, may well be the crown jewel of the creative collaboration between FX and producers Ryan Murphy and Brad Falchuk. Based on that most infamous of '90s court cases, the 10-episode season was the TV event of spring 2016. With Cuba Gooding Jr. in the title role and Emmy-winning turns by Sarah Paulson, Sterling K. Brown, and Courtney B. Vance, the gripping courtroom drama brilliantly revisited, dissected, and reframed the football player's trial as the media spectacle it was. For its follow-up season, the show switched coasts, enlisting Edgar Ramirez, Ricky Martin, Penelope Cruz, and breakout *Glee* star Darren Criss for its Miami-set *The Assassination of Gianni Versace*, which poignantly explored how sex, power, and shame led to a string of murders, including that of the famed Italian designer. After an announced-then-canceled Hurricane Katrina-focused season, the series's third season—releasing after we go to press—sets its eyes on yet another seminal '90s scandal: Bill Clinton's impeachment trial.

Five Ways HBO Changed TV Forever

Launched in 1972, Home Box Office is one of TV's great evolutionary stories. (OK, we know, it's "not TV, it's HBO"). The cable channel launched with a focus on sports, events, and feature films, before morphing into a hugely dominant original programmer and eventually a formidable force in today's streaming wars. So, HBO has changed a lot over five decades, but perhaps not so much as it has changed the world around it. Here's how.

1 It Let Creatives Do Their Thing

The first-ever premium cable channel, HBO turned into a powerhouse only after it expanded its scope beyond licensing movie blockbusters and entered the scripted space. Throughout the '90s, beginning with 1992's critically acclaimed late-night parody *The Larry Sanders Show*, HBO gave creators the freedom, trust, and control to produce what would become its calling cards: *Sex and the City* (1998), *The Sopranos* (1999), *Six Feet Under* (2001), and *The Wire* (2002), turning it into a prestige TV destination.

2 It Made Sex, Violence, and Saying F—king Anything Totally OK

With no advertisers (or broadcast FCC regulations) to answer to, explicit content was A-OK. And the network made that abundantly clear from the beginning of *The Sopranos*: Tony's office was in the back of a strip club, and he and his mob pals said *f—k* a whopping 437 times in the first season alone. Don't worry, pearl-clutchers—it's nothing you couldn't see in an R-rated movie.

3 It Put the Miniseries Back in the Cool Zone

Before there were "limited series," there were miniseries, a genre overrun with BBC book adaptations and pulp TV weekend events à la *The Thorn Birds*. Popular in the '70s and '80s, they'd fallen out of favor by the '90s. But starting with 1998's Tom Hanks–produced *From the Earth to the Moon*, about the US-Soviet space race in the '60s and '70s, HBO helped turn them into a prestigious American art form. The network would go on to perfect its strategy with short-run series, starring big-name talent like the World War II epic *Band of Brothers* and the presidential drama *John Adams* (both also Hanks-produced), Al Pacino and Meryl Streep in the Broadway adaptation of *Angels in America*, and Kate Winslet in *Mildred Pierce*. (Love a miniseries? Check out our guide to the best on page 148.)

4 It Inspired Imitators, and Lots of 'Em

Shows like *The Sopranos* and *The Wire* helped define what we think of as "prestige TV"—which became the blueprint for other cable networks that wanted to create their own critically lauded programming. As HBO earned accolades and Emmys, the likes of Showtime, FX, and AMC were forced to change their approaches as well, and TV viewers were all the better for it. (HBO notoriously passed on *Sopranos* writer Matthew Weiner's *Mad Men* and Vince Gilligan's *Breaking Bad*, both of which went to AMC.)

5 It Changed the Emmys Game

HBO's dedication to original scripted television paid off. Until 1993, when it took home seven prizes, HBO had typically won a couple of Emmys a year. In 1999, *The Sopranos* led all shows with 11 major nominations and Edie Falco became the first star from a cable network to win a major acting award. In 2003, HBO started a 17-year streak as the most-nominated network. Today, HBO holds dozens of Emmy records: most wins for a drama series and most wins for a series in a single year (*Game of Thrones*), most wins for single episodes (*Boardwalk Empire*, *GoT*), and many, many more.

COMMERCIAL BREAK

▶Tony, Walt, Don,

AND THE ANTIHEROES WE LOVED AND HATED

To say that one single show changed TV forever would be an exaggeration . . . if *The Sopranos* and its violent-but-lovable centerpiece, Tony, never existed. The HBO series, which premiered in January 1999 and went out with a bang—OK, more like a confusing blip—in June 2007, revolutionized the medium and almost single-handedly set the template for the kinds of stories, and, specifically, the kinds of characters, that would define the next few decades of television and streaming.

Sopranos creator David Chase knew what novelists, comic-book writers, and great filmmakers had known since virtually the dawn of storytelling: Everyone loves a villain. Or at least, someone whose morals are muddy, who rarely does the right thing, and hardly bothers trying to. While TV had long been obsessed with people saving lives and upholding the law (see the previous chapter), Chase and his mob-boss creation showed us the rich rewards of time spent with those who were breaking it. Enter the antihero.

We write specifically about the phenomenon of *The Sopranos* in this chapter, of course—how it swallowed up so much space in the pop culture, broke Emmys and ratings records, and made HBO a powerhouse. But it's in reading about the *other* titles we feature that the show's impact is truly felt. In the wake of HBO's success with *The Sopranos*, cable stations sought to imitate its strategy, spending lavishly on ambitious cinematic productions, bringing in creatives who reveled in the freedom to cuss and spill blood far from the broadcast network censors, and fully embracing the antihero.

So it was that Don Draper began pitching and sleazing on Fifth Avenue for AMC and serial killer Dexter Morgan stalked Miami over on Showtime; later, biker Jax Teller would break bones and hearts on FX, and Walter White would make the turn from science teacher to drug kingpin in the show that some say rivals, and even surpasses, *The Sopranos—Breaking Bad*. Eventually, our antiheroes became more diverse, with Netflix's *Orange Is the New Black*, Starz's 50 Cent–produced *Power*, and Carmela Soprano herself, Edie Falco, chugging drugs and saving lives in *Nurse Jackie.*

The writers creating TV's early antihero stories may not have known it at the time, but they were also creating a golden age for the medium—what's now commonly referred to as Peak TV. The phrase was actually first uttered in 2015 by FX chairman John Landgraf to describe a problem: That year, nearly 400 original series went to air, and the worry was that it was simply overwhelming for audiences and unsustainable for networks. But the phrase has taken on different shades of meaning, becoming shorthand for, yes, the shear *number* of shows being produced, but also the incredible quality that writers, producers, and actors were bringing to them.

Deciding what to watch is not just paralyzing because there are so many series spread across so many channels and apps; it's paralyzing because so many of them are must-sees. You can blame Tony and Carmela for that, if you dare—their exploits in suburban New Jersey led us here. Or you can use this rogues' gallery of a chapter, and this book, to start your journey to the summit.

Oz

▶ GAME-CHANGER

HBO / 1997–2003
6 SEASONS / 56 EPISODES

🍅 **92%** 🍿 **98%**

It's hard to overstate how shocking HBO's very first one-hour drama truly was. When it premiered back in July 1997, arguably announcing the cable network as a bona fide prestige television production company, *Oz* was a jolt to the American television landscape. Set in the "Emerald City" cell block of the Oswald Maximum Security Penitentiary (ergo "Oz"), where a rehabilitation program hoped to better serve its inmates, the prison drama made full use of cable TV's ability to feature coarse language, depict violence, and freely showcase nudity, giving viewers a chance to enter a world they had never seen quite like this. Narrated by a Black wheelchair-bound prisoner (Harold Perrineau's Augustus Hill), the pilot episode alone featured a gay man with AIDS pleading for a mercy killing, a Latino inmate getting shanked, and an Italian prisoner burned alive.

> *Creator Tom Fontana's bleak drama spent its unrelenting six-season run mining the darkest depths of its characters.*

Brutal, at times to a fault, creator Tom Fontana's bleak drama spent its unrelenting six-season run mining the darkest depths of its characters, which included gangsters and murderers as well as white supremacists with a penchant for sexual sadism (you'll never look at J. K. Simmons the same way again). Setting a template for the kind of Dickensian—if, alas, almost all-male—ensemble-driven storytelling that would characterize future HBO staples like *The Sopranos* and *The Wire*, *Oz* did find room for tenderness laced with its violence, as in the homoerotic love story featuring Christopher Meloni's Chris Keller, while also pushing for moments of narrative ingenuity, as with its season 5 musical episode "Variety."

The Sopranos

▶ GAME-CHANGER

▶ HIGHLY ADDICTIVE

HBO / 1999–2007
6 SEASONS / 86 EPISODES

🍅 **92%** 🍿 **98%**

Would there be a golden age of television, let alone this book, without *The Sopranos*? That's a hard no, boss. The accolades David Chase's boundlessly creative show has garnered—the most groundbreaking series of all time, according to too many outlets to count—hold up remarkably well more than two decades since its premiere. As Tony, the New Jersey mobster coping with panic attacks and suburban ennui, James Gandolfini gives an unmatched small-screen performance: broodingly self-loathing one moment, charmingly ball-busting the next, with chilling reminders throughout that we're witnessing the ebbs and flows of a monster. Yet Tony's wife, Carmela (Edie Falco, also excellent), might just be the most fascinating character over the show's eight-year run, as the homemaker inches toward freedom (intellectual, marital, and otherwise) in a culture that won't have it. *The Sopranos*'s influence can't be overstated, whether it was by upending its mob-movie genre (as *Deadwood* would do with the Western), breathing new life into the antihero

(*Breaking Bad*), or commenting profoundly on our sociopolitical moment (*The Wire*) and the existentialism of American life (*Sopranos* writer and executive producer Matthew Weiner's *Mad Men*).

James Gandolfini gives an unmatched performance: broodingly self-loathing one moment, charmingly ball-busting the next.

The Shield

FX / 2002–2008
7 SEASONS / 88 EPISODES

 90% 🗑 **96%**

This graphic drama put a new spin on the TV cop narrative, revolving around Detective Vic Mackey (Michael Chiklis) and his Strike Team, a special group within the LAPD devoted to getting the worst criminals off the streets. And the Strike Team is particularly successful in committing crimes themselves—including murder—which Mackey and Company not only get away with, but gain from financially. Their coworkers aren't blind to their ways, and some also profit from the Strike Team, like Captain David Aceveda (Benito Martinez), whose political ambitions are bolstered by Mackey's stats. Chiklis won an Emmy for his performance as one of Peak TV's earliest antiheroes, a man who believed he was justified in seeking his ill-gotten gains because he had to support his autistic children. The show's 2005 Peabody Award recognized the excellence of the entire production, including cast members Walton Goggins and Glenn Close, creator Shawn Ryan, and writer and producer Kurt Sutter.

Deadwood

 ▶ PERFECT CERTIFIED FRESH STREAK

HBO / 2004–2006
3 SEASONS / 36 EPISODES (AND A MOVIE)

 92% 🗑 **96%**

There is an artistry to the way *Deadwood*'s saloon owner/pimp Al Swearengen (Ian McShane, impeccably intimidating) spits insults so profane we don't feel comfortable printing them here. Indeed, there's an artistry running through all of *Deadwood*, David Milch's bloody, bleak, and sometimes bitingly funny upending of the Western, to the extent that we wouldn't look down on anyone for rewinding a particularly literary exchange and putting on subtitles to catch the linguistic nuances. Aside from McShane, there's Timothy Olyphant as Seth Bullock, a law-abiding yin to Swearengen's criminal yang, leading a truly impressive stable of actors, many playing historical figures from the Deadwood camp of gold-rush-era South Dakota—Robin Weigert is a standout as hard-drinking Calamity Jane. The initial run of *Deadwood* was cut short, resulting in an unresolved season 3 finale in 2006. Luckily, 13 years later, the coda *Deadwood: The Movie* surfaced to satisfy fans by tying up some loose ends.

Dexter

SHOWTIME / 2006–2013
8 SEASONS / 96 EPISODES

 71% **80%**

This Showtime hit, based on Jeff Lindsay's *Darkly Dreaming Dexter* novels, is bumpy TV. There are dizzying, Certified Fresh highs, including a darkly comic first season that introduces lovable serial killer and Miami Metro Police blood-spatter analyst Dexter Morgan (Michael C. Hall). There are also crashing, Rotten-as-hell lows: tune out the *moment* Dex starts hooking up with adoptive sister Debra (Jennifer Carpenter) to save yourself a ton of head-scratching and the pain of the show's 33% Rotten final season, something to which fans hope a revival series—released after we go to press—is a corrective. But those highs feature some of the 2000s' best TV moments. The show's strongest seasons see Dex, who wrestles with his urge to kill by targeting evildoers, squaring off with compelling adversaries, none so frightening as season 4 big bad Arthur Mitchell (John Lithgow), jovial suburban dad by day, "Trinity Killer" by night. Through it all, Hall is superb: Awkward, charming, frightening, he keeps a tight grip on this ultimate antihero even as the show struggles to provide him with a believable path forward.

Mad Men

▶ GAME-CHANGER

▶ PERFECT CERTIFIED FRESH STREAK

▶ HIGHLY ADDICTIVE

AMC / 2007–2015
7 SEASONS / 92 EPISODES

🍅 94% 🗑 96%

It's hard to think back to a time when "Don Draper" wasn't synonymous with the very best that prestige TV had to offer. But when *Mad Men* premiered in 2007, it was a gamble plenty of cable networks had passed on. Created by *The Sopranos* writer and executive producer Matthew Weiner, the period drama about Madison Avenue advertising execs in the 1960s seemed like a hard sell: It had no household names, its scripts were unabashedly literary, and its exacting visual style made it feel like a painstakingly re-created historical diorama, come to life. Finding a home on AMC, a network that hadn't produced original drama programming before, *Mad Men* quickly seduced anyone who watched its exquisite first season—and every one of the near-perfect six that followed. Here was a timely meditation on a history-changing decade in the trappings of a workplace melodrama. Jon Hamm's charming Don Draper may well have been the gravitational force of Weiner's drama, but as the show moved past his murky backstory plot and allowed characters like Elisabeth Moss's Peggy Olson to come into their own, *Mad Men* established itself as an ensemble piece that captured a seismic generational shift one Kodak (or Heineken, or Lucky Strike) ad campaign at a time. Delivering instantly classic episodes like "The Suitcase," "The Other Woman," and "Guy Walks into an Advertising Agency" amid intricately plotted season-long story lines, the show's critical reception was rapturous. Sixteen Emmy awards later—four in the Outstanding Drama Series category alone—there's no way to talk about television in the 21st century without bringing up not just Don and Peggy but Joan, Roger, and the rest of the Sterling Cooper crowd.

Breaking Bad

▶ GAME-CHANGER

▶ PERFECT CERTIFIED FRESH STREAK

▶ HIGHLY ADDICTIVE

AMC / 2008–2013
5 SEASONS / 62 EPISODES

🍅 96% 🗑 98%

The era of the antihero was well underway when Vince Gilligan first conjured up *Breaking Bad* in the mid-2000s, but he wanted to approach his central character from a fresh angle. Most other series introduced their so-called "villain protagonists" as fully formed sociopaths to some extent; Gilligan was more interested in the journey that might compel an otherwise normal person to abandon their morals. He came up with Walter White, an unassuming high school chemistry teacher who, upon learning that he has terminal cancer, decides to build a massive nest egg for his family by cooking and selling meth. It was a risky proposition to ask viewers first to sympathize with Walter, then gradually to dislike him—and even to fear him—as he descended deeper into the mindset of a ruthless drug kingpin.

Gilligan was more interested in the journey that might compel an otherwise normal person to abandon their morals.

Luckily, Gilligan knew a guy who would perfectly capture Walter's dual nature, and he called on Bryan Cranston, who had made a name for himself as the goofy dad on *Malcolm in the Middle*. Cranston dug deep and made Walter one of the most compelling, magnetic personalities on television, while Gilligan gracefully plotted Walter's rise and fall with meticulous attention to detail and a flair for creative storytelling. *Breaking Bad* wasn't a runaway hit at first, but once the first three seasons were made available on Netflix and viewers were able to mainline it, the floodgates flew open; in its fifth season, *Breaking Bad* almost tripled its viewership, and more than 10 million tuned in to the series finale. In his quest to deconstruct the TV antihero, Gilligan had not only given us one of television's finest dramas and most memorable characters, but he also helped usher in the era of the binge watch and proved that if you've got something good, fans will find it.

Sons of Anarchy

▶ **PERFECT CERTIFIED FRESH STREAK**

FX / 2008–2014
7 SEASONS / 92 EPISODES

 87% 🗑 80%

This ultra-macho bit of Shakespeare on wheels was, for much of its run, the biggest thing to happen to the cable network FX. And it's easy to see why the masses got so revved up for the goings-on of the Sons of Anarchy Motorcycle Club, Redwood Original (or SAMCRO for short). Masterfully tracking the interconnected lives of the members of a Hell's Angels–style motorbike club in California's Central Valley, *Anarchy*—created by Kurt Sutter, who wrote on *The Shield* and appears in the series as an imprisoned SAMCRO elder—has everything: rival gangs, white supremacists, crooked cops, shocking deaths aplenty, and even a baby kidnapping. Most crucially, though, it has Jackson "Jax" Teller (Charlie Hunnam), his mom Gemma (Katey Sagal), and Clay (Ron Perlman), her new husband, his new stepdad, and the club's Machiavellian president. Their grabs at power and betrayals are complicated brilliantly by their family ties, which center a series that could have easily swerved off-road. As Jax, who is haunted Hamlet-like by letters from his late father and former club head, Hunnam gave us TV's definitive damaged bad boy on the brink of redemption.

Their grabs at power and betrayals are complicated brilliantly by their family ties, which center a series that could have easily swerved off-road.

The Americans

FX / 2013–2018
6 SEASONS / 75 EPISODES

 96% **93%**

CRITICS CONSENSUS ▶ *The Americans* is a spy thriller of the highest order, with evocative period touches and strong chemistry between its leads. (Season 1)

WHAT IT'S ABOUT ▶ It's Cold War America, and Philip and Elizabeth Jennings (Matthew Rhys and Keri Russell) are the Reagan-era ideal: parents to two plucky kids, owners of a successful small business, friendly casserole-toting neighbors. They also happen to be Soviet KGB officers planted here years ago to ferret out government secrets, send them back to Moscow, and brutally execute anyone who tries to get in their way.

For a chunk of the 2010s, it was something of a badge of honor to be a fan of Joe Weisberg's once criminally under-seen and under-awarded spy thriller, *The Americans*—and to send out a flurry of angry tweets when the show was inevitably ignored by the Emmys and Globes. You were part of a small group of in-the-know fans who saw Weisberg's mix of sophisticated spy thriller and pointed—sometimes devastating—family drama for what it was: potentially the very peak of Peak TV.

The series's espionage-focused arcs are as gripping as anything you'll see in the spy TV genre. Weisberg focuses on the "craft" of spycraft, rather than too many Jack Bauer–style set pieces—*The Americans* frequently mines tension out of the placement of listening devices, and the series revels in the complications of becoming too involved with a human "mark." But there is fun to be had, too. On a few thrilling occasions, the show jolts us with a moment of brutal action, and the costume department clearly delighted in the task of conjuring up the roster of '80s disguises. (The couple's wigs would develop their own fan base.)

But the genius of *The Americans* is the core relationship between Philip and Elizabeth, whose arranged marriage has evolved from unchosen duty to something loving and messy and fraught and somehow still solid—a very American kind of marriage. As we watch them navigate business troubles, nosy neighbors, and hormonal teens, and struggle with their changing loyalties, the show becomes deeply involving, and Rhys and Russell—who became a real-life couple during the making of the show—are fully convincing.

The other genius of the show is in its supporting cast: Noah Emmerich as Stan, an FBI agent and the Jenningses' neighbor; Costa Ronin as Oleg, a Russian agent; and especially Holly Taylor as daughter Paige, whose journey from young evangelical to potential operative drives the show's later seasons. Look out, too, for Alison Wright as gullible secretary Martha, who falls for one of Peter's aliases, "Clark," and *Ozark* standout Julia Garner as the teenage daughter of a CIA agent who becomes infatuated with the worldly "James." Margo Martindale, as the Jenningses' KGB handler Claudia, rightfully won two Emmys for Outstanding Guest Actress for the series.

The Emmys finally did catch on to *The Americans* overall, with the show earning nominations for Best Drama for its fourth and sixth seasons, and Russell and Rhys earning acting nods every year for the final three seasons. (Rhys won in the show's final year and would be cast in HBO's splashy *Perry Mason* reboot.) By the time it wrapped, with one of the most heartbreaking, yet satisfying, season finales of the decade, *The Americans* was no longer a secret; those outside the fandom finally realized that, much like the Jenningses themselves, something truly remarkable had been hiding there in plain sight—on FX—for years.

BEST EPISODE ▶ Season 6, Episode 10—"Start." The rare series finale that manages to surprise, thrill, and devastate—and never feel too artificially "neat." You'll never listen to U2 the same way again.

CHARACTER WE LOVE ▶ Nina Krilova (Annet Mahendru), the young KGB officer, stationed in DC, whose heart and loyalties are tested when FBI agent Stan Beeman (Emmerich) enters her life. In a series that can be cold, Krilova brings warmth and heart.

DEEP ▼
▼ DIVE

Jack Bauer

24

FOX / 2001–2014

9 SEASONS / 204 EPISODES (PLUS 1 TV FILM)

 87% 🍿 85%

Where you stand on the heroism of Counter Terrorist Unit (CTU) agent Jack Bauer will largely depend on where you stand on coercive interrogation tactics. (Hint: If you feel we should have just come out and said *torture*, you're probably not Team Jack.) Played by Kiefer Sutherland—who would pick up an Emmy, a Golden Globe, and two SAG awards for his efforts—Bauer took an anything-to-get-the-job-done approach to thwarting the terrorist plots that shaped each season of this real-time thriller in which every episode was one hour of a full day. The urgency of the threats he faced—assassination attempts on a presidential candidate, a planned nuclear attack on LA—left little time to talk about the ethics of staging, say, the fake execution of a suspect's family in order to get crucial info. But in *our* world, there was plenty of time to dissect Bauer's methodologies, and as the War on Terror raged, *24* and Bauer, in particular, became a focal point for debates about the moral cost of modern war and how that should and shouldn't be depicted in popular entertainment.

Hero or Antihero? We'll leave this one to *24* fan Stephen King, who in a 2007 piece for *Entertainment Weekly* wrote: "There's also a queasily gleeful subtext to *24* that suggests, 'If things are this bad, why, I guess we can torture *anybody we want!*' . . . Yet Jack Bauer's face—increasingly lined, increasingly haggard—suggests that extreme measures eventually catch up with the human soul."

HERO or ANTIHERO ?

Annalise Keating

HOW TO GET AWAY WITH MURDER

ABC / 2015–2020

6 SEASONS / 90 EPISODES

 88% 🍿 85%

Audiences may not have *liked* Annalise Keating, the tough-minded, manipulative, and likely alcoholic Philly law professor who—over the course of six corpse-heavy seasons of this Shonda Rhimes-produced favorite—lies and schemes and kills to cover her ass and the asses of some of her top students. But audiences did fall in love with her. (Need evidence? The first season of *Murder* broke DVR playback records.) Part of that love came down to the actress who gave us those fabulously derisive Annalise Keating stares: Viola Davis became the first Black woman to win the Primetime Emmy for Outstanding Lead Actress in a Drama for a

Carrie Mathison

HOMELAND

SHOWTIME / 2011–2020

8 SEASONS / 96 EPISODES

 85% 🍿 85%

THE JURY'S STILL OUT ON THESE COULD-BE HEROES WITH A DARK SIDE.

If you watched the first zeitgeist-capturing season of *Homeland*—an adaptation of the Israeli series *Prisoner of War*—and didn't stick around after that, you might want to pick it back up: It stays good, twisted, and finishes strong. (The series's final season is Certified Fresh at 85%.) Its wide-eyed protagonist, on the other hand, *well*, she certainly stays twisted. CIA operations officer Carrie Mathison (Claire Danes) gave us hints of how far she was willing to go in season 1, in which she suspects a Marine rescued from capture in Iraq (Damian Lewis) has been turned and is plotting an attack in the United States, and alternately spies on and seduces him to get to the bottom of things. In the following seasons, she would help a wanted man escape the country and coolly order a bombing raid on a wedding, killing dozens of civilians. All as she continues her battle with bipolar disorder and struggles with alcohol. It makes for riveting antihero-era TV—and Danes's Emmy-winning turn is certainly intense—but as *Homeland* went on, many began to wonder if the character we're told over and over again is "brilliant" is actually good at her job at all. Others asked: Is Carrie just another reinforcement of the tired TV trope that women in the workplace are hysterical loose cannons?

Hero or Antihero? A nervy, hard-to-pin down, sometimes-brilliant, sometimes-terrible character trying to do the right thing and blowing up her world—and parts of ours—in the process? Merriam-Webster, you know what to do with Carrie's photo.

performance we rarely saw on TV—a professional woman of color as charismatic, damaged, sexual, and multidimensional as Don Draper, Walter White, Tony Soprano, or any other tortured and celebrated Peak TV white guy. Part of it was also that, while Keating could be a monster, she mostly used her claws to protect the folks around her that she loved. (Not that she'd ever tell them that.)

Hero or Antihero? A hero, with a little shady history. And whenever she gets to steam it up with lover Nate—a ridiculously well-sculpted Billy Brown—she's frankly a *queen*.

Nurse Jackie

SHOWTIME / 2009–2015

7 SEASONS / 80 EPISODES

  81% **86%**

When Edie Falco won the Emmy for Outstanding Actress in a Comedy for the first season of *Nurse Jackie,* she was shocked: "I'm not funny." Her disbelief was understandable. For all intents and purposes, her Jackie Peyton, an ER nurse with a substance abuse problem, was an antiheroine whose self-destructive behavior would be right at home in any gritty cable drama. Surrounded by an odd group of hilarious supporting characters at a fictional New York City hospital (including Merritt Wever's bubbly student nurse and Anna Deavere Smith's no-nonsense hospital administrator), Falco's Jackie emerged as the dramatic cornerstone of an otherwise sunny comedy. Yes, this sometimes uneven—especially in its later seasons—half-hour show let its female protagonist be a screw-up whose affairs and work-related recklessness had very real consequences, but it also found the light amid so much dark material.

House of Cards

▶ CERTIFIED FRESH STREAK

NETFLIX / 2013–2018

6 SEASONS / 73 EPISODES

 77% **76%**

To include or not to include? That was the question we faced when it came to this David Fincher–produced political thriller that put Netflix on the map as an original programming force. The seven-time Emmy winner, adapted by creator Beau Willimon from a BBC series of the same name, is an undeniably propulsive and knotty binge, tracking the rises, falls, and maneuvers of ruthless congressman—and sometimes murderer—Frank Underwood (Kevin Spacey) and his ambitious wife Claire (a formidable Robin Wright). (Watching its flawless first season, in particular, you can see why Netflix outbid HBO for the DC-based series, ordering up 26 episodes in 2011 for a cool $100 million.) And its influence has been mighty: Following muted response to *Lillyhammer* in 2012, this was Netflix's first hit and the show that proved a full-season drop was the way of the future. But accusations of sexual assault against Spacey that came to light toward the show's end—resulting in the actor's removal from the series and a final season that focused entirely on Claire—make *House of Cards* an uncomfortable watch, especially after Spacey released a video defense in the style of Underwood's fourth wall–breaking monologues. Still, love it or hate it—or just feel icky about it—few shows have had more impact on TV as we know it, and watch it, today.

Hannibal

▶ PERFECT CERTIFIED FRESH STREAK

NBC / 2013–2015

3 SEASONS / 39 EPISODES

 92% **94%**

The greatest trick *Pushing Daisies* creator Bryan Fuller ever pulled off was summoning psychiatrist Dr. Hannibal Lecter from the pages of Thomas Harris's novels to the small screen for this psychedelic crime drama about an FBI profiler's eerie partnership with the serial killer. Danish superstar Mads Mikkelsen portrays elegant Hannibal the Cannibal with debonair verve; Hugh Dancy stars as FBI consultant Will Graham, who unwittingly invites his prey to join the chase when he starts seeing Dr. Lecter for work-related psychological issues; and Laurence Fishburne plays Will's boss, Jack Crawford, the head of the FBI's Behavioral Sciences Unit who pushes Will into assignments that test his sanity. The horror series introduces other characters that fans of Harris's works or their feature film adaptations—*Manhunter*, *Silence of the Lambs*, *Hannibal*, *Red Dragon*—will be very familiar with, including "Tooth Fairy" killer Francis Dolarhyde (Richard Armitage), Rinaldo Pazzi (Fortunato Cerlino), Freddie Lounds (Lara Jean Chorostecki), Frederick Chilton (Raúl Esparza), and Mason Verger (played by Michael Pitt in season 2 and Joe Anderson in season 3). The series specialized in beautifully rendered murder, as in the season 2 episode "Futamono," in which a city councilor, responsible for the destruction of a rare songbird's natural habitat, is found grafted onto a tree with his chest cavity filled with poisonous flowers. But perhaps the most mesmerizing aspect of the series is the dance between Dr. Lecter and his pursuers; Mikkelsen performs a gory waltz with killer moves.

Orange Is the New Black

▶ GAME-CHANGER

▶ PERFECT CERTIFIED FRESH STREAK

NETFLIX / 2013–2019
7 SEASONS / 91 EPISODES

🍅 90% 🍿 82%

Like *House of Cards*, *OITNB*, as it is affectionately abbreviated, was an early factor in establishing Netflix as a player on the originals front. From *Weeds* creator Jenji Kohan and based on Piper Kerman's memoir of the same name, the show initially centered around a white woman (Taylor Schilling) sentenced to 15 months in Litchfield Penitentiary after being convicted of transporting a suitcase full of drug money for her smuggler girlfriend (Laura Prepon). By its seventh and final season, the series centered on Black and Brown women (led by Uzo Aduba, Danielle Brooks, Selenis Leyva, and Dascha Polanco), and was widely applauded for its entertaining and frank approach to addressing the ills of the prison-industrial complex and for humanizing its inmates. The show was also a jumping-off point for trans icon Laverne Cox who, for her role as inmate Sophia Burset, became the first known trans person to be nominated for a Primetime Emmy in any acting category.

Peaky Blinders

BBC, NETFLIX / 2013–
5 SEASONS / 30 EPISODES

🍅 93% 🍿 94%

When creator Stephen Knight's cinematic crime drama, based on a true-life band of razor-wielding army vets turned gangsters, debuted on the BBC in the fall of 2013, it was only a modest hit—mostly discussed for the muddled Romani accents that stars Cillian Murphy, Joe Cole, and the late Helen McCrory sported. When Netflix scooped it up, it would become one of the streaming service's most popular shows. (So popular it inspired its own fan festival in Birmingham, where it is set.) The show is a slow burn, and while the pilot and first season have noteworthy moments, *Blinders* takes off in season 3 and beyond when gang leader Thomas Shelby (Murphy) cements his rule as the head of the series's racketeering empire. (The *peaky* of the title comes courtesy of the razors the men have sewn into their flat caps—just a hint of the show's fashionably violent aesthetic.) *Blinders* plays like *The Sopranos* set in 1919: It's got the twisted story-telling, powerhouse performances, and gruesome violence, but at its heart is a damaged family whose members care about one another deeply.

Power

STARZ / 2014–2020
6 SEASONS / 63 EPISODES

 81%   82%

Just when he thought he was out, they pull him back in. That paraphrase of Michael Corleone's famous lament from *The Godfather Part III* is an apt one, not just because *Power* is about a New York mob family (a predominantly Black one in this instance), but also because, like Al Pacino's iconic movie figure, *Power*'s James "Ghost" St. Patrick (Omari Hardwick) is a brilliant businessman who, having accumulated his wealth via illegal activities, now wants to leave crime behind to be a nightclub mogul and forge a political career. Unlike Michael, Ghost doesn't have the benefit of a father who laid down an upwardly mobile path for him, and there are myriad complications on his way to legitimacy—many that come courtesy of those closest to him.

Six seasons of twist-filled developments and seriously scorching love scenes

---

James's wife Tasha (Naturi Naughton) and his life-long best friend and business partner Tommy (Joseph Sikora) are concerned about what will happen to them if Ghost ghosts the past, while a deep dive back into a relationship from high school spells even more trouble. Those complications delivered six seasons of twist-filled developments, seriously scorching love scenes, and a cliff-hanger that, once revealed in the series finale, sets up the first of four planned *Power* spin-offs. Among those are standout series revolving around Tommy's post-*Power* life, and Michael Rainey Jr. as Ghost and Tasha's son Tariq. These spin-offs all but ensure that viewers will continue to be pulled back in to this 50 Cent–produced Starz franchise.

Better Call Saul

▶ PERFECT CERTIFIED FRESH STREAK
▶ HIGHLY ADDICTIVE

AMC / 2015–2021
6 SEASONS / 63 EPISODES

 97%   96%

Better Call Saul had impossibly big shoes to fill when it premiered less than two years after the finale of the series that spawned it, *Breaking Bad* (considered the "Best TV Show Ever" by many). Thankfully, the creative team that gifted us with the latter was the same that came up with *Saul*, both a spin-off and a prequel that explores how Bob Odenkirk's fast-talking attorney Jimmy McGill became Saul Goodman, the slippery shyster we know and love. *Saul* is less pulpy and a slower burn, and it's anchored by career-best work from Odenkirk, not to mention a stellar supporting cast of familiar faces (Jonathan Banks as Mike Ehrmantraut, Giancarlo Esposito as Gus Fring) and brilliant new characters (Michael McKean as Jimmy's antagonistic older brother Chuck and Rhea Seehorn as Jimmy's girlfriend Kim Wexler, the voice of reason in his life). Somehow, series creator Vince Gilligan and writer-producer Peter Gould managed to take a minor source of comic relief from *Breaking Bad* and turn him into a tragic hero whose backstory rivals—and even surpasses, some would say—the saga of Walter White.

Ozark

▶ HIGHLY ADDICTIVE

NETFLIX / 2017–2021
4 SEASONS / 44 EPISODES

🫐 **81%** 🍿 **89%**

Today, *Ozark* is one of Netflix's landmark series, but the jury was out when the show (which is executive-produced—and regularly directed—by its star, Jason Bateman) first arrived. In the first season, Bateman's money-laundering Marty Byrde, in over his head with a Mexican cartel, moves his family from the suburbs of Chicago to the Missouri backwaters to start a new enterprise that he promises his crime bosses will more than make up for recent mistakes. For some, the premise was too close to nice-guy-goes-bad drama *Breaking Bad*, and while *Ozark* had promising elements—a stylishly drab aesthetic and a deft hand with sudden brutality—*Breaking* was quite the shadow to stand in. But by season 3, *Ozark* had stepped into its own light, mostly by homing in on a couple of major aces in its sleeve: Julia Garner's Ruth, the local girl with the foul mouth and sharp brain, and Laura Linney's Wendy Byrde, together two of our era's most intricately painted antiheroines. Linney's journey from tacit accomplice to ruthless expansionist is thrilling and, in her relationship with her brother Ben (Tom Pelphrey), leads to some of the most heartbreaking TV of the decade.

Barry

HBO / 2018–
2 SEASONS / 16 EPISODES

🫐 **99%** 🍿 **91%**

SNL alum Bill Hader loves film—and we're talkin' the good stuff. You can catch him discussing Essentials on TCM, spoofing 'em in *Documentary Now!*, and listing 'em (in lieu of an interview) in *Poking a Dead Frog*, a collection of conversations with comedy writers. So it's not shocking that his HBO vehicle—which he co-created, stars in, and writes and directs for—owes more than a bit to the best of the silver screen, and in particular the Coen brothers.

NoHo Hank, a cheerful and chatty Chechen mafioso, steals the show.

In *Barry*, flashes of violence and a propulsive cat-and-mouse game balance out the comedy as an aspiring actor (Hader) hides his reluctant profession as an assassin. On-screen, Hader shows the most range he has to date as Barry—his meek personality belying an anger that can snap, racking up the series's body count—but it's Anthony Carrigan as NoHo Hank, a ridiculously cheerful and chatty Chechen mafioso, who steals the show episode after episode.

Know Your
Very Special Episodes

Every now and then your favorite show will do something different: A character will burst out in song ("WTF?"), or flub a line ("Wait, is this live?"), or appear in an entirely different show altogether ("Wait, wasn't she in…"). Want to know what to call it when it happens and where it all started? We've got you with this guide to episodes that break the mold.

The Crossover Episode

Characters popping up on other series on the same network is a common way to get viewers to follow their favorites to new series or to tune in for a full night of programming. The CW's Arrowverse, aka the DC Comics superhero universe created by Greg Berlanti, evolved the concept with a massive multi-episode event featuring characters from six series and a dozen more DC properties that aired in 2019.

First-Ever Crossover Ep: "Lucy and Superman"—season 6, episode 13, *I Love Lucy.* The classic sitcom (and later *The Lucy-Desi Comedy Hour*) actually staged frequent crossovers between several shows—*The Adventures of Superman, Private Secretary, The Danny Thomas Show*—starting with a meta-appearance by George Reeves as Superman in this 1957 episode.

Best Crossover Ep: "Something Good Coming, Part 2"—season 2, episode 22, *Cougar Town.* Sure, it's great when related shows team up for a major story line that runs through both series. But the meta-version is even better: After *Community*'s Abed (Danny Pudi) told a story about being an extra on his favorite show, *Cougar Town*, the producers made it happen, leading to Pudi (as Abed) appearing as an extra in an actual episode of *Cougar Town*.

The Live Episode

All television was once live, but since the '70s live content has been mostly restricted to news, sports, and events. In the '90s, live episodes of dramas and comedies began to pop up as ratings stunts, with the cast performing versions for American audiences on the East Coast and West Coast.

First-Ever Live Ep: **"The Hand That Rocs the Cradle"—season 1, episode 18, *Roc*.** The Fox sitcom, which starred Charles S. Dutton as the titular Baltimore garbage collector, aired a live episode in 1992 that was so successful the network then aired the entire second season live.

Best Live Ep: **"Live Show"—season 4, episode 4, *30 Rock*.** Though the live episode is not relegated to sitcoms, it's a better showcase for the inevitable gaffes that come with the medium. Case in point: This first live episode of *SNL* vet Tina Fey's late-night spoof, which featured cameos from Matt Damon and Julia Louis-Dreyfus.

The Actual "Very Special Episode"

Originally used in advertisements to alert viewers that the episode being promoted would tackle a tough, controversial, or sensitive issue like drugs, racism, sexism, or abuse, the term soon became a way to refer to any episodes that touch on those topics.

First-Ever VSE: **"Maude's Dilemma"—season 1, episodes 9 and 10, *Maude*.** All of Norman Lear's '70s sitcoms tackled social issues head-on, but the most standout early example came with this two-part episode that saw Maude (Bea Arthur), a 47-year-old grandmother, discover that she was pregnant and ultimately decide to have an abortion.

Best VSE: **"Papa's Got a Brand New Excuse"—season 4, episode 24, *The Fresh Prince of Bel-Air*.** While plenty of VSEs in the '80s and '90s could occasionally veer silly (see: Jessie Spano's caffeine pill freakout on *Saved by the Bell*), the reunion between Will (Will Smith) and his absentee dad (Ben Vereen) resulted in a dialogue breaking down Will's abandonment issues and leading him to realize that Uncle Phil is his true father figure.

COMMERCIAL BREAK

The Bottle Episode

Originally developed as a cost-cutting measure to stretch a series's budget further over the course of a season, a bottle episode typically uses just one or two sets and a handful of actors to tell a self-contained story.

First-Ever Bottle Ep: "Controlled Experiment"—season 1, episode 16, *The Outer Limits*. While many attribute the phrase to *Star Trek* episodes that would contain all the action to the spaceship ("Ship in a bottle," get it?), others credit sci-fi anthology creator Leslie Stevens for figuring out a way to shoot an entire episode—about aliens studying a murder on Earth by playing and replaying the incident—in less than five days, like pulling a genie out of a bottle.

Best Bottle Ep: "The Suitcase"—season 4, episode 7, *Mad Men*. Ad man Don Draper and his protégé Peggy Olson hash out a pitch for Samsonite—and reveal their darkest truths to each other—at a diner in one of the most resonant hours of a series that was never lacking for budget or pathos.

The Backdoor Pilot Episode

Oftentimes, when a network wants to introduce a spin-off but isn't quite ready to commit, executives will commission one episode of an existing show to focus on the new characters and serve as proof of concept for the new series.

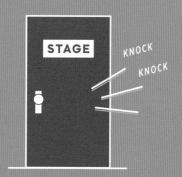

First-Ever Backdoor Pilot: "Love and the Television Set"—season 3, episode 22, *Love, American Style*. Not as jarring as an episode of a serialized show that abruptly focuses on a new set of characters, this episode of the early-'70s comedy anthology introduced the premise for what would become *Happy Days*.

Best Backdoor Pilot: "Assignment: Earth"—season 2, episode 26, *Star Trek*. The USS *Enterprise* crew travels back in time to 1968 Earth, where they meet a mysterious agent claiming to have been sent by otherworldly beings to save the planet—the setup for an "Assignment: Earth" TV series that was ultimately never made.

The Clip Show

Clip shows would introduce a conceit allowing characters to fondly recall past events—aka previous funny or memorable scenes—for the duration of the episode.

First-Ever Clip Show Ep: Clip shows have been around since radio serial days, so it was a common occurrence as television grew into a popular medium. An early example is the 1936 Republic Movie serial ***Robinson Crusoe of Clipper Island***, which added two extra installments using previously shot footage to recoup money lost from production delays.

Best Clip Show Ep: *"The Simpsons* 138th Episode Spectacular"—season 7, episode 10, *The Simpsons*. The first *Simpsons* clip show, in season 4, was practically apologetic, titled "So It's Come to This: *A Simpsons* Clip Show." But in season 7 the writers discovered a way to make it feel fresh: by airing deleted scenes, clips from *The Tracey Ullman Show*, and an alternate ending to a popular story line that viewers hadn't seen before.

The Musical Episode

Typically introduced well into a show's run when producers are looking to shake things up, musical episodes often take advantage of its cast's hidden talents.

First-Ever Musical Ep: "Lucy Goes to Scotland"—season 5, episode 17, *I Love Lucy*. The classic sitcom often had musical elements—Ricky was a singer and bandleader, after all—but this 1957 episode featured Lucy dreaming a full *Brigadoon*-inspired musical about visiting her family's ancestral village in medieval Scotland.

Best Musical Ep: "Once More, with Feeling"—season 6, episode 7, *Buffy the Vampire Slayer*. The episode that ushered the musical episode into the modern TV era, this season 6 event became such a cult classic that movie theaters held sing-along screenings before legal issues put an end to the episode's public showings.

COMMERCIAL BREAK

The ►Biggest LOLs

GAME-CHANGING SITCOMS AND THE KINGS AND QUEENS OF CRINGE

How do you capture the best and most influential TV comedy of recent times in one single chapter? By making that chapter absolutely huge. Which is only appropriate for a genre that has been the most popular among TV viewers since the medium's earliest days. Back then, families would gather to laugh along with variety shows like *Texaco Star Theater*, which had originated on radio and dominated ratings in the early 1950s, or America's first TV sitcom, *Mary Kay and Johnny*, about a New York City husband and wife played by real-life spouses Mary Kay and Johnny Stearns.

Comedy has been a staple in our TV-watching diets for 70-plus years, but it's never been a singular thing—and it's never been static. Under the umbrella of "TV Made to Make You Laugh," you'll find variety and sitcoms, but also sketch shows, late-night and news commentary, stand-up, game shows, category-defying "dramedies," and, in the last few decades, a can't-look-away brand of "cringe comedy" that revels in the painful hilarity of social awkwardness. And each is constantly evolving with new forms, sensibilities, and talent.

Nearly all those subgenres are present and accounted for in these pages, but two dominate, just as they do on networks, cable, and streaming: the sitcom and the cringe.

In some ways, the situation comedy of 2021 looks very similar to the situation comedy of 1951. Likable families solving weekly problems? Check. Quirky neighbors and work colleagues? Check. *Really* big couches? Check again! In other ways, 2021 sitcoms can be unrecognizable from those broadcast seventy years ago. There have been countless experiments with form—*Scrubs*'s embrace of the cutaway gag, *The Office*'s popularization of the mockumentary. And the families and workplaces at the center of our sitcoms have changed, too. The socially conscious creations of Norman Lear, outlined in chapter 1, paved the way for the families you meet in these pages: the Johnsons in *black-ish*, the Huangs of *Fresh Off the Boat*, and the Alvarezes of *One Day at a Time*—hilarious and binge-worthy shows featuring and run by Black, Asian, and Hispanic Americans, respectively.

As the sitcom evolved, the cringe comedy emerged, ushered in by comedians like Garry Shandling (*The Larry Sanders Show*), Jerry Seinfeld, and Ricky Gervais (*The Office* UK), before being perfected by Larry David (*Curb Your Enthusiasm*), and taken in fascinating directions by the likes of Phoebe Waller-Bridge (*Fleabag*). Perhaps two of the *most* fascinating variations on the genre are Issa Rae's *Insecure* and Donald Glover's *Atlanta*, both profiled in depth in this chapter and both of which blur the lines between cringey laughs, impactful drama, searing social commentary, and joyous celebration of the communities and cultures they feature.

Are they strictly "cringe comedies"? Or even *pure* comedies? It's hard to say, as it is with a number of the titles in this section. Don't think about it too hard, though: They *will* make you laugh.

Murphy Brown

CBS / 1988–1998, 2018
11 SEASONS / 260 EPISODES

Created by Diane English, this sitcom about sharp-tongued female investigative journalist Murphy Brown (Candice Bergen) ruffled plenty of feathers during its initial decade-long run, including then–Vice President Dan Quayle's. The VP called the working single mother Bergen portrayed a scourge on traditional family values, who was "mocking the importance of fathers." Quayle's speech became a plot point on the series, which would also work in real-life references to Donald Trump's presidency when it was revived 20 years after its cancellation for a single season on CBS. The sitcom also focused on Murphy's colleagues at the fictional newsmagazine *FYI* (and later, in the revival, cable news show *Murphy in the Morning*), featured a running gag about the character's revolving door of secretaries, and ultimately provided a role model for any career-focused women wondering if it really was possible to have it all.

Seinfeld

▶ GAME-CHANGER

▶ HIGHLY ADDICTIVE

NBC / 1989–1998
9 SEASONS / 180 EPISODES

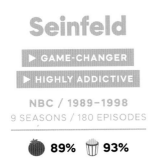 89% 🗑 93%

Is there anything left to say about the show about nothing? Larry David and Jerry Seinfeld's sitcom is that rarest of TV gems: something that seemingly everyone watched—it reached the number 1 spot in the Nielsen ratings for two of its seasons and 1998's final ep is the fourth most-watched finale ever—with Big TV Moments that somehow still managed to push the envelope and not water things down for the masses. The scripts shimmer with wit and originality, chronicling Jerry (Seinfeld playing a fictionalized version of himself) and his trio of friends—the bestie (Jason Alexander), the ex (Julia Louis-Dreyfus, playing, in retrospect, arguably the greatest character on the show), the "hipster doofus" of a neighbor (Michael Richards)—and changing the genre in the '90s and yada, yada, yada…

Saturday Night Live

NBC / 1975–
46 SEASONS / 900+ EPISODES

It's been said that if you were at a party in the mid-'70s, people would turn off the record player and huddle around the TV when *SNL* was on to witness what madness the late-night sketch and variety show had up its sleeves. That's probably not the case anymore, of course—too much has happened to comedy over the last 45-plus years—but *Saturday Night Live* has remained a constant in American life more than perhaps any other TV show. The task of creating an hour-and-a-half show from whole cloth each week sounds grueling, to put it mildly, but the payoff is tough to deny: Lorne Michaels's juggernaut has launched the careers of Bill Murray, Amy Poehler, Adam Sandler, Kristen Wiig, Eddie Murphy, Will Ferrell, Tina Fey, and on and on. To this day, *SNL* continues to capture the moment with must-see shareable sketches—even if you have to catch 'em on Sunday because you were at a party last night.

BEYOND SNL

Got a sketch show itch to scratch? Try these gems.

Key & Peele

COMEDY CENTRAL / 2012–2015

5 SEASONS / 53 EPISODES

 97%   94%

Mad TV alumni Keegan-Michael Key and Jordan Peele created and starred in this Peabody Award–winning series that offered some of the 2010s' sharpest satire. Consider Luther (Key), President Obama's (Peele) "anger translator," whose tirades tell us what the cool and collected commander-in-chief *really* feels.

Chappelle's Show

COMEDY CENTRAL / 2003–2006

3 SEASONS / 28 EPISODES

 96%   100%

Comedian Dave Chappelle hosts and features in most of the sketches on this acclaimed series, which dug deep into issues of race, gun violence, and sexuality. Look out for standout skits involving Rick James ("Bitch!") and Lil Jon ("Yeah!").

I Think You Should Leave with Tim Robinson

NETFLIX / 2019–

2 SEASONS / 12 EPISODES

 96%   73%

Created by and featuring *Detroiters* star and *SNL* alum Tim Robinson, and produced by Lonely Island, the bite-sized and often bizarre sketches found here are for those with a high tolerance for cringe. Stick with them, though: Skits like "Baby of the Year" are demented, inspired, and great.

A Black Lady Sketch Show

HBO / 2019–

2 SEASONS / 12 EPISODES

 100% 61%

TV all-rounder Robin Thede created this Emmy-nominated newcomer, starring Thede, Gabrielle Dennis, Quinta Brunson, and Ashley Nicole Black. It's suitably hilarious—witness guest star Angela Bassett leading a support group for "Bad Bitches"—but it's also notable as the first sketch show with a cast and writers room of all Black women, and with a Black woman (Dime Davis) directing every episode.

Tim and Eric Awesome Show, Great Job!

ADULT SWIM / 2007-2010

5 SEASONS / 50 EPISODES (PLUS TWO SPECIALS)

Tim Heidecker and Eric Wareheim's series is completely boundary-free. Beloved bits include the duo yelling at an unseen man named Jim to pick up the keys to his free house (it's free real estate!); a commercial for a board game challenging its players to name things that are not Jackie Chan; and Paul Rudd at his Cerebro-like computer creating dancing digital versions of himself.

It's Always Sunny in Philadelphia

FX, FXX / 2005–
15 SEASONS / 164 EPISODES

 94% 🍿 93%

▶ **CRITICS CONSENSUS** *It's Always Sunny*'s winning formula keeps the laughs rolling and the stomachs turning . . . topical, triumphant, and toxic in the best way. (Season 13)

▶ **WHAT IT'S ABOUT** A sitcom revolving around four pals: Delusional Mac (Rob McElhenney), deranged Charlie (Charlie Day), violent Dee (Kaitlin Olson), and predatory Dennis (Glenn Howerton)—though, really, all those descriptions are interchangeable—who hatch morally bankrupt plans to get rich, famous, or salvage the fortunes of the underpatronized Philly bar, Paddy's Pub, where the majority of the show is set.

There is no indignity, taboo, or humiliation too degrading for the "The Gang" that hangs out at the flailing Philadelphia bar in *It's Always Sunny*, and that's just fine with us because, well, they bring it on themselves. Virtually every scheme they cook up to save Paddy's Pub or improve their standing in normal society falls to pieces through their petty jealousies and backstabbing chicanery. (In one episode, Charlie literally cuts the brakes on their own van to prove he's the wild card of the group.) And the season 2 addition of Danny DeVito as Dennis and Dee's equally sociopathic father was that extra final ingredient to turn the show into consistent, sustainable comedy gold. The sitcom veteran is absolutely game for anything the four throw at him, from peeping into bathroom glory holes to wriggling naked, drenched in sweat, out of a couch during a Christmas party.

It's Always Sunny is a micro-aggression–filled universe that displays only the most aberrant behavior in people. And people, in return, can't get enough. The show became the longest-running live-action comedy show in TV history after its 15th season renewal in 2020; it's since been renewed through season 18.

In addition to all that terrible and terribly watchable bad behavior, its popularity is largely thanks to the eternally durable chemistry between its stars—friends in real life who were all struggling actors when they shot the pilot on what must've been barely three figures. Keeping that principal cast together for 15 seasons was due in large part

patrons . . .), or the series's use of Mac's noticeable weight gain/mass cultivation in season 7 to mock the sitcom standard of trying to keep stars looking as young and presentable as they were from the start.

It was one of several relatively radical developments for a comedy this long-running, but *It's Always Sunny* has always prided itself on barrelling over any boundaries you may throw up.

▶ **BEST EPISODE** Season 4, Episode 13—"The Nightman Cometh." The show has a love for amateur-production musicals, from Mac's coming-out ballet in a prison to Charlie's surprising gift as a songwriting savant. This leads to the production of "The Nightman Cometh," with hilarious and grim numbers about a young boy molested by creatures of the dark. It's these twisted peeks into the characters' inner lives that ironically give the show its most humane touch.

to only airing 10 episodes for most seasons, a workload that has kept them creatively engaged with the show while free to pursue other projects. Olson starred in her own show *The Mick;* Glenn Howerton has *A.P. Bio;* McElhenney created the excellent Apple TV+ series *Mythic Quest: Raven's Banquet;* and Charlie Day has starred in feature comedies like *Horrible Bosses* and *Fist Fight.*

It's Always Sunny is not *just* a safe space for douchebags and malcontents to witness the fantasy fulfillment of saying and doing all the things society prohibits them from. The show is a satire of shortsighted, arrogant narcissists, deriding all levels of hypocrisy. It comes out in surprising ways, as when the gang's attempt to garner better standing with a bar association becomes a metaphor for chasing Emmys (more sex appeal, token Black

▶ **CHARACTER WE LOVE** Mac, played by series creator and co-developer McElhenney. The actor is the show's MVP as the earnest and, therefore, more corruptible rogue; he put on and worked off those pounds in real life, and had his character come out as gay in season 13, after many years of allusions.

The Fresh Prince of Bel-Air

NBC / 1990–1996
6 SEASONS / 148 EPISODES

  93%

Before he became a Grammy Award–winning global superstar, Will Smith was "The Fresh Prince," a Grammy Award–winning rapper from West Philadelphia who first broke into acting with this Quincy Jones–produced and Andy and Susan Borowitz–created sitcom. As its instantly iconic theme song explains, the NBC family comedy followed "Will Smith," a brash teen who's been shipped out west to live with his wealthy family members in Bel-Air after his mom got worried about a "couple of guys who were up to no good" in their Philly neighborhood. Through its six-season run, *The Fresh Prince* explored the clashes between street-smart Will and his bougie cousins, straight-laced uncle, and doting aunt to craft a show that never took itself too seriously, even as it painted as trenchant (and hilarious) a portrait of race and class as you were likely to find on network TV. Like, did we mention that Will's family has a Black butler whose zingers were even fresher than Will's?

The Larry Sanders Show

 GAME-CHANGER

HBO / 1992–1998
6 SEASONS / 90 EPISODES

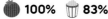 100% 83%

Nearly 30 years after its premiere, *The Larry Sanders Show* remains arguably the best series—or book

or film, for that matter—to skewer Hollywood vanity, backstabbing, and general pettiness. The single-camera ensemble comedy—which follows the goings-on at a fictional late-night talk show hosted by a whiny narcissist (Garry Shandling), produced by an indefatigable bulldog (Rip Torn), and sidekicked by an aloof man-child (Jeffrey Tambor, truly hilarious)—was hugely influential: It would set the playbook for groundbreaking comedy to come both across the pond (*The Office*, *The Thick of It*) and in the States (*Arrested Development*, *30 Rock*). It would also prove to be HBO's first capital-G great show, not to mention a career springboard for behind-the-camera talent like Judd Apatow and Paul Simms, as well as on-screen ones like Bob Odenkirk, Sarah Silverman, Janeane Garofalo, and Jon Stewart.

Absolutely Fabulous

BBC ONE, BBC TWO / 1993–2012
5 SEASONS / 39 EPISODES (INCLUDING 7 SPECIALS)

 96% 94%

Unlike the garish fashion trends its two leads chase, *Absolutely Fabulous* was a sitcom that refused to die. The series, which creator Jennifer Saunders developed from a recurring skit in her BBC sketch show, *French and Saunders*, initially took the tried-and-true Britcom path: three short, critically acclaimed, BAFTA-winning seasons, and then out on a high note with an "event" season finale, "The Last Shout." So far so *Fleabag*. But then came 2001 and a two-season revival—followed by a trio of specials—with Saunders back as London PR rep Edina Monsoon, the moneyed-up fame-chaser who never encountered an ill-fitting pair of pants she could refuse, and Joanna Lumley once more stepping into the thigh-highs of Patsy Stone: fashion editor, sex fiend, cokehead, and Eddie's "darling" co-dependent bestie. Three *more* specials came a decade later, and in 2016, a long-promised feature film in which the duo is suspected of killing model Kate Moss. While Saunders says she's done with the concept, you'll forgive our skepticism—and our *hope* that she might once more change her mind. Full of over-the-top physical comedy and savage one-liners—most directed at Eddie's serious and long-suffering daughter (Julia Sawalha)—it's utterly rewatchable and, with its tilts into the surreal and relentlessly cynical outlook, groundbreaking. Eddie and Patsy, now LGBTQ+ icons and Halloween costume faves, were nothing like the sitcom heroes who came before: They were wholly irredeemable. (Beware *any* shows of maternal instinct; it's not going where you think it is.) Long before Don Draper was indulging his vices on Fifth Avenue, these two friends were laying TV's antihero foundations in a basement kitchen in Kensington, one evil cackle, stubbed-out cigarette, and bottle of "Bolly" at a time.

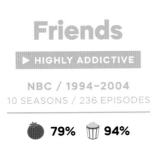

▶ HIGHLY ADDICTIVE

NBC / 1994–2004
10 SEASONS / 236 EPISODES

🍅 79% 🗑 94%

Three guys, three girls, and a coffee place. When you boil it down like that, *Friends* doesn't sound like much. But its ace ensemble—we'd name them, but we also assume you live under a roof rather than a rock—turned this quintessential '90s sitcom into the crown jewel of NBC's "Must-See TV" Thursdays. The ratings hit didn't just make superstars (and millionaires) of its main actors, but also turned "The Rachel" haircut into a worldwide phenomenon and made catchphrases like "How *you* doin'?" part of our shared cultural lingo. With episode titles that echoed the very water cooler chatter they fueled, the sitcom gamely tracked its characters' growth from bumbling twenty-somethings ("The One Where No One's Ready") to partnered and child-rearing thirtysomethings ("The One Where Rachel Has a Baby"), all while perfecting the "Thanksgiving episode," making season finale cliff-hangers work for a sitcom (one word: London), and proving that critical and ratings success need not wane with time (hi, Emmy-winning season 8!).

▶ GAME-CHANGER

HBO / 1998–2004
6 SEASONS / 94 EPISODES

🍅 70% 🗑 85%

"Are you a Carrie or a Samantha? A Miranda or a Charlotte?" To this day, the four principal characters from Darren Star and Michael Patrick King's *Sex and the City* remain a hip take on a Myers-Briggs test. The half-hour sex comedy, based on Candace Bushnell's book by the same name, starred Sarah Jessica Parker as Carrie Bradshaw, a "single and fabulous" New York City writer whose dating misadventures fueled six seasons' worth of glittering story lines. Often mistakenly reduced to its punny voice-over and raunchy banter over Cosmos, the groundbreaking hit swung wildly between being a swooning rom-com (see: Carrie and Mr. Big), an R-rated sex romp (aka any and all of Kim Cattrall's Samantha's subplots), a caustic comedy of errors ("He's just not that into you!"), and an absurdist dramedy (watch out for Kyle MacLachlan's Trey in season 3). With its high-fashion wardrobe, courtesy of Patricia Field, and glitzy vision of New York City, the banner HBO series was a zeitgeist-seizing hit that, two movies and two decades later, remains endlessly addictive.

Will & Grace

NBC / 1998–2006, 2017–2020
11 SEASONS / 246 EPISODES

 -- 🗑 87%

Will & Grace premiered at a time when a primetime network sitcom with a gay lead—even a well-to-do New York City lawyer (Eric McCormack) who has an all-too-close friendship with his straight female BFF (Debra Messing)—was a controversial proposition. And while the NBC hit, developed by Max Mutchnick and David Kohan, became a flag bearer for a more inclusive television landscape, it endures on the strength of its comedy.

The show's campy humor found room to develop serious emotional arcs.

The show's campy humor, best encapsulated by Sean Hayes's fey working actor Jack and Megan Mullally's boozy socialite Karen, found room to develop serious emotional arcs about surrogacy, coming out, and long-term relationships amid its many quotable one-liners ("Honey, tact is for people who aren't witty enough to be sarcastic") and high-quality physical comedy (see season 2's "Das Boob"). Just don't let those guest star–riddled later seasons (or the arguably ill-conceived post-2016 revival) deter you from revisiting this trailblazing Emmy-winning comedy.

Spaced

CHANNEL 4 (UK) / 1999–2001
2 SEASONS / 14 EPISODES

⚫ 100% 🗑 97%

Spaced was the breakout hit for the team of director Edgar Wright and actors Simon Pegg and Nick Frost, who went on to collaborate on what's become known as the Three Flavours Cornetto trilogy of genre satire films: *Shaun of the Dead*, *Hot Fuzz*, and *The World's End*. In *Spaced*, co-created by and starring Pegg and Jessica Stevenson, that adored trilogy's signatures are all present and accounted for. Wright (who directed every episode) infuses the story of two North London ne'er-do-wells who trick their way into a lease just shortly after meeting, with surreal fantasy sequences, frequent cinematic flourishes—the series became famous for its inventive panning shots—and so many pop-culture references that DVDs of the series came with the option of subtitles that point out every homage. Series 1 episode "Art," which paid tribute to zombie legend George A. Romero, put the bug in Wright and Pegg's ear that would one day become *Shaun of the Dead*.

Curb Your Enthusiasm

▶ GAME-CHANGER
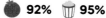

HBO / 2000–
10 SEASONS / 100 EPISODES

⚫ 92% 🗑 95%

How do you make 11 seasons of TV about a person you wouldn't want to spend 5 minutes with?

Leave it to Larry David, who made a hit out of a show about nothing, to find a way. In *Curb Your Enthusiasm*, David plays a version of himself who, like the real-life David, co-created *Seinfeld*, and who spends his semi-retirement golfing, tending—and not tending—to his wife Cheryl (Cheryl Hines), and pinballing from one awkward social interaction to another throughout Los Angeles (and for one season, New York). These encounters—like when Larry hires a prostitute in order to use the carpool lane and get to a game on time or kills a golf club's beloved black swan in self-defense—kick off intricate, butterfly-effect plots and subplots that are, inevitably, and ingeniously, tied together by episode's end . . . rarely to David's benefit. The show's semi-fictional approach and heavy cringe factor have influenced two decades of comedy; without *Curb*, do we get *Master of None*, *Ramy*, *The Comeback*, and so many more? More remarkable than that, though, is that it's still on the air and remains as difficult to watch, and as hilariously watchable, as ever.

Scrubs

NBC, ABC / 2001–2010
9 SEASONS / 182 EPISODES

 83% 🗑 87%

In the wake of so many celebrated and game-changing 2000s comedies—*30 Rock*, *Arrested Development*, *The Office*, and more in this chapter—it's sometimes easy to forget just how innovative Bill Lawrence's *Scrubs* was. And it predates all those heavy hitters. The premise itself was familiar: John "J. D." Dorian (Zach Braff) is an up-and-coming medico at Sacred Heart Hospital, along with ambitious Elliot Reid (Sarah Chalke) and college roommate and bestie Christopher Turk (Donald Faison). Over eight seasons, he rises up the ranks while dealing with a grumpy mentor (John C. McGinley), his feelings for Elliot, and life as the target of the hospital's prank-happy "Janitor." The execution, though, was fresh. Shot single-camera before it was cool, *Scrubs* was packed with surreal fantasy vignettes, signature episode-ending montages, a surprising thwack of heart, and was always consistently surprising. (Perhaps never more so than when it completely reinvented itself for its final season, moving to a medical school setting and introducing new leads.) Amid all the slapstick surrealness and formal invention, the core relationships were always the draw, especially between Turk and head nurse Carla (a wonderfully dry Julie Reyes), and Turk and J. D. Great friends to this day, Braff and Faison's *Scrubs* rewatch podcast "Fake Doctors, Real Friends," is a must-listen for fans.

Arrested Development

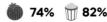
▶ GAME-CHANGER

FOX, NETFLIX / 2003–2019
5 SEASONS / 84 EPISODES

🍅 74% 🗑 82%

Arrested Development follows—start reading in your Ron Howard voice—"the story of a wealthy family who lost everything, and the one son who had no choice but to keep them all together," and felt like something entirely new when it arrived on Fox in the early 2000s. It was edgy, and, of course, very funny, which was frankly a real aberration when you looked at what else was playing on mainstream television at the time. (If you guffawed at *8 Simple Rules* and the final seasons of *Dharma and Greg*, feel free to send us a letter.) Overseen by creator Mitchell Hurwitz, the scripts sizzled with quick wit, Easter eggs, callbacks, and ridiculous cutaways that inspired multiple viewings, and *(Continued on page 66.)*

BINGE BATTLE

THE THICK OF IT ◄ VS ► VEEP

While HBO's *Veep* isn't a direct remake of the BBC's *The Thick of It*, the two famously crude and brutal political satires share the same DNA, courtesy of creator Armando Iannucci and his team of master insulters . . . er, we mean *writers*. Let's see which is the mother-bleeping best.

The Thick of It

BBC / 2005–2012
4 SEASONS / 23 EPISODES

 85% 🍿 95%

▶ **WHAT IT'S ABOUT** Set in the fictional UK Department of Social Affairs, Iannucci's breakout hit first centered on inept British minister Hugh Abbot (Chris Langham) and the scathing Malcolm Tucker (Peter Capaldi), sent by the prime minister's office to keep an eye on things—and step in where needed. As seasons progressed, more bureaucratic bumblers entered Tucker's profanity-laden line of fire.

Veep

HBO / 2012–2019
7 SEASONS / 65 EPISODES

 93% 🍿 89%

▶ **WHAT IT'S ABOUT** Former Maryland Senator Selina Meyer (Julia Louis-Dreyfus) is the ruthlessly ambitious vice president of the title, who claws her way up to the presidency and back down again as the series progresses. She's aided—and more frequently hindered—by a staff that includes communications head Mike McLintock (Matt Walsh) and doting "body man" Gary Walsh (Tony Hale).

BINGE BATTLE

◄ MOST SCATHING LINE ►

"He's useless.
He's absolutely useless.
He's as useless as a
marzipan dildo."

—Malcolm Tucker, *The Thick of It*

(We told you they shared DNA.)

"That's like trying to use a
f—ing croissant as a dildo.
It doesn't do the job and
it makes a f—ing mess."

—Selina Meyer, *Veep*

◄ AWARDS ►

5 BAFTAs

17 Emmys
(including 6 for Louis-Dreyfus)

► OUR PICK   We're casting our ballot for **Veep**. Ultimately, it's *Veep*'s ensemble cast and pure savagery that gives it the edge. Iannucci raised the comedy bar—and the height of the swear jar—substantially with *The Thick of It*, but he raised it again when he brought his talent stateside.

the main ensemble cast—Jason Bateman, Jeffrey Tambor, Jessica Walter, Michael Cera, Will Arnett, Portia de Rossi, Tony Hale, and David Cross—played off each other so well that it seems unfair to single out any one performance. While *AD* peaked in its first two seasons (the third is good, albeit messier, and the years-later Netflix revival unfortunately just didn't click), there's still nothing quite like it.

The Comeback

▶ GONE TOO SOON

HBO / 2005, 2014
2 SEASONS / 21 EPISODES

🍅 73% 🍿 91%

On paper, *The Comeback* didn't sound like much. In her first big role since *Friends,* Lisa Kudrow was to play Valerie Cherish, a red-headed TV has-been, hoping to revive her career with a bit part in a youth-skewing sitcom and an accompanying behind-the-scenes reality docuseries. Yet the comedy, co-created by Kudrow and Michael Patrick King (*Sex and the City*), soon proved to be more than the cringe-worthy study in desperation its logline suggested. Arriving just as the mockumentary took off on American TV (*The Office* premiered mere months before), the HBO show presented itself as found footage from Valerie's reality show. Such a meta concept mined the central tension at play: How does comedy thrive in the age of reality TV? Kudrow's Emmy-nominated performance went further. She leaned into her character's most grating qualities to paint a damning portrait of the rampant Hollywood sexism that women like Valerie internalize and fight against in equal measure, all while eliciting plenty of (all-too-awkward) laughter from one-liners and pratfalls alike. Arguably

ahead of its time, the show debuted to modest reviews and low ratings, and was canceled soon after. Slowly, though, audiences caught on. Valerie's catchphrases ("I don't want to SEE that!" "Jane? Am I being heard?") followed Kudrow around for years, making the show a beloved cult hit that, against all odds, earned a second season order close to a decade later. Taking on dark cable dramas and featuring Seth Rogen in a plum guest role, Valerie's belated return was a resplendent, bittersweet send-off to one of television's most captivating "It" girls.

Flight of the Conchords

▶ GONE TOO SOON

HBO / 2007–2006
2 SEASONS / 22 EPISODES

🍅 94% 🍿 98%

In the mid-aughts, American audiences were introduced to "New Zealand's fourth most popular guitar-based digi-bongo a capella-rap-funk-comedy folk duo"—Jemaine Clement and Bret McKenzie, portraying fictionalized versions of themselves—as they tried to scrape by in modern-day NYC. The musical interludes in the scrappy comedy were equally catchy and funny; in real life, the Conchords even released two LPs on Sub Pop Records and toured the States. And the deadpan interplay between the two hipster everydudes didn't overstay its welcome, especially when they interacted with their manager (Rhys Darby, flexing some amazing comic timing) and their only fan, the obsessed and stalkerish Mel (Kristen Schaal, ably straddling the line between bubbly and creepy).

Community

  ▶ HIGHLY ADDICTIVE

NBC, YAHOO! SCREEN / 2009–2015
6 SEASONS / 110 EPISODES

🍅 88% 🗑 88%

Creator Dan Harmon's feel-good show, about a group of community college outcasts who reluctantly form a study group, boasted a fierce independent streak that helped it stand out from the sitcom pack. While its network contemporary, *30 Rock*, had already proven that American audiences were ready for sharply written absurdist meta-comedy, *Community* turned sitcom conventions upside down, skewering the medium with razor-sharp parodies, laced with pop-culture references. But even as it spoofed *Law & Order*, Ken Burns's *The Civil War*, and the *G.I. Joe* cartoon with gleeful abandon, the series never diminished the human relationships that were its foundation, best captured in the odd-couple bromance of Donald Glover's Troy and Danny Pudi's Abed. *Community*'s flights of fancy ultimately proved too niche for mainstream audiences, and it finished its six-season run on the short-lived Yahoo! Screen platform. Its anything-goes spirit is visible everywhere in contemporary comedy.

30 Rock

NBC / 2006–2013
7 SEASONS / 138 EPISODES

🍅 78% 🗑 93%

The rapid-fire comedic rhythms of Tina Fey and Robert Carlock made *30 Rock* the most absurd workplace comedy on broadcast television. In her first gig since her tenure as head writer and cast member of *SNL*, Fey played Liz Lemon, the ever-frazzled showrunner of an NBC live sketch show headlined by two wildly unpredictable stars. She starred opposite Alec Baldwin's Jack Donaghy, the exec in charge of making the peacock network profitable again. *30 Rock*—named for 30 Rockefeller Plaza, home to NBC's New York HQ—remained a ratings-starved critical darling that was highly regarded by industry insiders who knew this scathing portrait of TV corporate culture was both ridiculous and spot-on. Moreover, the Emmy-winning comedy made Liz, with her valiant attempts at having it all, into a goofy yet relatable role model for single working women everywhere. Whether it was going highbrow to tackle New York City politics and women-in-comedy debates or going low, calling its ace ensemble to land jokes about werewolf bar mitzvahs, fart machines, and muffin tops, *30 Rock* was the definition of must-see TV—and still is.

Modern Family

  ▶ HIGHLY ADDICTIVE

ABC / 2009–2020
11 SEASONS / 250 EPISODES

🍅 85% 🗑 87%

The title of ABC's five-time Emmy Award winner for Outstanding Comedy Series, *Modern Family,* is a bit of a misnomer. Sure, the multigenerational show featured a gay couple and their newly adopted daughter as well as Ed O'Neill married to Sofía Vergara. But, as a whole, the extended Pritchett family—which also included a fumbling middle-aged husband, his lovably uptight wife, and embarrassed kids—was full of familiar archetypes that have populated family sitcoms for generations. What made the long-running hit feel fresh was its mockumentary format. This blend of old and new infused the show's decidedly well-trod comedy of errors–style plotlines with a, yes, *modern* sensibility. Its solid ensemble, which included eventual two-time Emmy winners Eric Stonestreet, Ty Burrell, and Julie Bowen, mastered both the sitcom's signature heartwarming humor as well as its penchant for physical comedy, turning birthday clowns and Valentine's Day dates, Vegas getaways and Disney trips, into some of the best choreographed comedic set pieces seen on broadcast TV.

Parks and Recreation

NBC / 2009–2015

7 SEASONS / 126 EPISODES

 93% 89%

After the runaway success of *The Office*, series creators Greg Daniels and Michael Schur decided to repurpose the mockumentary formula for another workplace comedy, this time set in the world of local politics. *SNL* alum Amy Poehler was tapped to lead the ensemble cast as the unflappable do-gooder Leslie Knope, the eternally optimistic head of a small-town Parks and Recreation department with an unmatchable work ethic and, eventually, ambitions for higher office. Though it initially struggled to set itself apart from *The Office* and suffered a somewhat rocky start—fans will tell you *how much better* the show gets after the season 2 departure of Paul Schneider's Mark Brendanawicz—*Parks and Rec* hit its stride in season 3. It didn't reinvent the genre, but it spawned some of 2010s TV's most memorable characters (Nick Offerman's anti-establishment Ron Swanson), catchphrases ("Treat yo self!"), and soon-to-be stars (Aubrey Plaza, Aziz Ansari, the Marvel Cinematic Universe's Chris Pratt). And it even gave us Galentine's Day.

Brooklyn Nine-Nine

FOX, NBC / 2013–2022

8 SEASONS / 153 EPISODES

 95% 94%

Not many shows can survive a cancellation and a network change. Then again, Fox's *Brooklyn Nine-Nine,* the zany sitcom about a fictional police precinct led by *SNL* breakout star Andy Samberg, always seemed better suited to NBC's brand of humor. Its move to the Peacock's Thursday lineup in its sixth season felt like a return home and a creative reboot for the Golden Globe–winning show (it would last three seasons there, with NBC announcing an eighth and final 10-episode season for 2021–2022).

Its move to the Peacock's Thursday lineup felt like a return home and a creative reboot for the Golden Globe–winning show.

Samberg's Jake Peralta may well be the clownish anchor of the *Brooklyn* crew, but few ensembles can rival the one Dan Goor and Michael Schur assembled, which makes room for Andre Braugher's deadpan delivery, for Stephanie Beatriz's badassery, for Chelsea Peretti's oddball energy, and for every kind of physical pratfall its cast is willing to milk for laughs. Wearing its silliness with pride—see: its classic annual Halloween heist episodes, and its many running gags ("Bingpot!")—*Brooklyn Nine-Nine* constantly finds ways of making a cop show a laugh riot.

Broad City

 PERFECT CERTIFIED FRESH STREAK

COMEDY CENTRAL / 2014–2019
5 SEASONS / 50 EPISODES

🍅 99% 🎫 86%

Broad City's Ilana and Abbi—played by real-life friends and co-creators Ilana Glazer and Abbi Jacobson—live in such a specific little weirdo vision of 21st-century New York City that you can't help but want to get lost in it. Glazer and Jacobson's idiosyncratic ode to female friendship, developed from their own web series with the help of executive producer Amy Poehler, was a breath of fresh air when it premiered on Comedy Central in 2014. Capturing a freewheeling and weed-infused brand of humor that felt authentic precisely because it was so outlandish, *Broad City* was equally at home making jokes about pegging, turning wisdom teeth recovery into a hysterical drug-fueled Whole Foods trip, and capping off a seasons-long gag with a Shania Twain cameo. The chemistry of its two leads was key to its stellar five-season run, but don't sleep on its equally hilarious supporting cast. (Arturo Castro as Jaimé? *Yas queen!*)

black-ish

  GAME-CHANGER

ABC / 2014–
7 SEASONS / 156 EPISODES

🍅 92% 🎫 63%

black-ish announced its intentions from its very first episode: Yes, the Johnson family was going to make you laugh, but they were also going to challenge you. In the show's pilot, patriarch Andre (Anthony Anderson) grapples with two forces that would define much of the series's run: Concern that his middle-class family, living in a mostly White suburb, is losing touch with its Black roots; and, on the flip side, stereotyping in the workplace—an exciting promotion at his ad agency turns out to be an elevation to senior vice president of the Urban Division, prompting Dre to ask, "Did they just put me in charge of Black stuff?" Through Dre, wife Rainbow (Tracee Ellis Ross), and their kids Zoey (Yara Shahidi), Andre Jr. (Marcus Scribner), Jack (Miles Brown), and Diane (an ice-cold Marsai Martin), creator Kenya Barris unapologetically *digs in* to controversial topics, most markedly in landmark episodes like "Hope," in which the family gathers around their TV to watch coverage of a police brutality case, or 2017's heartbreaking "Please, Baby, Please," which addressed NFL players' kneeling protest and the policies of President Trump. That episode was shelved at the time, only to be eventually released on Hulu in the summer of 2020, as Black Lives Matter protests swept the country.

Silicon Valley

 PERFECT CERTIFIED FRESH STREAK

HBO / 2014–2019
5 SEASONS / 53 EPISODES

🍅 94% 🎫 92%

In 2014, as the IT sector in California's Bay Area was booming, Mike Judge (*Office Space*, *Idiocracy*) brought his sharp observational comedy to bear on HBO's *Silicon Valley*. Focusing on a team of misfit programmers who found a tech company, the series thrived on its authentic—if frequently over-the-top—presentation of the industry's cutthroat culture, thanks in part to (Continued on page 72.)

BINGE BATTLE

THE OFFICE (UK) ◀ VS ▶ THE OFFICE (US)

Ricky Gervais and Stephen Merchant's award-winning mockumentary sitcom about the mundane lives of the employees at a paper company was so popular that it eventually spawned localized versions in several other countries, but its most well-known offshoot was the one produced in the United States. Which side of the pond did cubicle life best?

The Office (UK)

BBC TWO / 2001–2003
2 SEASONS / 14 EPISODES

 96% 86%

▶ **WHAT IT'S ABOUT** The original *Office* takes the form of a faux docuseries, chronicling the everyday lives of the employees of a local branch of a paper company in Slough, England. Starved for the admiration of his employees, the branch's delusional, self-involved manager David Brent (Ricky Gervais) repeatedly commits monumental social blunders for which he attempts to make amends by committing even more awkward gaffes.

The Office (US)

NBC / 2005–2013
9 SEASONS / 204 EPISODES

 81% 90%

▶ **WHAT IT'S ABOUT** The American *Office* takes the form of a faux docuseries chronicling the everyday lives of the employees of a local branch of a paper company in Scranton, Pennsylvania. The branch's oblivious but well-meaning manager, Michael Scott (Steve Carell) is also prone to monumental social blunders, but he's a big softie at heart, and while his lack of self-awareness frequently makes life more difficult for his employees, they come to understand each other in ways that make redemption possible.

BINGE BATTLE

◀ MOST CRINGE-WORTHY MOMENT ▶

Season 2, Episode 4—"Motivation." David Brent is paid to make a management presentation that amounts to a motivational speech in which he rambles aimlessly, cracks terrible jokes, invokes Native American wisdom, laughs alone onstage, and exits the room as a boom box plays "The Best" by Tina Turner. The seminar attendees offer no reaction to his antics, but he's only too confident he nailed it.

Season 6, Episode 12—"Scott's Tots." Michael Scott is obliged to fulfill a promise he made a decade prior to pay the college tuition for an entire class of underprivileged third graders. Of course, he doesn't have that kind of money, so he's forced to come clean at a "thank-you" party thrown by the students, who are now high school seniors. It does not end well.

 ◀ AWARDS ▶

6 BAFTAs
2 Golden Globes
1 Peabody Award

5 Emmys
1 Golden Globe
1 Peabody Award

▶ OUR PICK *The Office* (UK) was groundbreaking in many ways, helping to establish the mockumentary format as a potent sitcom formula and ushering in the era of cringe comedy, but we've got to side with the Scranton branch on this one. The ***The Office*** **(US)** waded into similar comic territory but gave its central narcissist a softer edge, which makes the series a feel-good binge. We may love to hate David Brent, but we actually love Michael Scott, and that's always more powerful.

own early experiences working at a start-up. Even those who weren't privy to the inner workings of Silicon Valley found plenty to laugh at, whether it was the games of petty one-upmanship between Gilfoyle (Martin Starr) and Dinesh (breakout star Kumail Nanjiani), or the frequently futile efforts of Pied Piper CEO Richard Hendricks (Thomas Middleditch) to outdo his corporate nemesis Gavin Belson (Matt Ross). It cemented Judge as a master satirist and helped to demystify a niche community for a wider audience, who wondered what exactly those nerds at Facebook and Google were up to.

Catastrophe

▶ PERFECT CERTIFIED FRESH STREAK

▶ HIGHLY ADDICTIVE

CHANNEL 4, AMAZON PRIME VIDEO / 2015–2019
4 SEASONS / 24 EPISODES

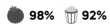 98% 🗑 92%

Stars and co-creators Sharon Horgan and Rob Delaney's comedy starts with what sounds like a gimmicky premise—Can two strangers make it work after a hookup during a business trip results in a surprise pregnancy?—and ends up being a jaded-yet-heartfelt attack on the institution of marriage. Irish comedian Horgan's on-screen alter ego can be selfish (she's upset that his coming home late means she'll have to watch *Game of Thrones* alone "like a pervert") and American Delaney's can be childish (his wife's number remains saved in his phone as "Sharon London Sex"). But each partner's honest feelings of respect and concern for the other—such as when she worries that every car accident she sees will involve him after he has a lapse in sobriety—makes us hope these two kids can make it work. It's also one of the reasons the ambiguous series finale is one of Peak TV's most debated.

Fresh Off the Boat

ABC / 2015–2020
6 SEASONS / 116 EPISODES

 94% 🗑 77%

Fresh Off the Boat was always going to be landmark TV. When it debuted, this adaptation of Eddie Huang's autobiography, about a Taiwanese American family settling in Orlando after moving from DC, was the first US sitcom to center on an Asian American family since Margaret Cho's *All American Girl* 20 years earlier. But the show didn't last six seasons (or weather several controversies, including Huang abandoning all involvement after its first season and breakout star Constance Wu infamously tweeting that she was "so upset" when the show was renewed for its last season) because it was history-making. *FOTB* went the distance because it was genuinely funny (see: every moment involving sharp-tongued grandma Lucille Soo); heart-warming (see: season 4's premiere, in which neighbor Nicole comes out to hip-hop–obsessed oldest son Eddie); and studded with standout performances from the likes of Randall Park as patriarch Louis Huang, Ian Chen as gifted young mama's boy Evan, and especially Wu as the overbearing "mama" in question, Jessica, a tactless comic creation for the ages.

Master of None

NETFLIX / 2015–2017
2 SEASONS / 20 EPISODES

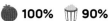 100% 🗑 90%

Created by comic and *Parks and Recreation* alums Aziz Ansari and Alan Yang, *Master of None* stars Ansari as Dev, a 30-year-old actor living and loving in New York. Though a simple, common premise, the comedy diversified the representation of immigrants on television with a particular focus on Ansari's Indian American identity and balancing the traditional motivations of his parents with his decidedly nontraditional desires. Perhaps the show's best episode, "Thanksgiving," which comes in season 2, centers on Dev's best friend, played by Lena Waithe. Based on Waithe's own coming out to her family as a lesbian woman, the episode stars Angela Bassett as her mother and Kym Whitley as her aunt, and in 34 minutes unfurls the multi-year journey of a Black family growing to accept and love their queer child. Waithe became the first Black woman to win the Primetime Emmy for comedy writing for co-penning the episode with Ansari. Awards voters also recognized Ansari for his acting: For his work on season 2, he became the first Asian American to win a Golden Globe for best actor in a TV series—comedy or musical.

Schitt's Creek

▶ GAME-CHANGER

▶ HIGHLY ADDICTIVE

CBC, POP TV / 2015–2020
6 SEASONS / 80 EPISODES

🍅 93% 🍿 93%

When it began airing on CBC Television and Pop TV in 2015, no one could've predicted what a cultural phenomenon *Schitt's Creek* would become. Ostensibly about a privileged family navigating their newfound poverty while living in the derelict if affable small town they once bought on a lark, the comedy boasted the talents of two legends: Catherine O'Hara (instantly iconic as wig enthusiast Moira Rose) and Eugene Levy (co-creator of the show with Dan Levy, his son both on- and off-screen). O'Hara

and Levy's pitch-perfect pairing elevated *Schitt's* early seasons, helping the Canadian series slowly amass a cult fan base that would keep growing well into its sixth and final season, which historically swept the 2020 Emmys comedy categories. Neither cutting satire nor zippy sitcom, the show paved its own way, embracing earnestness as a vehicle for laughter, offering endlessly quotable one-liners ("Ew, David!"), fleshing out its lovable townie weirdos, and anchoring its late seasons on one of television's most beloved queer couples.

Superstore

NBC / 2015–2021
6 SEASONS / 113 EPISODES

 92% 🍿 79%

Superstore's arrival in late 2015 was met with little fanfare. Slowly, though, what began as a conventional comedy became one of the bravest, most thoughtful sitcoms on network TV in decades. Boasting a very funny ensemble that gave life to the kooky employees of its titular Cloud 9 store (with executive producer America Ferrera as its anchor), its plots were at first mostly formulaic takes on workplace story lines about pranks and price scanners; no surprise given creator Justin Spitzer's tenure at *The Office*. The comedy slowly found its groove in season 2. Beyond acing the ongoing will-they/won't-they romance between Ferrera's Amy and Ben Feldman's Jonah, *Superstore* began using its wide array of working-class characters as a springboard to tell ever more daring—while still very funny—stories. This is perhaps best exemplified by the season 4 finale in which a visit by ICE to detain an undocumented worker, at the behest of corporate, leads to a push to unionize Cloud 9 employees.

Insecure

▶ GAME-CHANGER

▶ PERFECT CERTIFIED FRESH STREAK

HBO / 2016–

4 SEASONS / 36 EPISODES

● 96% 🗑 81%

▶ **CRITICS CONSENSUS** *Insecure* uses star Issa Rae's breakout web series *Awkward Black Girl* as the basis for an insightful, raunchy, and hilarious journey through the life of a twentysomething Black woman that cuts through stereotypes with sharp wit and an effusive spirit. (Season 1)

▶ **WHAT IT'S ABOUT** In the final days of her twenties, we follow Issa Dee (Issa Rae), an awkward Black millennial, as she and her friends have misadventures in friendship, love, careers, and sex, in addition to the everyday struggles of being Black and "trying to adult" in South-Central Los Angeles.

In 2016, Issa Rae translated her wildly popular YouTube web series *The Mis-Adventures of an Awkward Black Girl* into a half-hour sitcom, a move that marked a watershed moment in television. At the time *Insecure* premiered on HBO, Rae became the first Black woman to helm a show on premium cable. Today, countless Black women have followed, populating HBO, Showtime, and others with identity-focused series that chronicle the messiness of modern-day adulthood from a previously rarely seen vantage point.

The series follows Issa's closest friendships, her bumpy relationship with on-again-off-again boyfriend Lawrence (Jay Ellis)—and the men and women who create those bumps—as well as her career ups and downs in the nonprofit space. The Issa-Lawrence story line provides for some of the show's best and swooniest moments; many millennials would mark Issa and Lawrence's season 4 montage of mind-blowing orgasms, Chinese food, tender kisses, and share-sipping from the same wine bottle as #RelationshipGoals.

From the first season, though, it's the bond between Issa and career-focused lawyer Molly (Yvonne Orji)—best friends since their days at Stanford—that anchors *Insecure*. Following their journey, from the joys of innocuous self-care Sundays to epic season-long tensions that will force you to print your Team Molly or Team Issa shirts, will break you down and build you back up again. As a bonus: All the drama plays out in some of the best (previously) hidden gems of South-Central Los Angeles, and is underscored by some truly well-chosen R&B tracks.

Documenting the lives of complicated, smart, and flawed female friends is nothing new for television, but *Insecure* stays fresh—more precisely, Certified Fresh for all seasons—by addressing serious Black issues through the group. Postpartum depression, mental health in the Black community, the fetishization of Black women (and men), and the perils of interracial dating are all explored with insight, and yet never overwhelm the comedy: When things threaten to get too deep, the series will bring in the scene-stealing Natasha Rothwell (the good-times–loving Kelly), hood profit Thug Yoda, and freestyle raps about "Broken P-ssy."

Rae, co-creator Larry Wilmore, and cowriter/executive producer Prentice Penny enlisted directors like Regina King, Kerry Washington, Debbie Allen, and *Queen & Slim* helmer Melina Matsoukas—who shot the unapologetically Black pilot and several episodes of the first season—to steer the series. Matsoukas also famously shot Beyoncé's "Formation" music video, and it is perhaps at the

intersection of *Insecure* and Queen B where the series hits its peaks. No episode synthesizes the essence of what many love about *Insecure* more than season 3's "High-Like." In the now-iconic 39 minutes, the crew travels to the Coachella music festival to see Beyoncé's historic performance, a journey that is at turns hilarious (Kelly's ill-timed edible) and poignant (love interest Nathan and Issa bonding on the Ferris wheel).

It is also distinct, with every laugh and heart flutter filtered through the vibrant lens of the Black female experience.

HBO's *Girls* was one of the first shows to pair female friendship, raunchy sex, and deep . . . well, *insecurity* with quarter-life angst and crisis, but *Insecure* stands apart from that series and others because it chose to center and celebrate the characters, culture, and locations that shows like *Girls, Sex in the City,* and *Gossip Girl* largely left in the margins or entirely ignored.

▶ **BEST EPISODE** Season 1, Episode 8—"Broken As F**k." Season 3's "High-Like," mentioned above, makes a strong case, but we're going with this late first-season gem, another road-trip episode in which the girls head to Malibu to escape the realities of life—and particularly the revelation that Issa cheated on Lawrence.

▶ **CHARACTER WE LOVE** Story editor–turned–writer and star Natasha Roswell's Kelly is the heart of *Insecure*; blunt, hilarious, and always slightly tipsy, she juggles as many bed partners as she does one-liners, and gives the "hilarious sidekick" role, usually played by a man, a feminist and empowering twist.

Atlanta

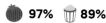

FX / 2016–
2 SEASONS / 21 EPISODES

🍅 **97%** 🍿 **89%**

The millennial generation's most inventive Renaissance man might just be the musician, actor, writer, and comic Donald Glover, and this trailblazing television series might just be his crowning achievement. The Certified Fresh and Emmy-winning absurdist dramedy about three friends trying to make it in the music industry in Atlanta, Georgia, thrives by finding the humor in the everyday. *Atlanta*'s writing team—including Donald and brother Stephen Glover—serves rich, character-driven drama, even as they tap into the hilarity of a lost day at the barbershop, a meandering night out at the club, or a misadventure to the house of a bizarre childlike celebrity shut-in (also played by Glover; we did say he was a Renaissance man). The series's strength also lies in its focus on the unseen corners of the African American experience. Nerdy and soft-spoken, our hero Earn, played by Glover, is a couch-surfing Ivy League dropout who has a child with his ex and makes a living managing his cousin Alfred (Brian Tyree Henry), better known as the up-and-coming rapper Paperboi, a man who seems as put off by his new fame as he is hungry to achieve more. The cousins are frequently joined on the couch, in the club, and in their ride by Alfred's eccentric but surprisingly profound and prophetic best friend Darius (a star turn from LaKeith Stanfield). Every episode, the trio continues reaching for the greatness they feel they're destined for. Each season has its own particular tone and tenor, but they're stitched together seamlessly by the city

in which the drama takes place, something of a contradiction in itself: a city rich in Black culture nestled in one of the more Conservative states in the South. This is where our leads strive to "stay woke," as the chorus of Glover's hit song "Redbone" implores listeners to do, and ignore the undiagnosed depression and PTSD they feel living on the wrong side of being young, Black, and gifted.

Better Things

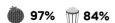

FX / 2016–
4 SEASONS / 42 EPISODES

🍅 **97%** 🍿 **84%**

It's impossible to talk about *Better Things*—Pamela Adlon's semi-autobiographical series about a single mom and actress juggling work, auditions, love, bills, and her three demanding daughters—without talking about the off-screen drama that left the "show dangling from a precipice," according to its star, following season 2. It was while that season was airing in 2017 that Adlon's co-creator, cowriter, and executive producer, Louis C.K. was accused of and admitted to multiple instances of sexual misconduct against women, leading FX to sever ties with the comic completely. Suddenly, Adlon was alone, but in a vindicating feminist twist, *Better Things* only got, well, *better.* For season 3, Adlon pulled together a writers' room and directed all 12 episodes herself. The season was universally acclaimed, Certified Fresh at 100% on the Tomatometer, and cemented Adlon's place as one of Peak TV's great dramedy auteurs. Her on-screen alter ego, Sam Fox, does it all, too, showrunning an often-chaotic LA life that zigzags between making lunches, motel hookups, and hilarious exchanges with her dotty mom (and across-the-street neighbor), played by the great British actress Celia Imrie. While the laughs are sharp and frequent, the series is at its best when it slows down and zooms in on Sam's relationship with her daughters, listening in as she shares a laugh with her rebellious eldest Max (Mikey Madison), discusses new ideas with androgynous middle child Frankie (Hannah Alligood), or dozes off next to her ridiculously sweet youngest, Duke (Olivia Edward). Adlon had been stealing scenes for decades from the likes of *Grease 2*, *Californication*, *Louis*, and with her Emmy-winning turn voicing Bobby Hill in *King of the Hill*, but in *Better Things*'s flustered, frank, and fiercely caring Sam Fox she delivered what the *New Yorker* called "possibly the most poignant love letter to single motherhood that has ever aired on TV." And she did it on *her* terms.

Fleabag

 **GAME-CHANGER**

BBC THREE, AMAZON PRIME VIDEO /
2016–2019
2 SEASONS / 12 EPISODES

 100% 🍿 **94%**

It is the rare TV show that boasts a 100% Certified Fresh season. That the dark comedy *Fleabag* manages it twice is a testament to the fresh new voice that creator and star Phoebe Waller-Bridge brought to international audiences in 2016. The series—which began its life as a one-woman stage show at the Edinburgh Festival Fringe—tells the story of a London-based café owner, her tragicomic romantic entanglements, and strained relations with family. Season 1 slowly unfurls the underlying dysfunction that has turned "Fleabag" (Waller-Bridge)—who never goes by any other

name—into a dry-witted narrator who addresses her audience directly in the fourth wall–smashing asides the series is famous for. In season 2, her inappropriate love interest (shout-out to internet-dominating "hot priest" Andrew Scott) takes note and questions her audience-as-therapist habit—"What was that?"—recognizing the deeper emotional disconnect that afflicts Fleabag. Waller-Bridge won three Emmys in 2019 for *Fleabag*'s second season: Comedy Series, Lead Actress, and Writing for a Comedy Series. Costars Sian Clifford and Olivia Colman and guest stars Fiona Shaw and Kristin Scott Thomas were also nominated. The show turned its creator/star into one of the most in-demand voices around: Waller-Bridge would soon develop the hit spy thriller *Killing Eve*, appear as a *Star Wars* droid, and be brought on like a modern-day Carrie Fisher to polish scripts for big-budget studio flicks like the James Bond movie *No Time to Die*. Next up: A lead role in the next *Indiana Jones* movie.

The Good Place

 PERFECT CERTIFIED FRESH STREAK

NBC / 2016–2020
4 SEASONS / 53 EPISODES

🍅 **97%** 🍿 **89%**

Mike Schur's follow-up to the relentlessly positive *Parks and Recreation* had lofty ambitions for a network sitcom: Explain complex philosophy, posit grand ideas about the afterlife, and investigate whether humans are inherently good . . . all in a 22-minute weekly package. Somehow, though, it worked, running for four Certified Fresh seasons, anchored by Ted Danson as the supernatural afterlife architect Michael who, along with all-knowing supercomputer Janet (D'Arcy Carden), ushers four (Continued on page 80.)

Ramy

 GAME-CHANGER

HULU / 2019–
2 SEASONS / 20 EPISODES

 97% 🗑 **89%**

▶ **CRITICS CONSENSUS** An insightful and hilarious glimpse into the life of a Muslim American family, *Ramy* perfectly articulates the precarious nature and nuances of identity and announces Ramy Youssef is a talent to watch. (Season 1).

▶ **WHAT IT'S ABOUT** The adventures (and misadventures) of Ramy Hassan (Youssef), a millennial Egyptian living with his family in New Jersey, trying to figure out love, sex, religion, career, and personal morality, all while deluged with the opinions of friends and family and the fellow worshippers in his mosque.

You will root for Ramy Hassan. He might even become one of your favorite TV characters. But you won't always *like* him or the things he does, which is no small thing for a program—a comedy, no less—that is the first scripted American series that revolves around a Muslim American character.

Comedian Ramy Youssef, who created, writes, and stars in the story that is a loose nod to his own life, might have felt pressure to make TV Ramy, TV Ramy's family and friends, and most of all, TV Ramy's actions, palatable to an audience that isn't used to seeing this character and culture on television. Be assured, though: He and the other writers on the show (a diverse group), resist that pressure at every turn.

Ramy, though always well-intentioned, can be self-involved and underappreciative, especially when it comes to his family. He professes to hold certain morals important, then acts in direct opposition to them. He makes one cringe-inducing bad decision after another—including, infamously, beginning a relationship with his first cousin—and sometimes those decisions hurt people. A lot.

But TV Ramy also has a big heart. He shows respect even for people who might not have earned it, and can exhibit an extraordinary level of concern for others, be it a drunk teenage stranger who could get him and his friend in serious trouble, or that friend, Stevie, Ramy's best pal since grade school, who gets around in a wheelchair.

In short, TV Ramy is a regular twentysomething, just like a twentysomething from any place, culture, religion, or ethnicity. It is thanks to the insight, sensitivity, and honesty of Youssef and the *Ramy* writers that the series so nimbly honors the universal truths of a person at this stage of being a young American. They also deliver a TV comedy that is undeniably funny, even if it isn't usually in a laugh-out-loud way. That shouldn't be such a revelation, but it is in the package of *Ramy*: There were many who'd never gotten the chance to see someone who looks like them—and prays like them—on television, leading a regular kind of life, before the series launched on Hulu.

But back to Stevie. Played by Youssef's real-life childhood best friend Steve Way, he is atop the lineup of terrifically drawn characters and actors that shape the nuanced world surrounding and supporting Ramy. May Calamawy and Laith Nakli are also outstanding as Ramy's sister and uncle, one a young woman unafraid to go after what she wants, the other a middle-aged man scared to death that people will find out who he really is, and both well aware they will never easily be able to take advantage of the kinds of choices Ramy takes for granted.

▶ **BEST EPISODE** Season 1, Episode 4—"Strawberries." The first installment Youssef directs flashes back to the September 11 attacks and how they changed life for elementary school student Ramy, who desperately wanted to be like the other boys. It's crushing, but in the end he finds something much sweeter.

▶ **CHARACTER WE LOVE** Maysa Hassan (Hiam Abbass), Ramy's lonely, unintentionally politically incorrect, and endearing mama. In another of the series's best, most poignant, episodes, season 1's "Ne Me Quitte Pas," Maysa tries to make new connections by entering the gig economy.

recently deceased humans into their new homes in the Good Place: sarcastic, selfish, potentially there by mistake Eleanor Shellstrop (Kristen Bell); neurotic philosopher Chidi Anagonye (William Jackson Harper); dim-witted break-dancing Florida man Jason Mendoza (Manny Jacinto); and snobby socialite Tahani Al-Jamil (Jameela Jamil). Come for the "forking" funny comedy and well-deployed twists, stay for the contemplation of morality and goodness in a post-Obama world.

One Day at a Time

▶ PERFECT CERTIFIED FRESH STREAK

NETFLIX, POP TV / 2017–2020
4 SEASONS / 46 EPISODES

🍅 99% 🍿 90%

This reboot of the classic Norman Lear series showed that a traditional multicam sitcom could feel as fresh as any of the cool-kid comedies that squeezed it out of Emmy contention year after year. The blueprint of Lear's socially conscious classic is there—a single mom raising two kids, trying to make ends meet, and dealing with a nosy-but-charming building superintendent—but it's the thoughtful modern spins that make *One Day* stand out. The Alvarezes are a Cuban American family living in LA's Echo Park neighborhood, in Trump's America, which adds rich cultural layers to the series's weekly and season-long story lines about immigration, PTSD, and coming to terms with one's sexuality. (The season 1 finale, in which teenage Elena [Isabella Gomez] comes out to her disapproving father, is one of the most moving episodes of TV we've seen in years.) The series's mix of big laughs and big feels is carried by a game cast, especially Justina Machado as the family's

tough-loving and huge-hearted mom, Penelope. The *biggest* laughs, though, come courtesy of screen legend Rita Moreno as the always-knows-better *abuela* (grandmother) Lydia. Moreno's line reads burst with excess flavor, her signature scene entrance is up there with Cosmo Kramer's iconic door-burst, and Lydia's withering treatment of pining would-be lover Dr. Leslie Berkowitz—the great character actor Stephen Tobolowsky—provides for a wickedly funny running joke. *One Day* rightfully earned a fiercely loyal following: When Netflix canceled the show following its third season, fans raised such a clamor that Pop TV stepped in to save the day and keep the Alvarez antics alive—if only for one more season.

What We Do in the Shadows

▶ HIGHLY ADDICTIVE

FX / 2019–
2 SEASONS / 20 EPISODES

🍅 97% 🍿 94%

It can't be easy adapting source material this good—that is, the 2014 New Zealand vampire mockumentary of the same name by writers-directors Taika Waititi (*Jojo Rabbit*) and Jemaine Clement (*Flight of the Conchords*)—without watering things down. Will the chemistry that made the movie sing translate? Will the setup—in the TV show's case, a quartet of ancient, oft-quibbling vampires and a human caretaker (mostly) holed up in a house in modern-day Staten Island—go stale after a season? Luckily, the FX series quells those fears. The casting is really what keeps viewers coming back, with Matt Berry (a fixture in UK comedy getting his much-deserved due stateside), Kayvan Novak, and

Natasia Demetriou all superb as the bloodsuckers. But the secret weapons might be Mark Proksch, playing a Wisconsin-accented vampire who feeds off people by boring them (he's an "energy vampire"), and fan favorite Harvey Guillén, who portrays the gentle, doting servant hoping to join the ranks of the undead.

Pen15

HULU / 2019–
2 SEASONS / 17 EPISODES

 97%  84%

Pen15's approach to mining laughs from middle school blues is as ingenious as it is simple: The show's co-creators, Maya Erskine and Anna Konkle, play versions of themselves as seventh graders—with nothing hiding the fact that they're obviously in their thirties—while their friends and tormenters are played by actual teens. If it sounds a bit cringeworthy, well, it is—this is the car-crash comedy of Larry David given a millennial makeover.

This is the car-crash comedy of Larry David given a millennial makeover.

Pen15 arrived on Hulu in 2019 with the kind of comedy pedigree that set expectations soaring: Erskine and Konkle were on-the-verge breakouts with credits on comedies like *Insecure* and *Maron* and the Lonely Island team were among a battalion of heavyweight executive producers. *Pen15* delivered the laughs, but surprised with unexpected heart: Season 1 episode "Posh," in which half-Japanese Maya is made to play Scary in a Spice Girls video because she's the non-White girl, packs the kind of complicated emotional punch that makes this slice of surrealness something special.

Ted Lasso

APPLE TV+ / 2020–
2 SEASONS / 22 EPISODES

 91%   97%

This breakout hit for new-ish streamer Apple TV+ has a success story as unlikely as that of its titular hero, a college football coach inexplicably brought to the UK to manage a soccer team with almost zero understanding of "the beautiful game." Ted Lasso—played with glass-half-full-and-then-some pluck by Jason Sudeikis—made his debut in NBC Sports promo ads for the English Premier League in 2013. When the spots proved popular, *Scrubs* creator Bill Lawrence was brought in to develop a series around the character. Unlike other ill-fated projects involving corporate mascots-turned-sitcom stars—we're looking at you, GEICO Cavemen—the show turned out great. Part of that is down to Lasso himself, as bright and optimistic (but never naïve) a goof as TV fans have ever been gifted. But where *Ted Lasso* really runs up the scoreboard is in its surprising emotional turns and deep bench of loveable supporting characters. The boys in the locker room are a lot of fun, but it's the women to look out for: Juno Temple shines as Keeley Jones, a WAG with a big heart (and even bigger brain). Hannah Waddinngham is stellar as team owner Rebecca Welton, whose slow realization that Ted might be just the thing her club needs to succeed—and how that may screw up her plans for it to fail—might be the first season's most complex, and moving, arc.

THE SCIENCE OF BINGE WATCHING

by Yasmin Tayag

IT HAD BEEN A LONG WEEK.

AND I KNEW EXACTLY HOW I WAS GOING TO SPEND MY WEEKEND.

FRIDAY NIGHT...

THE WITCHER

I JUST DIDN'T KNOW HOW EMOTIONALLY AND CHEMICALLY INTENSE IT WAS GOING TO BE.

I STARTED BY MAKING SOME NEW FRIENDS.

BINGE WATCHING LET ME START "PARASOCIAL RELATIONSHIPS" WITH INTERESTING (AND ATTRACTIVE) PEOPLE.

SOOO WHAT'S THE HOT GOSS IN CINTRA?

WE LAUGHED, CRIED, FOUGHT, DRANK, AND SANG TOGETHER.

PSYCHOLOGISTS SAY THESE RELATIONSHIPS ARE REAL...

... ALBEIT ONE SIDED.

WAIT UP!

WHO IS SHE?

SHE'S BEEN FOLLOWING US SINCE FRIDAY...

THEN, I GOT MY PLEASURE FIX.

EVERY TIME YOU DO SOMETHING PLEASURABLE,* A RUSH OF DOPAMINE FLOWS THROUGH YOUR BRAIN.

HO HO NH_2

* THIS INCLUDES SEX, DRUGS, AND OGLING BROODING MAGICAL HIMBOS.

DOPAMINE ACTIVATES THE BRAIN'S REWARD SYSTEM, WHICH ENCOURAGES YOU TO KEEP DOING WHATEVER YOU'RE DOING.

EASY ENOUGH!

▶ MORE DOPAMINE?

SHE HASN'T SHOWERED... ...IN 38 HOURS... ...AND COUNTING

ALL THE WHILE, I WAS MAKING MY ESCAPE.

EVERY HOUR I SPENT BINGE WATCHING...

...WAS AN HOUR NOT SPENT WORRYING ABOUT MY LIFE.

WHAT'S A WITCHER GOTTA DO TO GET SOME PRIVACY AROUND HERE?

Dramas We Can't. Stop. Watching.

Every great TV drama has a hook. Not necessarily a grabby and high-concept conceit — though mega-hit *This Is Us*, with its multiple time lines and nonlinear structure, certainly has that—but a key "something" that keeps viewers coming back for more, often despite the lack of a consistent mystery, the promise of big laughs, or big-budget explosions. For the best TV dramas, that hook is often a simple one: the people in it.

Drama, like comedy, is a broad category, and this chapter, like our comedy chapter, is quite the ride. It will take you from the court of King Henry (*The Tudors*) and the palace of Queen Elizabeth II (*The Crown*) to the boardrooms of Manhattan (*Succession*) and then onto its underground ballrooms (*Pose*). You'll spend time with families like the Gilmores of Stars Hollow (*The Gilmore Girls*); the Taylors of Dillon, Texas (*Friday Night Lights*); and the Granthams of Yorkshire (*Downton Abbey*); and then you'll make friends with the fierce women of *Claws* and the rich kids of *The OC*. You'll love many of them, love to hate some, and you won't be able to leave them alone.

While dramas about families, friendships, and workplaces have long been centerpieces of networks' primetime lineups—witness the *Dallas* versus *Dynasty* battle for '80s ratings supremacy in our first chapter—most of the titles from this chapter were broadcast or streamed in the last two decades. That's because our mission is not just to track TV's most influential titles but the most binge-worthy, and much of the most innovative and compelling work in drama has happened in the swirl of network, cable, and streaming competition, and with the freedom it has offered. The dramas highlighted here aren't just binge-worthy as hell, they pushed the genre forward.

That's how we get the likes of *In Treatment*, HBO's late-2000s hidden gem that showed that a short-form, five-nights-a-week series could play with the prestige cable big boys. Or *David Makes Man*, Oprah Winfrey Networks's lyrical story of a Miami teen trying to get out of the projects, rendered poetically by creator and mind behind *Moonlight* Tarell Alvin McCraney. And *Scandal*, the bat-s—t pedal-to-the-metal political thrill ride with which creator Shonda Rhimes upped the ante on the very concept of binge-ing and further established herself as *the* most powerful force in network TV. (Seriously, look her name up in our index!)

Want to see just how far TV drama has come? Look to the youth. In these pages, we also chart the evolution of the teen drama, from those thirtysomething-looking teens of *90210* right through to Netflix's diverse and sharp *Never Have I Ever* and on to HBO's hyperstylized, trauma- and drug-fueled *Euphoria*, a kind of repudiation of everything the genre had offered before.

Euphoria's intense sex scenes and distressing overdoses shock and compel, but its central appeal is the same as what appealed to fans of *Dawson's Creek* or *Gossip Girl*: the people at the center of all that drama.

There are a lot more characters to discover in these pages; we think you'll enjoy meeting them.

Freaks and Geeks

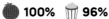 **GONE TOO SOON**

NBC / 1999–2000
1 SEASON / 18 EPISODES

 100% 🗑 **96%**

Will we ever see another show launch the careers of so many young stars after just a single season on air? Seth Rogen, James Franco, Linda Cardellini, Jason Segel, John Francis Daley, and Martin Starr all made their breakthroughs here as the titular weirdos and nerds navigating high school drama and turbulent family lives in suburban Michigan. *Stranger Things* may have more recently popularized a romantic nostalgia of yesteryear's small-town adolescence, but *Freaks and Geeks* presented a blunter truth: Listening to prog rock or being obsessed with Atari or comic books in the early 1980s repelled most people, rather than bringing them together. The show's chief creative forces, among them Paul Feig and Judd Apatow, compiled all the humiliating and mortifying events of their teenage years and, in filtering them through the fresh-faced cast, presented a kind of personal and unvarnished honesty never before seen on network television.

Gilmore Girls

THE WB, THE CW, NETFLIX / 2000–2007, 2015
7 SEASONS / 153 EPISODES

 85% **86%**

Lorelai Gilmore (Lauren Graham), a single working mother in the quaint town of Stars Hollow, Connecticut, is 32. Her daughter, Rory (Alexis Bledel), is 16. You do the math. To ensure her daughter's safe and successful passage into adulthood,

Lorelai strikes a deal with her wealthy estranged parents for tuition money, sending Rory to an upscale private school, where she mixes with higher society as she pursues her journalism dreams. After the blow-up success of *Dawson's Creek*, The WB launched *Gilmore Girls* to appeal to the newly coveted teenage audience. And while the show initially did offer the usual high school drama trappings, like self-discovery and relationships ("Team Jess" or "Team Dean" was very much a hook early on), it had cross-generational appeal for half-focusing on Lorelai's thirtysomething life and career. It had erudite, rapid, pop culture–laden conversations between mother and daughter (and whoever else could keep up within its vast lineup of quirky secondary characters, including Melissa McCarthy's lovable chef Sookie. Standout costar Kelly Bishop, as Lorelai's snobbish and distant mother, hilariously *cannot* keep up.) Creator and showrunner Amy Sherman-Palladino left after the first six years, leading to a seventh and final season that some fans say feels out of step with the series. In 2015, Sherman-Palladino partnered with Netflix for a revival series, *Gilmore Girls: A Year in the Life*, producing four feature-length episodes that find Rory the same age as Lorelai when the show first debuted, and reaching the ending its creator had envisioned since the beginning.

Queer As Folk

 GAME-CHANGER

SHOWTIME / 2000–2005
5 SEASONS / 83 EPISODES

 –– **98%**

With the Q word in its title, *Queer As Folk* was a radical proposition when it began airing on Showtime (and Canada's Showcase) back in 2000. The remake of Russell T Davies's UK series by the

same name was the first hour-long drama on American television to portray the lives of gay men and women. Equally racy and groundbreaking, the Pittsburgh-based cult hit gave insight into a wide variety of LGBTQ-specific issues at the turn of the 21st century, moving beyond just coming-out stories to tackle surrogacy, pornography, drug abuse, and much more. Even as its focus became ever more political (including a devastating subplot that ends with its Babylon gay bar being bombed), its glittering appeal was forever grounded in its lovable characters and its unlikely central couple, Brian and Justin (Gale Harold and Randy Harrison), who made sure we never listened to Darude's "Sandstorm" the same way ever again.

Six Feet Under

HBO / 2001–2005
5 SEASONS / 63 EPISODES

 81% 97%

Creator Alan Ball's drama about a family that runs (and lives in) a Los Angeles funeral home reminded us that, yes, death can be scary, sad, and painful—but it can also be beautiful and maybe even funny, just like life. One of the most famous lines from the show comes during the season 1 episode "Knock Knock": When eldest son Nate (Peter Krause) is asked why people have to die, he calmly responds "to make life important." Even *Six Feet*'s notorious cold opens, which featured a weekly rotation of the family's "clients," routinely mocked and subverted the "victim of the week" trope associated with procedural crime shows like *Law & Order*. There was the outlandish—a mountain lion attack!—but there were also somber deaths that addressed serious cultural problems, including a boy who accidentally shoots himself while his brother gets high.

Desperate Housewives

ABC / 2004–2012
8 SEASONS / 180 EPISODES

 72% 89%

"I spent the day as I spent every other day, quietly polishing the routine of my life until it gleamed," says Mary Alice, a picture-perfect housewife and the narrator of Marc Cherry's *Desperate Housewives* during the show's pilot episode. She then admits that what she did next—take a gun to her head—perplexed her neighbors on Wisteria Lane. The mystery surrounding Mary Alice's suicide drove the thrilling, near-perfect first season of this hit show, which focused, in turn, on the quiet desperation of her closest friends, single working mom Susan (Teri Hatcher), harried stay-at-home mother of four Lynette (Felicity Huffman), Stepford Wife incarnate Bree (Marcia Cross), and unhappy trophy wife Gabrielle (Eva Longoria). With a sudsy new mystery framing each new season—and a shocking post-tornado, five-year flash-forward-slash-much-needed narrative reset at the end of season 4—this campy take on modern suburban women all but revamped the primetime soap for the 21st century.

The L Word

 GAME-CHANGER

SHOWTIME / 2004–2009
5 SEASONS / 70 EPISODES

✳ 57% 76%

"Why shouldn't the lesbian nation have its own out/proud, kinda porny *Melrose Place*?" asked the *Austin Chronicle* in a review of *The L Word*'s first season. It was a question that summed up the dual appeals of this West Hollywood–set drama about a circle of LGBTQ+ friends, which hit Showtime just four years after the American version of *Queer As Folk* debuted on the same network. It was groundbreaking—the first ensemble cast featuring homosexual, bisexual, and transgender characters and actors—and, just as crucially, it was as deliciously soapy, sexy, and bitchy as anything Aaron Spelling had done. *L Word* showrunner Ilene Chaiken was keenly focused on that second factor ("I rail against the idea that pop television is a political medium," she told the *Times*), and so it was that Bette (Jennifer Beals), Jenny (Mia Kirshner), Kit (Pam Grier), Laurel (Tina Kennard), Shane (Katherine Moening), Dana (Erin Daniels), and a revolving door of newcomers swapped beds, raised children, battled sickness, came out, and even got murdered. The show was a notoriously bumpy ride—the whodunnit-focused sixth season is Rotten at 20%—but a sequel series, *The L Word: Generation Q*, did some redeeming, kicking off in 2019 with a new generation of talent and a Certified Fresh return to form.

Friday Night Lights

▶ HIGHLY ADDICTIVE

NBC, THE 101 NETWORK / 2006–2011
5 SEASONS / 76 EPISODES

🍅 **97%** 🍿 **93%**

While directing his film adaptation of H. G. Bissinger's nonfiction book about a small-town Texas football team's run toward the state championship, Peter Berg started early drafts of this television show of the same name, inspired by the same source. The series focuses on Eric Taylor (Kyle Chandler), new head coach of the famed Dillon Panthers and just one loss away from

being fired as the series opens, and his wife, Tami (Connie Britton), who has started work as the high school guidance counselor. And, of course, the members of the team itself. But for a show ostensibly about football, *Friday Night Lights* is less concerned with the sacks and gains those kids make than you would think; instead, *Lights* tackles race, class, unfulfilled dreams, abuse, and poverty as it empathetically paints its complex and close-knit community. Among the huffed-up future football superstars, damaged cheerleaders, and other teens we meet, two very different young men most fully capture viewers' hearts: Matt Saracen (Zach Gilford), the shy, stuttering backup QB thrust into the spotlight when the starter goes down, and Tim Riggins (Taylor Kitsch), the trouble-on-and-off-the-field fullback who drinks, smokes, and screws his way through high school, painfully aware that playing for the Panthers is likely the best his life will get. Gilford and Kitsch are just two of the A-list names whose careers would be kicked off by their runs on *Lights*: Jesse Plemons, Jurnee Smollett-Bell, Michael B. Jordan, Aldis Hodge, and Caleb Landry Jones all show up. Never a ratings winner, the series moved to DirectTV in its third season, where it would eventually retire with a fitting and poignant finale that left few eyes clear, but many hearts full.

The Tudors

BBC TWO, SHOWTIME / 2007–2010
4 SEASONS / 38 EPISODES

🍅 **69%** 🍿 **85%**

With its lustful King Henry VIII (Jonathan Rhys Meyers) and handsome, scheming courtiers, *The Tudors* gave the finger to its Masterpiece period-drama brethren and offered a rock 'n' roll historical soap opera. Michael Hirst, writer of Academy Award Best Picture nominee *Elizabeth*, unleashed the sexy and smart drama about Henry's excesses and revolving bedroom door to mixed reviews, but to almost universal acclaim for its period detail. The series, with multiple Emmy wins for costumes, was also recognized with nominations for casting, and no wonder: It features then up-and-coming performers like Henry Cavill and Natalie Dormer, as well as legends like Peter O'Toole as Pope Paul III. Rhys Meyers played King Henry in leather pants with a swagger to make nuns blush, and that sensuality and modern edginess would set the tone for historical TV dramas to come like *Reign*, *The White Princess*, *Da Vinci's Demons*, and *The Borgias*.

In Treatment

HBO / 2008–2010
3 SEASONS / 106 EPISODES

🍅 88% 🍿 96%

Unlike many contemporary HBO dramas, *In Treatment* didn't air weekly. Instead, when it premiered back in 2008, it aired five times a week. Viewers were able to follow, in real time, as psychologist Paul Weston (Gabriel Byrne) attended to his daily appointments, seeing a patient the same day every week (as well as visiting his former mentor for his own session on Fridays). Such self-contained storytelling—borrowed wholesale from *BeTipul,* the Israeli series it's based on—made every episode a mini-play, driven solely by conversation. With Byrne as its gravitational force, *In Treatment* mined the process of therapy for maximum dramatic potential, serving as an acting showcase for its supporting cast, which got to play everything from suicidal teen gymnasts (Mia Wasikowska) to fighter pilots dealing with PTSD

(Blair Underwood). Weston's own midlife crisis and the show's meta-narrative about the talking cure made this literate melodrama as gripping as anything else on cable in the Peak TV era.

▶ CERTIFIED FRESH STREAK

▶ HIGHLY ADDICTIVE

ITV, PBS / 2010–2015
6 SEASONS / 52 EPISODES

 86% 🍿 95%

Fans of the 2001 Julian Fellowes–penned film *Gosford Park* found much to love in *Downton Abbey*. Here again was an upstairs/downstairs drama, set in the early 20th century at a lavish British estate, with Dame Maggie Smith as a deliciously curmudgeonly dowager. Originally planned as a spin-off of the film, Fellowes reworked it instead as a standalone miniseries about the Earl and Countess of Grantham and their three daughters, all grappling with the prospect of losing the titular estate. The ITV drama was an instant global phenomenon. Gripped by Lady Mary's (Michelle Dockery) romantic life, by the dowager's witty one-liners, and by the series's sumptuous style, audiences instantly clamored for more—and Fellowes delivered. Ushering in a British invasion on US TV, courtesy of PBS, the gilded soap opera ended up running for six seasons (and a 2019 movie), using everything from the 1918 Spanish flu epidemic to the British election of 1932 as backdrops for class-conscious melodramatic stories about ill-fated marriages, salacious affairs, and endless criminal trials that captured the changing face of Britain's aristocracy. The series was eventually capped by a Certified Fresh 2019 film in which the Granthams welcome their most demanding guests yet: the king and queen of England.

BACK TO SCHOOL:

The best in class for televisions teen dramas

MOST LIKELY TO HANG OUT AT A COMIC-BOOK SHOP

Riverdale

The CW (2017–), 5 seasons
● 86% ⊟ 58%

And not just because *Riverdale* is an adaptation of the classic Archie comics. The series follows the local teens as they live murder-filled lives rife with pop culture influences: see the movie-reference episode titles, musical episodes, and, casting of late teen heartthrob Luke Perry as Archie's dad.

MOST LIKELY TO HAVE TEENS ACTING THIRTYSOMETHING

Dawson's Creek

The WB (1998–2003), 6 seasons
●-- 🏆 79%

Dawson (James Van Der Beek), Joey (Katie Holmes), Pacey (Joshua Jackson), and Jen (Michelle Williams) talk about themselves and everyone else with a self-awareness that might be annoying if they weren't otherwise still just a bunch of modern teens dealing with love, friendship, and, in one of the series's best story lines, sexuality.

MOST LIKELY TO HAVE TEENS THAT ACTUALLY ACT LIKE AVERAGE TEENS

My So-Called Life

ABC (1994–1995), 1 season
● 95% 🏆 95%

Few series so perfectly portray the raw angst of the teen years and the certainty that nothing will ever be as important as everything feels at this time of your life. And, thanks to Claire Danes's vulnerable turn as Angela Chase, few series of any genre remain as influential as this one-season favorite.

MOST LIKELY TO HAVE A THIRTYSOMETHING PLAYING A TEEN

Beverly Hills, 90210

Fox (1990–2000), 10 seasons
●-- 🏆 94%

Technically, Ian Ziering and Gabrielle Carteris were only in their late twenties when they started on this teen drama, and while that's good for a perpetual joke, no one was laughing about the phenomenon *90210* became. The series's Brandon/Kelly/Dylan triangle was also the model for many teen soap love rivalries to come (i.e., Dawson/Joey/Pacey).

MOST LIKELY TO LAUNCH THE CAREERS OF FUTURE MOVIE STARS

Skins

E4 (2007–2013), 7 seasons
●-- 🏆 74%

Oscar nominees Daniel Kaluuya and Dev Patel, and Nicholas Hoult are alums of this British hit (which spawned a less successful American counterpart), also known for its controversial portrayal of issues like abortion and violence and for keeping the stories fresh by swapping in new cast members in its seven-season run.

MOST LIKELY TO FEATURE ONE OF YOUR NEW FAVORITE TEENAGE HEROINES

Never Have I Ever
Netflix (2020–), 2 seasons

🍅 97% 🍿 89%

Mindy Kaling created this dramedy about super-smart Indian American high school junior Devi (Maitreyi Ramakrishnan), who's both proud and annoyed by her heritage, is obsessed with having a boyfriend, and butts heads with her mother. Tennis legend John McEnroe narrates Devi's life, which is less random, and far funnier, than it sounds.

MOST LIKELY TO TEACH REAL TEENS ABOUT POSTMODERNISM

The O.C.
Fox (2003–2007), 4 seasons

🍅 67% 🍿 72%

How meta is this drama about a troubled teen (Ben McKenzie) who's adopted by a wealthy Newport Beach family? Okay, concentrate: *The O.C.* inspired MTV's reality series *Laguna Beach: The Real Orange County*; meanwhile, in *The O.C.* itself, characters watch a show-with-in-the-show called *The Valley*, which also has a reality TV equivalent. Layers!

MOST LIKELY TO FEATURE TEENS MORE MATURE THAN THEIR PARENTS

Sex Education
Netflix (2019–), 3 seasons

🍅 94% 🍿 –

Otis (Asa Butterfield) is privy to the advice his sex therapist mother, Jean (Gillian Anderson), doles out, and despite his personal anxieties on that subject, uses his knowledge to launch a secret sex therapy service at school. Frisky teen adventures ensue, as does an enlightened effort by the young ones to genuinely respect themselves and each other.

MOST LIKELY TO HAVE TEENS WHOSE WARDROBES COST MORE THAN YOUR HOUSE

Gossip Girl
The CW (2007–2012), 6 seasons

🍅 84% 🍿 78%

For the Upper East Siders attending the Constance Billard School for Girls and St. Jude's School for Boys, the only dirty word in their vocabulary is "scholarship." That doesn't stop handsome middle-class prep student Dan Humphrey (Penn Badgley) from ingratiating himself right to center of the drama-soaked social scene and making a huge impact.

MOST LIKELY TO INTRODUCE TEENS YOU HAVEN'T SEEN ON TV BEFORE

On My Block
Netflix (2018–), 3 seasons

🍅 95% 🍿 91%

Four lifelong LA friends find their relationships shifting as they start high school, with gangs and violence as much a part of their lives as aspirations and quinceañeras. Tonal shifts may jar, but it's well worth the ride to see this candid portrayal of a diverse, endearing group of characters.

Pose

 GAME-CHANGER

 PERFECT CERTIFIED FRESH STREAK

FX / 2018–2021
3 SEASONS / 25 EPISODES

🍅 **98%** 🍿 **89%**

▶ **CRITICS CONSENSUS** Charged with energy, poise, and confidence, *Pose* pirouettes between artistic opulence and deliciously soapy drama to create a fresh new addition to Ryan Murphy's lexicon. (Season 1)

▶ **WHAT IT'S ABOUT** It's late 1980s New York and Blanca (Mj Rodriguez), tired of being mistreated by her chosen family, sets out to start one of her own. Modeling the type of motherhood she herself didn't receive, her goal is to make an impact on the underground ballroom scene—and the world.

When the history books look back at the 2010s in TV, *Pose* might be seen as the industry's most transformative show.

Created by Steven Canals and produced by powerhouse duo Ryan Murphy and Brad Falchuk, the series is set in the 1980s and 1990s New York ballroom culture, and mirrors the real-life world in which mainly Black and Brown LGBTQ+ people find community and family in the underground scene of competitions, or balls, in which they battle it out to see who can vogue the best, catwalk like Naomi Campbell, and more. (For most people, Jennie Livingston's documentary *Paris Is Burning* was their first introduction to this world; Livingston is a consulting producer on *Pose*.)

At its core, *Pose* is a family drama with all the bells and whistles of the genre. But these families are chosen, and the bells and whistles are literal (and extravagant). The story lines are not only relatable, they're rooted in the lived experiences of a community that doesn't often see themselves authentically reflected on screens large or small.

A culmination of decades of work by trans actors to prove their worth to an industry—and broader society—whose experiences were often relegated to transphobic story lines on cop procedurals or sensational segments on shows like *The Jerry Springer Show* and *Maury*, *Pose* was iconic before a single scene had been filmed.

The series made history by casting Black and Brown trans actors Mj Rodriguez, Angelica Ross, Indya Moore, Hailie Sahar, and Dominique Jackson as its leads. That gave *Pose* the largest cast of season regulars who are trans of any television production. And that distinction was important at the show's launch, given that it came at a time in which demands for authentic casting—selecting trans people to play trans characters, as opposed to the popular practice of hiring cisgender actors for trans roles—in Hollywood were at an all-time high. (And these calls were still coming after Laverne Cox ushered in what *TIME* called the "transgender tipping point" with her groundbreaking *Orange Is the New Black* role and Joey Soloway created their influential series, *Transparent*.)

Pose also smashed down barriers off-screen. Of particular note is Murphy's recruitment of journalist and author Janet Mock to join the writing team. While the decision in retrospect was an obvious one—to have a Black trans woman help craft the stories of Black and Brown trans characters—at the time it wasn't often that writers' rooms reflected the lived experiences of the often-marginalized characters whose stories they crafted. When Mock signed on, she became the first Black trans woman to write for television. She would add "first Black trans woman to direct for television" to her list of personal achievements when she helmed episode 6 of the first season, titled "Love Is the Message" and featuring the heart-wrenching death of Pray Tell's

(Billy Porter) lover to complications of AIDS. Based on her work on *Pose*, Mock signed a landmark production deal with Netflix.

Pose broke all this ground while delivering engrossing television, developing story lines for its cast of lovable characters that were pulled, in many instances, from LGBTQ+ history, among them: the lived experiences of trans model Tracey Africa; the organizing and activist efforts by ACT UP during the AIDS epidemic; and the ongoing, shockingly frequent killings of Black trans women. While undoubtedly creative fiction, *Pose* weaved in nods to the real-life happenings of the time period it reflects, creating a socially conscious, historically relevant piece of art that critics and fans alike applaud. And all of this was done amid a host of fantastically staged balls and parties that pay tribute to the vibrancy of the culture.

▶ **BEST EPISODE** Season 2, Episode 4—"Never Knew Love Like This Before." Featuring the death of one of the show's main characters, the episode raises awareness about the epidemic of violence against Black trans women.

▶ **CHARACTER WE LOVE** It's a tie between Blanca, the beating heart of the show, and Elektra (Dominique Jackson), the evil stepmother you hate to love and love to hate.

Girls

HBO / 2012–2017
6 SEASONS / 62 EPISODES

 89% 73%

Best known as the series that launched a million hot takes about millennials (and women's bodies, gentrification, sex on TV, and anything else you can think of), Lena Dunham's *Girls* was *the* show to talk about in 2012. Focused on Hannah Horvath (Dunham) and her circle of Brooklynite friends, the dramedy drew ire and admiration from all corners. Hannah's struggles with sex, money, men, and writing were nakedly observed under Dunham and co-showrunner Jenni Konner's unvarnished gaze, which never shied away from positing the show's characters as complex—and therefore oftentimes unlikable—people. Boasting an ensemble of up-and-comers that included Allison Williams and Adam Driver, *Girls* captured a youthful zeitgeist with aplomb, daring critics and viewers to go along on its ride of season-long arcs about friendships torn apart and artistic ambitions deferred. Instantly iconic bottle episodes like "American Bitch" and "One Man's Trash" took on prickly conversations about consent and desire.

Scandal

▶ CERTIFIED FRESH STREAK

▶ HIGHLY ADDICTIVE

ABC / 2012–2018
7 SEASONS / 124 EPISODES

 93% 74%

It's the rare TV drama that earns a Certified Fresh Tomatometer score for all but one of its seasons— especially when there are seven of them. But then *Scandal* was a rare breed. Executive producer Shonda Rhimes poured everything that had defined her soapy, totally addicting *Grey's Anatomy* and its spin-off *Private Practice* into this pulpy DC political thriller: head-spinning twists; steamy couplings; a pitch-perfect use of music and stylish camerawork to sustain our sugary rush; and a compelling and complex woman at the center of it all. Kerry Washington's Olivia Pope is the capital's best "fixer," a former White House director of communications who now manages crises—cover-ups, assassination attempts, her own affair with the president (Tony Goldwyn)—along with the associates of her firm. Just try to catch your breath as she and the team work to stay ahead of the next absurd and fitfully entertaining twist Shondaland throws at them.

Vikings

HISTORY / 2013–2020
6 SEASONS / 89 EPISODES

 93% 89%

HBO kicked off the sword-swinging historical drama fad with its 2005 series *Rome*, which paved the way for shows like Starz's gladiator series *Spartacus* (2010) and BBC America/Netflix's early Anglo-Saxon series *The Last Kingdom* (2015). But none has experienced the success of or generated the same level of gleeful fan fervor as History's *Vikings*. From Michael Hirst (*The Tudors*), the series tells the story of Ragnar Lothbrok (Travis Fimmel)—based on a legendary real-life Viking chieftain—his warrior wife Lagertha (Katheryn Winnick), and his brood of sons who fight for leadership of Kattegat, a center of commerce in medieval Scandinavia. Theirs is a rags-to-riches story, starting as a humble farming family that scrapes, fights, and plunders its way to the top of Viking society. But, as with many families, ambition can also be a curse when son-battles-son-battles-stepmom-battles-cousin and so on for dominance. A smaller network's response to *Game of Thrones*—and an opportunity for lovers of the genre to chase one with the other, or vice versa—*Vikings* delivered handsome stars and as much gore as HBO's massive hit. Fimmel set the standard for *Vikings*'s actors with his charismatic portrayal of ambitious warrior and leader Ragnar. The series became a fan favorite—its stars drew crowds to packed-out Comic-Con halls—and would spawn a spin-off: The Netflix series *Vikings: Valhalla* begins 100 years after the conclusion of the original series and focuses on famous Vikings like Leif Eriksson and Norman King (and Viking descendant) William the Conqueror.

Jane the Virgin

THE CW / 2014–2019
5 SEASONS / 100 EPISODES

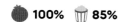 100% 85%

Jane the Virgin's premise sounds straight out of a telenovela: A happily engaged writer-in-the-making saving herself for marriage gets pregnant after a mishap at her ob-gyn's office—oh, and her boss, whom she might be in love with, is the father! And, well, that's because it is. But The CW's charming take on the hit Venezuelan series, *Juana la Virgen,* didn't just adapt its outlandish plot. Narrated by a Latin lover–type voice-over artist, the much-cherished bilingual postmodern drama embraced a meta-approach to its twisty storytelling, constantly winking at its audience even as it offered one of the most sweet-natured shows to premiere during the Peak TV era. Swinging wildly between its soapy love triangle, its broad comedy (courtesy

of scene-stealer Jaime Camil as Rogelio de la Vega, Jane's estranged father and telenovela leading man), and many an improbable subplot involving a criminal mastermind by the name of Sin Rostro, this hidden gem was always anchored by the winsome charm of Gina Rodriguez's central performance.

One of the most sweet-natured shows to premiere during the Peak TV era.

Transparent

▶ CERTIFIED FRESH STREAK
▶ GAME-CHANGER

AMAZON PRIME VIDEO / 2014–2019
5 SEASONS / 41 EPISODES

 90% 77%

The word *groundbreaking* gets thrown around a lot, but *Transparent*, to be sure, is just that. Joey Soloway's series follows Maura, a trans woman (Jeffrey Tambor, in a career-topping turn, which is saying something), her ball-of-energy of an ex-wife (Judith Light), and their grown-up children who are all, to varying degrees, lost: Sarah (Amy Landecker), Josh (Jay Duplass), and Ali (Gaby Hoffmann). But beyond its groundbreaking subject matter, what propels all the big ideas this show explores—about trans rights, Jewish identity, sex, ego, family, Los Angeles, and on and on—is a drama that's absorbing, moving, and, occasionally, sharply funny. Even when a character acts selfishly or shortsightedly (Spoiler: This happens often), it's hard not to pull for them and hope that they find their own little slice of happiness, if only for a spell—whatever that may entail.

BINGE BATTLE

SHAMELESS (UK) ◀ VS ▶ SHAMELESS (US)

Two houses, both alike in indignity, go head to head: the Gallaghers of Manchester and the Gallaghers of Chicago, the central families of British dramedy *Shameless* and its US adaptation. Both shows put a sharp focus on poor and marginalized people that neither nation's TV-makers frequently choose to focus on. Which did it better?

Shameless (UK)

CHANNEL 4 / 2005–2012
11 SEASONS / 139 EPISODES

▶ **WHAT IT'S ABOUT** This gritty dramedy plunged viewers into a world rarely seen on British screens: life among the families living in a run-down council estate in greater Manchester. Our tour guides are the Gallaghers, a dysfunctional but ultimately loving bunch, headed up by hard-drinking, long-rambling Frank (David Threlfall), who has a lot to say about discrimination against the working man, even though he has an aversion to work himself. As the series went on, focus shifted to other families in the Chatham estate, and beloved cast members—including Anne-Marie Duff as eldest daughter Fiona and a young James McAvoy as her boyfriend Steve—left.

Shameless (US)

SHOWTIME / 2011–2021
11 SEASONS / 134 EPISODES

 82% **79%**

▶ **WHAT IT'S ABOUT** This faithful adaptation, EP'd by the British series's creator Paul Abbott, shifts the action to the South Side of Chicago, but keeps the players—Frank (here William H. Macy), Fiona (Emmy Rossum), Steve (Justin Chatwin), and the rest—and the themes—the struggles of poverty, addiction, sexuality—largely the same. The show was originally developed by former *ER* and *West Wing* showrunner John Wells for HBO, but moved to Showtime before its launch, where it became the cable network's longest-running scripted series ever.

◀ AWARDS ▶

1 BAFTA
(for Best Drama Series in 2005)

4 Emmys
(3 for stunt coordination,
1 for Guest Actress Joan Cusack)

GALLAGHER

◀ STANDOUT SIBLING ▶

All six bring something to the table, but for us it's **Debbie Gallagher** (Rebecca Ryan, who started playing her at age 11). The weird little girl from season 1 is forced to grow up when Fiona leaves the next year, and her growth—and sweet connection with Frank—becomes the heart of the show.

The incredible Emmy Rossum as **Fiona,** who stuck around for 10 seasons of the US series, and gave us a resourceful, witty, deeply caring, and occasionally fallible heroine to root for as father Frank continued to f—k things up, over and over. Little wonder the series lost some magic when she left.

▶ **OUR PICK** We're raising a frothy one to the Americans. There's something to be said for the totally unvarnished, uncensored original, and if we were only judging its first few years, the Brit Gallaghers would take the win. But the series suffered by losing key characters early on, and from an ill-advised tonal shift around season 8—more of the cartoonish high jinks less of the social commentary. **Shameless (US),** with Rossum at its heart for nearly its entire stretch, only got better.

Empire

FOX / 2015–2020
6 SEASONS / 103 EPISODES

🍅 **84%** 🪣 **49%**

Sometimes described as a *King Lear*–inspired story set in the world of hip-hop, the Danny Strong– and Lee Daniels–created *Empire* helped redefine television. That was partly due to its focus: As with fellow mid-2010s groundbreakers, Shonda Rhimes's *Scandal* and *How to Get Away with Murder*, *Empire* was a major network drama centered on a Black woman. But it was the richness, and frankly eventual *iconicness* of that character that made *Empire* a smash as well as a milestone.

The show was the fastest-growing new drama on television in a decade. And deservedly so.

Oscar nominee Taraji P. Henson memorably played Cookie Lyon, the ride-or-die ex-wife of Terrence Howard's Lucious Lyon, who served 17 years in prison to protect her family. When she gets out at the beginning of the series, she returns to the lives of her three sons (Trai Byers, Jussie Smollett, and Bryshere Y. Gray) and to get her piece of the family's multimillion-dollar record label. With its mix of high drama (of the camp variety), flashy musical numbers, and sociopolitically charged story lines, the show was the fastest-growing new drama on television in a decade. And deservedly so.

The Crown

NETFLIX / 2016–
4 SEASONS / 40 EPISODES

🍅 **90%** 🪣 **90%**

The Crown brings England's royal family to the masses in an addictively bingeable format, humanizing Queen Elizabeth II; her husband Philip, duke of Edinburgh; their son Charles, prince of Wales; as well as the royalty and courtiers circling in their orbit in one of the most elaborate and expensive series ever made. Creator Peter Morgan, Oscar-nominated for his original screenplay for *The Queen*, treads familiar territory with the series, which for the most part treats the family sympathetically as it portrays their highs and lows. *The Crown* wowed critics and fans with its debut, garnering a Certified Fresh Tomatometer score for season 1 and attracting Emmy nominations like moths to a flame. Among the nominees: Claire Foy and Olivia Colman for their work playing the younger and then middle-aged Elizabeth II over the course of the first four seasons. (Veteran British actress Imelda Staunton steps in for season 5, and the rest of the core cast similarly trades out every two seasons.) The series interweaves the Windsors' family drama with major historical events—Elizabeth's coronation, the death of Winston Churchill (John Lithgow), Margaret Thatcher's (Gillian Anderson) stint as prime minister and the Falklands War, and Charles (Josh O'Connor) and Diana's (Emma Corrin in season 4) courtship, fairy-tale wedding, and ultimate estrangement. But Elizabeth is the star of the series, which charts her life from childhood and the warm relationship with her father and predecessor, George VI (Jared Harris), through to her marriage and on her way to becoming the United Kingdom's longest-reigning monarch.

This Is Us

> ▶ **CERTIFIED FRESH STREAK**

> ▶ **HIGHLY ADDICTIVE**

NBC / 2016–

5 SEASONS / 90 EPISODES

🍅 93%   🗑 73%

Even by the standards of soapy family dramas, *This Is Us* tugs the heartstrings in ways that make a box of Kleenex and a rehydrating beverage necessary viewing accompaniments. The NBC series is led by an excellent, diverse writing staff and a deep bench of on-screen talent that has given us one of primetime's *leading* leading men in Sterling K. Brown. In lesser hands, the decades-spanning story of triplets Kate (Chrissy Metz), Kevin (Justin Hartley), Randall Pearson (Brown), and their parents Rebecca and Jack (Mandy Moore and Milo Ventimiglia) could feel emotionally manipulative. Instead, even "The Big Three's" most frustrating life choices endear them to us, and the series's signature flashbacks and flash-forwards, key since the jaw-dropping pilot to unfolding the twist-filled saga, have allowed for gentle revelations and character development aplenty.

Queen Sugar

OPRAH WINFREY NETWORK / 2016–

5 SEASONS / 65 EPISODES

🍅 98%   🗑 91%

Ava DuVernay's *Queen Sugar* is a perfect example of what socially conscious, universally enthralling television looks like. Based on the 2014 novel of the same name by Natalie Baszile, this family drama follows the lives of three siblings (Rutina

Wesley, Dawn-Lyen Gardner, and Kofi Siriboe) grappling with what to do with the family's 800-acre sugarcane farm in Louisiana in the aftermath of their dad's sudden death. The Oprah Winfrey Network production (Winfrey also serves as an executive producer) masterfully addresses the legacy of chattel slavery, criminal justice inequality, and countless other issues of importance to Black Americans in a poetic, yet grounded fashion—all while packing an entertaining, sometimes jaw-dropping or tears-inducing punch. Featuring arresting supporting performances by the likes of Omar Dorsey, Tina Lifford, and Bianca Lawson, among others, the series is the first in which women direct every single episode.

Underground

> ▶ **GONE TOO SOON**

WGN AMERICA / 2016–2017

1 SEASON / 20 EPISODES

🍅 96%   🗑 87%

Before Misha Green investigated present-day racial horror through sci-fi terror in *Lovecraft Country*, she and co-creator Joe Pokaski fearlessly tackled slavery in the bingeable melodrama *Underground*. Set in antebellum Georgia, the series follows blacksmith Noah (Aldis Hodge) and house slave Rosalee (Jurnee Smollett) as they pursue freedom and secretly shuttle slaves to the North with the help of Harriet Tubman (Aisha Hinds). The series chronicles the legend of the Underground Railroad in an original way: not solely by dramatizing vicious racial violence, but by using modern music and visuals to spotlight the characters' transcendence from oppression. We see this approach from the pilot's opening sequence, featuring fragmented shots of Noah running from slave catchers as

Kanye West's "Black Skinhead" thumps hard in the background. Imbuing a slave narrative with blockbuster thrills was a big risk, but in Green's *Underground*, it paid off.

Claws

TNT / 2017–2021
4 SEASONS / 40 EPISODES

 90% 🗑 82%

This dark comedy from creator Eliot Laurence made a deliberate point of focusing on characters—and performers—often relegated to the margins. The stacked and diverse cast of *Claws* features players who had seen supporting success elsewhere, but not yet gotten their chance to lead, among them *True Blood*'s Carrie Preston, *Scrubs*'s Judy Reyes, *Oz*'s Harold Perrineau, *Breaking Bad*'s Dean Norris, and, crucially, *Reno-911* standout Niecy Nash as Desna Simms, the owner of a South Florida nail salon whose artists get involved in organized crime when they start laundering money. The swampy, campy, tele-novela-style drama is a turn of the page from the likes of *Breaking Bad* and *Sons of Anarchy*, moving the antihero genre in a sex-positive, body-positive, female-forward direction with welcome ethnic, sexuality, and gender representation. It's less about guns and nails—though they're spectacular—than it is a riff on authentic female friendship. And, among the women, you will find your favorite new curvy champion in Nash's Desna. This dedicated boss with a soft heart simultaneously balances Russian mobster vendettas while caring for her mentally challenged brother and maintaining her friendships and business—nails sharp, face beat, hair flawless, and waist cinched the whole time.

The Marvelous Mrs. Maisel

▶ PERFECT CERTIFIED FRESH STREAK

AMAZON PRIME VIDEO / 2017–
3 SEASONS / 26 EPISODES

🍅 88% 🗑 89%

There is no character quite as quick and snappy as the titular heroine of Amy Sherman-Palladino's *The Marvelous Mrs. Maisel.* Played by the winsome (and Emmy-winning) Rachel Brosnahan, "Midge" speaks fluent Sherman-Palladino, the mile-a-minute screwball-meets-Sorkinese dialogue the writer perfected with *Gilmore Girls*. A 1950s New York City housewife who forsakes her life as a homemaker to make it as a comedy star, Midge is the kind of magnetic presence whose stand-up bits—about her divorce, her fastidious but loving Jewish parents, her kids—are thrilling precisely because they harken back to the Hepburns and Lombards of yore. Designed and directed like a musical, with sweeping, choreographed, long takes, anchored around its stylish feminist lead, the series was an instant critical darling and an audience favorite, serving as a whimsical re-creation of midcentury comedy clubs that spoke all too urgently to 21st-century concerns. (Spoiler alert: Yes, women *are* funny!)

Succession

HBO / 2018–
2 SEASONS / 20 EPISODES

🍅 92% 🗑 88%

In 2018, just when we thought movies and shows about families of filthy-rich a-holes had been done to death, along came this dramedy, which, along with being devilishly fun to watch and wonderfully cast and plotted, also happened to be the best-written show on television. *Succession* follows a Murdoch-like media mogul (Brian Cox, in arguably his greatest performance) and his children, Jeremy Strong's Kendall (the problematic heir apparent), Sarah Snook's Shiv (the political black sheep), Kieran Culkin's Roman (the smart-ass man-child), and Alan Ruck's Connor (the oblivious eldest). To be in this family—and its business—is to swim in a sea of well-dressed sharks, and creator Jesse Armstrong (of the beloved British comedy *Peep Show*) and Company's scripts are packed with dialogue so vitriolic and funny that they're almost poetic.

Vida

STARZ / 2018–2020
3 SEASONS / 22 EPISODES

 100% 80%

Inspired by Richard Villegas Jr.'s short story "Pour Vida," Tanya Saracho's drama follows two Latinx sisters (Melissa Barrera and Mishel Pradawho) who return to their East Los Angeles neighborhood home after their mother dies; upon doing so, they discover that their mom was in a relationship with another woman. Applauded for centering such a narrative against a decidedly Mexican American backdrop, the show continued to be an inclusive, intersectional experience throughout all three of its seasons, mixing English, Spanish, and Spanglish—sans subtitles—in almost every scene, and earned rare critical acclaim along the way: Every season is 100% Fresh on the Tomatometer. An added bonus was its steamy sex scenes of the variety only a premium cable network like Starz can deliver, in which its leads unapologetically courted men, women, and nonbinary folks.

David Makes Man

OPRAH WINFREY NETWORK / 2019–
2 SEASONS / 20 EPISODES

 100% 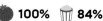 84%

Any time a young, fresh face in Hollywood wins an Oscar, the industry wants to know what they're going to do next. For playwright Tarell Alvin McCraney, who shares an Academy Award with writer-director Barry Jenkins for penning the play that inspired 2016's *Moonlight*, his answer was the coming-of-age drama *David Makes Man*. The show follows a 14-year-old prodigy named David from the projects (Akili McDowell), who is haunted by the death of his closest friend. Bused out of his community to a mostly white school, David is forced to don two personas: one to navigate the streets that raised him and another to succeed in the education system that may offer him a way out. (Season 2—which premiered after we went to print—follows David in his 30s, now played by Kwame Patterson.) The South Florida–set series, which also stars Alana Arenas, Isaiah Johnson, and icon Phylicia Rashad, among others, is a thoughtful interrogation of what it means to survive the circumstances into which one was born. Its cast of largely fresh faces—led confidently by 17-year-old McDowell—breathes life into the show's vividly nuanced writing, which elevates the series from what could be a running "very special episode" to a rich, expansive exploration of the many ways the "American dream" evades Black and poor communities. It's lyrical and poetic (thanks to incredible cinematography), unlike anything else on television, but it's not didactic. And with fan favorite, gender nonconforming character Mx. Elijah (Travis Coles), there's plenty of levity to keep you coming back for more complex storytelling.

Euphoria

HBO / 2019–
1 SEASON / 8 EPISODES + 2 SPECIALS

 90% 85%

Sam Levinson's risqué HBO series *Euphoria* broke ground in two key ways: by being possibly TV's most unflinchingly bleak meditation on the teen experience to date, as well as the rare example of a teen drama led by a Black woman. Primarily following Rue (Zendaya), a teenage girl suffering from a crippling drug habit, *Euphoria* radically updated and upended the high school TV show formula, taking it to the dark side and diving headfirst into the sex, drugs, and insecurities swirling around late 2010s millennials.

Euphoria upended the high school TV show, taking it to the dark side.

Consider Rue's love interest, transgender teen Jules (played by trans actress Hunter Schafer), whose backstory slowly reveals the factors that led to her dangerous attraction to older homophobic men. The show has a look all its own—the camera is spontaneous and dynamic—which can sometimes sit uneasily with its subject matter. But Levinson's frank exploration of the impact of trauma, and the diverse cast that plays it out, mark this as essential—if uncomfortable—viewing. As does Zendaya's history-making performance: In 2020, at age 24, she became the youngest person to ever win Best Actress for a Drama at the Emmys.

You

▶ HIGHLY ADDICTIVE

LIFETIME, NETFLIX / 2019–
2 SEASONS / 20 EPISODES

 90% 81%

You brilliantly morphed *Gossip Girl*'s "Lonely Boy" Dan Humphreys, played by heartthrob Penn Badgley, into a sinister sex symbol that had many—including the man who plays him—strangely conflicted: Badgley is fond of reminding people that *You*'s Joe Goldberg is a murderer and a sociopath, and definitely *not* boyfriend material. The deliciously bingeable drama, based on Caroline Kepne's novel of the same name about a New York City bookstore clerk who stalks/seduces aspiring writer Guinevere Beck (Elizabeth Lail), debuted to little fanfare on basic cable channel Lifetime in 2018, but attracted a staggering international fan base when episodes became available on Netflix. (The streamer converted it to a Netflix Original for season 2 and beyond.) The fact that many find Joe—who breaks into Beck's house, hacks her phone, follows her, and kills her friends and exes—so alluring, speaks to the show's smart balance of charm and malevolence. And it speaks to Badgley's masterful performance, captured in his yearning and ever-present voice-over narration and unassuming demeanor, which grounds the show even as its twists stretch credulity further and further, particularly in the LA-set second season. Badgley may not want you to fall for evil Joe, but he makes it awfully hard not to. (And season 3 promises wilder times, still.)

Like HBO, Netflix's is a story of transformation: from Blockbuster-killing snail-mail DVD service, launched in 1997, to innovative video-on-demand provider to original content producer and on to global king of "streaming." Now, that familiar dah-dum heralds our nightly "Netflix and chill." Like HBO, too, Netflix changed the industry around it as it shook out of its old-tech cocoon. Here's how.

1 It Paid Up

Netflix execs knew that in order to compete in the prestige TV arena they were going to have to foot the bill as well as give creatives the freedom HBO was known for. That's why the fledgling streaming service outbid the cable network for David Fincher's *House of Cards*—a reported $100 million for two 13-episode seasons. It would go on to strike mega-deals with big TV names including Ryan Murphy and Shonda Rhimes, and, by 2020, upped its original content budget to a reported $16 billion.

2 It Began the Binge

Netflix had always planned to release the entire first season of *House of Cards* at once—shot as cinematically as possible to lure a feature director, like Fincher, perhaps—but when it did so, it changed the TV release model forever. We now have a term for the way *HoC* was meant to be watched in a couple of sittings: binge-watching. It's a model other streaming services, like Amazon Prime Video, and even some cable networks, like Syfy and youth-skewing Freeform, have now embraced for some of their programming.

3 It Sparked the Streaming Wars

Much as HBO inspired networks like Showtime and FX to move into scripted television, Netflix inspired studios to move into streaming. Competitors like Hulu, Amazon Prime Video, Disney+, NBCUniversal's Peacock changed the way they consume TV—cutting the cord and not subscribing to cable at all. Essentially, Netflix has changed the business model of an entire industry. (Though, as the competition starts to bundle, you might say the more things change, the more they stay the same . . .)

4 It Said, "Screw Ratings"

By withholding viewership data and making it difficult to even determine what the company considers a win, Netflix has also changed the way TV networks define success. This has been a boon for the company in that it can selectively promote whatever stats it wants to put forward—the Henry Cavill–led video game fantasy adaptation *The Witcher* got "76 million views in four weeks," though a "view" can be just two minutes. But it's also a bust in the eyes of fans when their beloved series are canceled with very little explanation.

5 It Introduced Us to the Algorithm

If Netflix were in a job interview, it would definitely say its flaw is that it has perhaps *too many* shows. It's *too* dedicated to providing viewers with ultra-tailored experiences! But the company also knows how to deliver those shows to the viewers who will enjoy them most, thanks to its proprietary, hyperspecific (and kinda terrifying, if you think about it) recommendation algorithm. Don't ask how it works, just trust the robot and click PLAY on another episode of *The Great Briti*

Genre Grows Up

NEXT-LEVEL HORROR, HEROES, SCI-FI, AND FANTASY

Science-fiction, horror, and fantasy series have been delivering some of the most sophisticated storytelling since the dawn of this once very sci-fi–seeming thing called TV. Consider *The Twilight Zone*. Or *The Outer Limits*. Or the very long-running and very prosperous *Star Trek* franchise. And yet viewers, critics, and awards voters haven't always given "genre" television—a blanket term we'll use to cover tales of aliens and monsters, ghosts and ghouls, magic and murderers and caped crusaders—the respect it deserves.

Game of Thrones, with its witches and dragons and White Walkers, may have broken umpteen Emmy records in the 2010s, but in the decades before its reign, *genre* was a dirty word. Some series cut through with awards voters: *Star Trek* picked up Emmy noms in the 1960s; *The X-Files*'s Gillian Anderson collected hardware for her portrayal of Dana Scully. For the most part, though, shows roundly considered groundbreaking today were ignored in their day, made to be content with nominations for special effects and makeup, and, very occasionally, for writing or direction.

Because the best thing on TV *couldn't* be that show about the high schooler killing vampires, *right*? (Spoiler: In 1997, it was, and you can read about it and its complicated legacy in this chapter.)

How did genre grow up and command the respect it gets today? By being completely undeniable. While 20th-century genre gems were often outliers—a lot of genre TV *was* pretty bad—in today's era of Peak TV, great sci-fi, fantasy, and horror series are produced at a clip, and by some of the most creative minds working in the medium. Consider that, in 2019 alone, three of the most inventive and acclaimed comic-book adaptations ever—*The Umbrella Academy*, *Doom Patrol*,

and *The Boys*—premiered just months before what many consider the best of all time, *Watchmen*, with names like *Lost* co-creator Damon Lindelof and Seth Rogen attached. Peak TV is not purely the domain of *anti*heroes.

Technology, appropriately, played its part: Spend-happy cable and streaming companies are only too glad to throw money at special effects teams to bring to life monsters and worlds once reserved for big-screen projects. But it also played its part in another way. The DVR and streaming's reshaping of our viewing habits—our collective shift to the "binge"—allowed creators to embrace the complexity inherent in the best literary works of genre. Suddenly, source material considered "unfilmable" in a time of episodic weekly chapters was being crafted into attention-demanding serialized epics, ready to be consumed by fans in big glugs, like the hefty science-fiction and fantasy novels bricking their bookshelves.

Not all the shows in this chapter were produced in this recent environment; some laid the groundwork back when magic and beasties pigeonholed a show in the "not serious" zone. They broke the ground, and we're happy to conjure some light to shine on them here.

Doctor Who

BBC / 1963–1989, 2005–
38+ SEASONS / 800+ EPISODES

 92%* 69%*

*2005– REVIVAL

Centuries from now, the BBC's *Doctor Who* could be as foundational as King Arthur and Robin Hood—the character is just that mythical. The series follows the wanderings of a mysterious alien—the human-looking title character—who travels through time and space in a machine disguised as a police call box (the TARDIS), and changes its appearance when seriously harmed. This in-universe twist means the lead character is regularly recast, and has helped enable its longevity. The show is loved, though, because of the Doctor (never "Doctor Who"), a children's hero who's charmed generations of adults with wit, ingenuity, and reluctance to use violence as a solution. Whether watching the original series (1963–1989) or its continuation (2005–)—or any of the 13 people to star as the Doctor—the essential appeal of the character shines through beyond cast changes and the march of time. The Doctor's antagonists, which include the mini-tanks known as Daleks and the emotionless Cybermen, are also an oft-terrifying draw.

The X-Files

▶ HIGHLY ADDICTIVE

FOX / 1993–2002, 2016–2018 (REVIVAL)
11 SEASONS / 218 EPISODES

 74%* 86%*

*1993–2002 SERIES

The X-Files's iconic opening theme—dance remixes of the track raced up the charts in Europe in the mid-'90s—announced from episode 1 what audiences were in for. As composer Marc Snow's whistle repeats, we see grainy UFO footage, a warping human face, and then those now-famous words: "The Truth Is Out There." Like that montage, creator Chris Carter's series was weird, disturbing, conspiracy-obsessed—and the world could not look away. The "X-Files" in question were a set of marginalized FBI cases, usually of the paranormal variety, investigated by agents Fox Mulder (David Duchovny), a *very* open-minded believer, and Dana Scully (Gillian Anderson), his skeptical partner and a medical doctor. Mostly, the duo faced monsters of the week, among them creations that took TV horror to terrifying new levels: Think the murderous inbred family of season 4's "Home," the first television episode to be slapped with a TV-MA rating. But what kept true believers on the hook and spawned two films, two spin-offs, and a 2016–2018 revival was the series's complex and ongoing "mytharc," which followed the discovery of a government conspiracy featuring little green men, a mysterious black oil, and a man with a *serious* smoking habit. That and the chemistry between Duchovny and Anderson, which was almost, well, *supernatural*.

Xena: Warrior Princess

SYNDICATED / 1995–2001
6 SEASONS / 134 EPISODES

 –– 🗑 86%

It's a testament to Lucy Lawless and her portrayal of Xena that the character began as a minor guest star on the fantasy series *Hercules* and inspired such an overwhelming fan reaction that she was given her own show. For six seasons, Xena and her farm girl–turned–warrior sidekick Gabrielle (Renee O'Connor) dished out justice across ancient Greece, eventually surpassing *Hercules* in ratings and popularity. But *Xena* offered more than just the campy pleasures of its predecessor; it tackled big issues without being preachy, explored LGBTQ-positive themes before it was cool, and proved it was just as much fun to watch women kick ass on TV as their male counterparts—maybe more so. The writing was often deeper than it needed to be, with genuinely complex characters and a fair share of narrative risks—including a fabulous musical episode—which helped solidify its cult classic status years before Buffy made girl power fashionable.

Alias

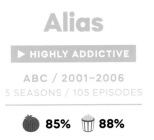

ABC / 2001–2006
5 SEASONS / 105 EPISODES

🍅 **85%** 🍿 **88%**

If you want a taste of what J. J. Abrams's signature "Mystery Box" storytelling looked like pre-*Lost* and *Fringe*, look no further than *Alias*. The spy thriller followed a seemingly ordinary young woman leading a double life as a secret, globe-trotting spy for a black-ops team called SD-6. Only, in the first of many (oh so many!) twists, Jennifer Garner's Sydney Bristow finds out she'd been recruited not by the CIA, but by a shady organization led by an eccentric former agent obsessed with a Renaissance prodigy whose inventions, if discovered, are said to hold untold power. Still with us? Because the show only got more outlandish from there (arguably spiraling out of control in its later seasons), as Sydney's attempts to bring down SD-6 from within were filled with plenty of double crosses, MacGuffins, retcons, doomed love affairs, amnesia bouts, explosive action sequences, a young Bradley Cooper (yes, really), and one of TV's greatest wig collections.

Firefly

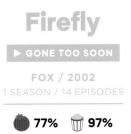

FOX / 2002
1 SEASON / 14 EPISODES

🍅 **77%** 🍿 **97%**

Firefly is the definition of cult TV. Created by *Buffy the Vampire Slayer*'s Joss Whedon, the sci-fi Western set on a smugglers' ship in the year 2517 had a famously bungled rollout. If you were a fan of the Fox show when it premiered back in 2002, there's a chance you didn't see its episodes in order, were confused about its East-meets-West sensibility (characters curse in Mandarin?), awed by its witty dialogue, and disappointed when the low-rated drama was unceremoniously canceled. There were enough vocal fans back then (Hi, "Browncoats"!) that by 2005 Universal released *Serenity*, a follow-up film about Captain Mal Reynolds (Nathan Fillion), his ragtag crew, and the superpowered girl who's as much an asset as a liability to their ship. Like the best of Whedon's work, *Firefly* endures for how it playfully subverts the well-worn tropes it calls forth; Mal, if you must know, is the kind of space cowboy who actually rides a horse on land.

Battlestar Galactica

SCI-FI CHANNEL (LATER SYFY) / 2004–2009
4 SEASONS / 76 EPISODES

🍅 **95%** 🍿 **93%**

In rebooting the 1978 space opera series for the mid-aughts, writer and executive producer Ronald D. Moore, collaborating with executive producer David Eick, swept away the *(Continued on page 110.)*

Buffy the Vampire Slayer

▶ GAME-CHANGER

▶ HIGHLY ADDICTIVE

THE WB, UPN / 1997–2003
7 SEASONS / 144 EPISODES

🍅 82%   🍿 92%

▶ CRITICS CONSENSUS *Buffy* slays her way into the pop-culture lexicon in a debut season that lays the groundwork for one of TV's greatest supernatural teen dramas. (Season 1)

▶ WHAT IT'S ABOUT When she transfers to Sunnydale High, party-happy popular girl Buffy Summers (Sarah Michelle Gellar) discovers she is the "chosen one" and spends the next seven years working with her Watcher (Anthony Head) and a group of friends (played by Alyson Hannigan, Seth Green, Nicholas Brendon, and others) to fight off a weekly influx of vampires, demons, and monsters drawn to the local Hellmouth.

For Joss Whedon, the TV series *Buffy the Vampire Slayer* was a correction to the movie *Buffy the Vampire Slayer*. The 1992 comedy was a flop that had lost a lot of its bite on its journey from Whedon's script to the big screen: Jokes that would one day become the writer's trademark were removed because they were too obscure and darker elements of the story were sliced away to keep things light. Whedon famously walked off the set in frustration during production.

He was determined that the same thing would not happen with the series—and it didn't. The *Buffy the Vampire Slayer* that premiered on The WB in March 1997 was Whedon's *Buffy* as intended: a surprisingly dark, supernatural tale that inverted the "blonde in distress" horror trope by putting her at the center of the action, stake in hand. (And, yes, it had obscure jokes aplenty: The stake's name was "Mr. Pointy.")

The first season's monsters look a bit cheesy these days—think men-in-suits and bargain-bin late-'90s CGI—but there was something about them, the show, and the characters that made audiences and critics realize that something different was going on here. The ghoulies were born from dark teenage realities, and the Scooby Gang, as Buffy and her friends would come to be known, fended them off as they grappled with their own burgeoning hormones and relationships.

The special effects got better, the stories more complex and increasingly serialized—each season has its overarching Big Bad, the best of which was season 3's jovial and terrifying mayor—and the performances richer. Gellar threw herself into the career-defining role, alternately nailing those obscure jokes with a self-knowing grin and breaking hearts as she agonized over her relationships with sometimes-reformed vampires Spike (James Marsters) and Angel (David Boreanaz).

It's little surprise that so many of the writers and producers on *Buffy* went on to big things—not just Whedon, who would define the MCU, and another kind of Scooby Gang, with *The Avengers*—but Marti Noxon (*UnReal*, *Sharp Objects*), Drew Goddard (*Cabin in the Woods*), and more. It was *Buffy*'s voice, as scripted by these minds, that came to define the series, a pop culture–fused and stylized patter that was the peak of the "high schoolers don't really talk like this" approach to 1990s teen movies and shows.

The legacy of Buffy has, in recent years, been complicated by the man whose mark it so indelibly bears. Charisma Carpenter (who plays fan favorite Cordelia), publicly accused Whedon of being "casually cruel" during production, playing favorites, and creating a toxic environment—other cast members came out in support. Gellar herself said that while proud to be associated with Buffy Summers, "I don't forever want to be associated with the name Joss Whedon." Its sexual and racial politics have also come under scrutiny.

Whedon would get the *Buffy* he always wanted, one that fans adored, but at a seemingly heavy cost.

▶ BEST EPISODE Season 5, Episode 16—"The Body." This departure in pace features the death of a major character in an incredibly quiet and raw 44 minutes of television.

▶ CHARACTER WE LOVE Willow Rosenberg (Alyson Hannigan), the smartest girl in school—and then college—whose journey from quirky naïf to powerful witch is one of the series's most compelling throughlines.

DEEP ▼ ▼ DIVE

corniness of the original to set the stage for a grittier, character-driven story of human survival among the stars. Starting with a 2003 three-hour miniseries that was a ratings hit for what was then known as the Sci-Fi Channel (now Syfy), the premise succeeded and the miniseries would serve as a backdoor pilot for the four-season series about humans fleeing war with their own android creations. The new creative team's most controversial move was a gender-flip on two of its lead characters, Starbuck and Boomer; male in Glen A. Larson's original late-1970s series, the characters were played by Katee Sackhoff and Grace Park, respectively, for the miniseries and the show. The rest of the crew was populated by actors familiar to TV genre fans and those who would go on to become synonymous with their roles: Edward James Olmos portrayed Commander Adama with Jamie Bamber as Captain Lee "Apollo" Adama, James Callis as Dr. Gaius Baltar, and Tricia Helfer as Cylon "Number Six." *Battlestar Galactica* wrapped up its main story in season 4 after winning critical acclaim and later landed on many best-of lists—including Rotten Tomatoes's own "Best Sci-Fi TV Shows of All Time"—but the rebooted series's universe kept giving even after the show's cancellation; in 2010, short-lived prequel spin-off *Caprica* aired on Syfy, where it traced the development of Cylon androids and starred Eric Stoltz, Esai Morales, and Paula Malcomson.

Supernatural

THE CW / 2005–2020
15 SEASONS / 325 EPISODES

🌑 **93%** 🗑 **78%**

The CW's longest-running series stars Jensen Ackles and Jared Padalecki as two hunky brothers, the Winchesters, who road-trip across the country in their 1967 Impala and hunt supernatural beings while searching for their missing father (Jeffrey Dean Morgan). Aside from looking good in Henleys—a prerequisite of the CW casting contract, we assume—Sam and Dean defeated countless demons, saved the world *soooo* many times, and brought each other back from the dead on multiple occasions over 15 seasons. Created by *The Boys*'s Eric Kripke, it is a large undertaking with plenty of ebbs and flows in quality (as you'd expect over a decade and a half). Overall, though, it's funny, scary, and a beautiful tribute to family—both blood and chosen.

Pushing Daisies

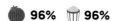
▶ GONE TOO SOON

ABC / 2007–2009
2 SEASONS / 22 EPISODES

🌑 **96%** 🗑 **96%**

There is something quite macabre about the premise of Bryan Fuller's *Pushing Daisies.* As its playful narrator informs viewers in the Barry Sonnenfeld–directed pilot episode, Ned, played by the affable Lee Pace, has the ability to bring people back from the dead with just a touch of his finger. Only, should he touch them again, they're dead forever. Such a "gift" has made the young pie-shop owner a guarded individual who nevertheless operates a side hustle solving increasingly improbable murder cases. (It helps, after all, when you can question the victims themselves.) What happens, though, when Ned is called to wake his deceased childhood crush Chuck (Anna Friel), knowing full well that even a chaste kiss may thereafter kill her permanently? Despite the morbid-sounding plot, this self-described "forensic fairy tale" was vibrant and colorful. In keeping with Fuller's previous work

(*Dead Like Me, Wonderfalls*), it existed in a hyper-real world where striking visuals and off-kilter story lines lived in harmony: Where else could you see Kristin Chenoweth re-creating a *Sound of Music* moment in an episode all about a bee-stinging–related murder plot at a honey-based cosmetics company? Alas, *Pushing Daisies'* queer and quirky sensibility never quite broke through. Its truncated first season (courtesy of the Writers Guild strike of 2007–2008) guaranteed that it came back for an even stronger if, again, curtailed second season (courtesy of ABC's cancellation notice). Ever since, the Emmy-winning show has been perennially dubbed a "gone too soon" gem, kept alive by its devoted fans who, to this day, hope to see what Ned and Chuck's happily ever after could have looked like. Listening, Netflix?

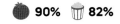

Fringe

FOX / 2008–2013
5 SEASONS / 100 EPISODES

🍅 90% 🗑 82%

Series creators J. J. Abrams (*Lost*), Alex Kurtzman (*Star Trek*), and Roberto Orci gave sci-fi fans a next-generation *X-Files*–like drama with *Fringe*. Newcomer Anna Torv played FBI Special Agent Olivia Dunham, who taps institutionalized genius Walter Bishop (John Noble) and his son Peter (Joshua Jackson) to help investigate what unfolds into a time-traveling, mind-bending multiverse mystery, in which scientist "Observers" from the future (like Michael Cerveris's "September") attempt to take over 2015 Earth. As if the show's sci-fi cred needed a boost, Leonard Nimoy (the *Star Trek* universe's Spock) appears as Dr. William Bell, founder of technology and pharmaceutical conglomerate Massive Dynamic. The series was critically acclaimed, but suffered during a time when networks were still figuring out how to make money off time-shifting viewership—DVRs were in about one-third of American homes and Netflix had just debuted its streaming service—which *Fringe*'s devoted fan base favored.

Terminator: The Sarah Connor Chronicles

 ▶ GONE TOO SOON

FOX / 2008–2009
2 SEASONS / 31 EPISODES

🍅 85% 🗑 87%

There is no story better suited to endless reboots and remakes than *The Terminator*. It's all about that time-travel conceit, which James Cameron first introduced in his seminal 1984 film in which Arnold Schwarzenegger's titular cyborg assassin was sent back in time to kill Sarah Connor in order to prevent her son John from leading the resistance against the terrifyingly self-aware A.I. known as Skynet. Since then, the long-running franchise has found countless ways of resetting its plots. With *Terminator: The Sarah Connor Chronicles,* Fox hoped to take the best bits of Cameron's lore and create a grounded drama centered on the mother-son duo. Developed by Josh Friedman, the short-lived series began with its own time-jumping premise, transporting an on-the-run Sarah (a pre–*Game of Thrones* Lena Headey) and a teenage John (Thomas Dekker) from 1999 to 2007, along with a new cyborg from the future (Summer Glau's always compelling Cameron), who's equal parts John's protector and love interest. The show did not have the big budgets of the Cameron films—which actually led to quite inventive action sequences, like a Johnny Cash–scored poolside FBI/Terminator showdown—but it had their *(Continued on page 114.)*

(Continued on page 114.)

CHOOSING THE RIGHT ARROWVERSE SHOW FOR YOU

Getting into The CW's so-called "Arrowverse"—a collection of interconnected series based on DC Comics characters and executive-produced by superproducer Greg Berlanti—can be an intimidating experience. With seven multiple-season shows on various networks and streaming outlets, there is a lot of superhero content to watch. Let this simple guide steer you toward the right show for you.

Are you in the mood for more Drama or more Comedy?

DRAMA!

ARE YOU A FAN OF ONE TREE HILL?

STARTS LIGHT

COMEDY!

HA HA HA

✗ NO   YES ✓

CHOOSE A PATH

ADORKABLE & NERDY

TALKING APES

TIME TRAVEL

STARTS DARK

SARCASTIC & GOOFY

SUPERSONIC FEET

SUPERSONIC FLIGHT

PICK A CITY

FREELAND

GOTHAM

So . . . dark & broody, what else?

DC HISTORY IN THE MAKING

BATARANGS

BROODY WITH A SIDE OF COMIC RELIEF . . .

PICK A STRENGTH

ARCHERY

DC'S LEGENDS OF TOMORROW

🍅 87% 🍿 70%

The CW | 2016– | 6 seasons

Though the show had a famously rough first season, it quickly found its voice when it leaned into the comedy chops of its cast. In the process, it became about a group of lesser-known DC characters—like the perpetually optimistic but unlucky-in-love Ray Palmer (Brandon Routh) and goofy history-bro Nate Heywood (Nick Zano)—whose time-traveling hi-jinks force them to become better people.

SUPERMAN & LOIS

🍅 87% 🍿 64%

The CW | 2021– | 1 season

The newest of the DC superhero shows sets out to re-frame the Man of Steel (Tyler Hoechlin, who also played Superman on *Supergirl*) as a concerned father. Both he and Lois (Elizabeth Tulloch) try their best to balance the demands of their family with their jobs as journalists and heroes. At the same time, the show gives their sons Jonathan (Jordan Elsass) and Jordan (Alex Garfin) meaty teen story lines, which may remind you of the days when The CW had more family dramas than spandex adventures.

THE FLASH

🍅 89% 🍿 66%

The CW | 2014– | 7 seasons

The cheery answer to *Arrow*'s moodiness—a point made whenever the shows cross over—is stuffed with nerdiness, thanks to its main location at S.T.A.R. Labs, heroic scientists like Cisco Ramon (Carlos Valdes) and Dr. Caitlin Snow (Danielle Panabaker), and, of course, its dorky main character, Barry Allen (Grant Gustin). The show also knows its DC Comics history and makes full use of it. From telepathic talking apes to multiversal crises, *The Flash* will scratch an itch to see some of the comics' wildest ideas realized on TV.

BLACK LIGHTNING

🍅 92% 🍿 49%

The CW | 2018–2021 | 4 seasons

Through its first three seasons, it pulled from events like the Tuskegee experiment to the CIA's deployment of crack cocaine (transformed into the show's fictional drug, Green Light) in the 1980s to give the community of Freeland's superpower problem a complicated and thought-provoking origin. And though the themes are heavy, the show cuts loose every now and again, with Black Lightning's (Cress Williams) headstrong younger daughter Jennifer (China Anne McClain) offering a teenager's viewpoint on the community's troubles.

SUPERGIRL

🍅 88% 🍿 51%

CBS and The CW | 2015–2021 6 seasons

Initially devised as a romantic comedy, the program scored a victory when it cast Melissa Benoist in the title role. The romantic element eventually fell by the wayside, but that adorable leading-lady energy makes Benoist a pleasure to watch when battling invading aliens, ordinary humans terrified of peaceful alien immigrants, or just trying to live her life as a young single professional.

ARROW

🍅 86% 🍿 63%

The CW | 2012–2020 8 seasons

The Arrowverse's debut program can be aggressively dark—particularly in its first season—as Oliver Queen (Stephen Amell) wages a one-man war against those who failed his city. His war eventually attracts other warriors, and the interplay between them offsets the bleak city streets and general broodiness of the lead character. And when the comedic byplay starts to get old, the show offers you a brutal (by network standards, anyway) fight scene.

BATWOMAN

🍅 84% 🍿 16%

The CW | 2019– | 2 seasons

The most high-profile LGBTQ+ hero in the DC Comics canon made a splashy debut in 2019 with an equally dramatic shift in its second season, thanks to the disappearance of Kate Kane (original series star Ruby Rose) and the arrival of Ryan Wilder (Javicia Leslie). But no matter who wears the cowl, *Batwoman* continues to chart TV superhero history with its focus on LGBTQ+ issues and its willingness to carry on after the departure of its original star.

same propulsive storytelling. In fact, its episodic pacing slowly made *The Sarah Connor Chronicles*, amid its banging action sequences and various takes on villainous Skynet fiends (including one played by *Garbage*'s Shirley Manson during the show's second season), a fascinating meditation on the toll it takes to constantly fight for a future that may well rest on your every choice.

Misfits

E4 / 2009–2013
5 SEASONS / 37 EPISODES

🍅 **92%** 🗑 **80%**

Superheroes aren't always pillars of moral clarity and goodness. Sometimes they're juvenile delinquents who get caught up in a freak electrical storm while doing community service and emerge with superpowers. This BAFTA-winning sci-fi dramedy launched the careers of many of your faves—*Game of Thrones*'s Iwan Rheon, *The Umbrella Academy*'s Robert Sheehan—as they played teens attempting to repent for their past mistakes, come to terms with their new powers, and cover up the accidental murder of their probation officer. You know, typical high school stuff. The first two seasons are nearly perfect, but the show never really recovers after the charismatic Sheehan's season 3 departure. (The addition of Joseph Gilgun's equally chaotic troublemaker helps a little.) *Misfits* premiered at the dawn of the Marvel Cinematic Universe, and while the flawed superhero is a common sight a decade-plus later, its reluctant working-class heroes helped pave the way for the imperfect supes of Sheehan's next series, *The Umbrella Academy*, Amazon's *The Boys*, and plenty more comics-inspired TV.

The Walking Dead

▶ **GAME·CHANGER**

▶ **CERTIFIED FRESH STREAK**

▶ **HIGHLY ADDICTIVE**

AMC / 2010–2022
10 SEASONS / 153 EPISODES

🍅 **81%** 🗑 **78%**

Stellar world-building, clever writing that nods to its graphic-novel origins with twisty plot remixes, and a cast that comes to play—none more so than one-time series lead Andrew Lincoln—have made this AMC genre hit a show that appeals to even the most zombie-indifferent. In fact, the series's season 5 premiere drew 17.3 million viewers, making it the most watched episode of a cable TV series ever at the time. And *TWD* has since became such a phenomenon that it sparked its own talk show, fan conventions, and a pair of spin-offs, with more to come. That's because *The Walking Dead* Powers That Be—including comic-book creator Robert Kirkman, special effects whiz and director Greg Nicotero, and chief content officer Scott Gimple—capitalize on all the gory possibilities of a tale about a group of apocalypse survivors trying to escape the living dead, while also remembering that any good narrative, no matter how high the concept, is about simply telling good stories. Stories about trying to maintain humanity when it may cost us dearly; about how labels like "hero" and "villain" are sometimes a matter of perspective; and about sustaining the motivation to forge ahead when the only certainty greeting you is loss. The pace ebbs and flows across the seasons, but the slowdowns leave time for humor among so much darkness, like Carol's (Melissa McBride) happy homemaker distribution of pink beet cookies, and Eugene's (Josh McDermitt) mullet maintenance. The spaces between the constant escapes from throngs of zombies (aka "walkers"), and brushes with the often-even-more-dangerous living, are open for poignant episodes that flash back to a dejected Morgan's (Lennie James) meetup with the friend who pushes him to rejoin the living, and the one where Michonne (Danai Gurira) reveals the tragedy that led her to become the warrior she is.

Game of Thrones

▶ **GAME-CHANGER**

▶ **CERTIFIED FRESH STREAK**

▶ **HIGHLY ADDICTIVE**

HBO / 2011–2019
8 SEASONS / 73 EPISODES

🍅 89% 🗑 85%

HBO's adaptation of George R. R. Martin's *A Song of Ice and Fire* fantasy book series became a worldwide phenomenon—but you already know that. On a weekly basis, millions of fans cheered Khaleesi Daenerys Targaryen (Emilia Clarke) and her dragons; he-who-drinks-and-knows-things Tyrion Lannister (Peter Dinklage); and, of course, Ned Stark (Sean Bean), his wife Catelyn (Michelle Fairley), and their brood—Robb (Richard Madden), Sansa (Sophie Turner), Bran (Isaac Hempstead Wright), Arya (Maisie Williams), and even young Rickon (Art Parkinson), who tragically never learned to zigzag. They also jeered villains like Queen Cersei Lannister (Lena Headey), her evil spawn Joffrey Baratheon (Jack Gleeson), and the magical Night King (Vladimir "Furdo" Furdik/Richard Brake) of the icy North. Showrunners David Benioff and D. B. Weiss got off to a rocky start with $10 million sunk into a pilot that was scrapped, but somehow convinced network executives to give them a do-over. Recasting some major roles—including Daenerys,

originally played by Tamzin Merchant—and reshooting paid off in a series that is now a near-perfect binge (if you can forgive the clearly rushed and notoriously Rotten final season). From the gates of Winterfell, to the frozen North beyond the Wall, through the bustling streets of King's Landing, and east across the Narrow Sea to the great cities, deserts, and vast grass plains of Essos, *Game of Thrones* not only gave viewers beloved heroes like the not-a-bastard man of the Night's Watch Jon Snow (Kit Harington), but also exotic locations to stoke the imagination. The series set Emmy records (59 Emmy Awards on 165 nominations) and sent every other streamer raiding the fantasy bookshelves, hoping to replicate HBO's success. Look to stand-out episodes like season 1's penultimate "Baelor," which delivers the series's first distressing character death (something it would become notorious for); season 3's "And Now His Watch Is Ended," in which Daenerys taught viewers to never underestimate her; or the same season's shocking ninth episode, "The Rains of Castamere," known to the show's fandom as "The Red Wedding." All provide evidence of what a 100%-Tomatometer-score episode looks like, why *Game of Thrones* remains one of the most pirated TV shows of all time, and why that extra $10 million was worth it.

American Horror Story

▶ **CERTIFIED FRESH STREAK**

FX / 2011–
9 SEASONS / 103 EPISODES

🍅 76% 🗑 71%

When *American Horror Story* premiered on FX in 2011, the Ryan Murphy– and Brad Falchuk–created drama about a family haunted by the many spirits living in their new home struck *(Continued on page 120.)*

Watchmen

HBO / 2019
1 SEASON / 9 EPISODES

 96% 56%

▶ **CRITICS CONSENSUS** Bold and bristling, *Watchmen* isn't always easy viewing, but by adding new layers of cultural context and a host of complex characters, it expertly builds on its source material to create an impressive identity of its own.

▶ **WHAT IT'S ABOUT** Tough-minded Angela Abar (Regina King), a Tulsa, Oklahoma, detective known as Sister Night when wearing her black hood and pursuing vigilante justice, investigates the death of her friend, familial bloodlines tracing back to the 1921 Tulsa Massacre, and a white supremacist group known as the Seventh Kalvary.

For Damon Lindelof, adapting Alan Moore and Dave Gibbons's seminal graphic novel *Watchmen* presented a substantial challenge. An earlier cinematic adaptation of the gruesome, deconstructive, superhero story, directed by Zack Snyder, had been a disappointment, and, complicating matters further, the famously adaptation-averse Moore wanted nothing to do with the televised reimagining.

Lindelof, a creative force behind mind-benders like *Lost* and *The Leftovers*, was never going to be in for a conventional approach. His task was to take a groundbreaking graphic novel—one that intricately utilized an alternative history to probe how world-changing events like World War II, the Cold War, and Watergate influenced the brutality inherent in comics from those eras—and create something related to, different from, and as politically ambitious as the sacred source text.

HBO and the showrunner accomplished this feat by fearlessly eschewing the comic's most famous characters, such as the Comedian, Nite Owl II, and, to a point, Rorschach. (The character's famous Rorschach Test mask does appear, but not on anyone you'd call a hero.) In meta-fashion, some of the most tangible elements of the graphic novel featured are shown in a television series that the characters watch called *American Hero Story*, which plays as a sort of parody of what this adaptation *could* have been in different hands. Other remnants from the book include the ever-present legend of Dr. Manhattan; the exiled Ozymandias (Jeremy Irons); the Silk Spectre, now FBI agent Laurie Blake (Jean Smart); and an ode to the comic's killer squid by way of random, goopy, squid rainshowers.

But for his central focus, Lindelof dreams up rich new characters—chief among them police officer Angela Abar/Sister Night (Regina King). The pilot opens with a young Black boy, whose importance becomes apparent later, witnessing his parents' deaths during the 1921 Black Wall Street massacre in Tulsa. By the end of the episode, nearly a century later, the death of Tulsa Police Chief Judd Crawford (Don Johnson), kicks off a complex nine-episode story—the fewer details we reveal, the better—that will bring Abar, Blake, Ozymandias, Dr. Manhattan, and others together in devastating ways.

The show's generational pain becomes a repudiation of police brutality and white supremacy, and an examination of how those twin scourges have influenced each other. The subjects aren't native to Moore's graphic novel, but the contemporary existential fears they explore are akin to the terror nuclear power wrought on those living through the Cold War. The Seventh Kalvary evoke images of tiki torches on the streets of Charlottesville, and the fervor of the Black Lives Matter movement courses through the show's veins, which was released just half a year before the deaths of Breonna Taylor and George Floyd and the protests they inspired.

Watchmen is a breathtakingly radical adaptation of a nearly unadaptable text. Lindelof and company succeeded by making an interpretation that barely looks like its source—one that challenges conventional narrative arcs by forcing us to confront the existential threats of our time while being deliriously entertaining. With *Watchmen*, HBO showed that one of the best ways to adapt a sacred text is to show zero fear. And if he ever sees it, we think Moore might approve.

▶ **BEST EPISODE** Season 1, Episode 6—"This Extraordinary Being." Written by Damon Lindelof and Cord Jefferson, and directed by Stephen Williams, "This Extraordinary Being" inventively manipulates time for 60 minutes through its evocative cinematography.

▶ **CHARACTER WE LOVE** Abar is the standout, but maybe-villain Lady Trieu (Hong Chau) is just as compelling. The head of an unstoppable drug corporation, the dangerously intelligent Trieu arrives in Tulsa in search of Dr. Manhattan, and, in the process, coldly manipulates the main players for her own power-hungry ends.

The Expanse

 CERTIFIED FRESH STREAK

SYFY, AMAZON PRIME VIDEO / 2015–
5 SEASONS / 56 EPISODES

🍅 **94%** 🍿 **93%**

▶ **CRITICS CONSENSUS** *The Expanse* blends sci-fi elements and detective noir into a visually compelling whole, though it takes a few episodes for the story to capture viewers' intrigue. (Season 1)

▶ **WHAT IT'S ABOUT** An epic space opera, *The Expanse* is based on the critically acclaimed series of sci-fi novels about the crew of the ship *Rocinante* and their role in interplanetary politics of a future solar system colonized by humans.

The novels, collectively known as *The Expanse*, winner of the 2020 "Best Series" Hugo Award, have a fan in Amazon CEO and founder Jeff Bezos. For one thing, his online mega-retailer featured one of the novels in the premiere of the Kindle Fire in 2011. For two, it was Amazon Prime Video that snatched up the TV adaptation after Syfy canceled the series following season 3, which had set off an enormous #SaveTheExpanse fan campaign, directed at streaming rivals Amazon and Netflix. Bezos announced the news himself.

Written by James S. A. Corey, the pen name of authors Daniel Abraham and Ty Franck, *The Expanse* universe presents a rich future of human space travel, colonization, alien technology, and far-off worlds waiting to be conquered by human hubris. The vastness of the book series resulted in an expensive TV show with a multi-perspective story line and complex interplanetary politics that initially overwhelmed some viewers, including a few critics, but made fans of others.

Season 1 is a master class in world building, focusing on two stories that ultimately come together and introduce viewers to a slew of characters, regions, and castes. The first begins on the ice-hauling ship *The Canterbury* and presents the series's core characters as a ragtag shuttle crew sent on a mission: former UN Navy officer James Holden (Steven Strait); chief engineer Naomi Nagata (Dominique Tipper), a "Belter" native to the asteroid belt between Mars and Jupiter; Martian Navy vet and pilot Alex Kamal; and engineer Amos Burton. On their return, the shuttle crew watches in horror as a stealth ship destroys *The Canterbury*, setting the stage for a flare-up in tensions between militarized Mars, UN-governed Earth, and Belter terrorist group/governing body the Outer Planets Alliance (OPA).

The first season focuses on the shuttle crew's journey from space flotsam to hunted avengers aboard an inherited Martian gunship they name *Rocinante* and their collision course with the investigation of Detective Joe Miller (Thomas Jane), a Belter working on Ceres Station for an Earth-based security firm and tasked with probing the disappearance of heiress-turned-activist Julie Mao (Florence Faivre). Seasons 2 and 3 see destruction caused by alien technology, called the "protomolecule," as well as war between the three main factions as they and others try to control it. In season 4, corporations fight Belters over the spoils of war, while political intrigue and military action continues.

Abraham and Franck serve as executive producers, along with showrunner Naren Shankar, who started his career as a writer and science consultant for *Star Trek: The Next Generation* and holds a PhD in physics and engineering from Cornell, lending the show an enviable level of scientific legitimacy. The series is celebrated in scientific circles to such a degree that the journal *Physics Today* even used an image of an *Expanse* space station on the cover of its December 2016 issue to illustrate the speculative article "Physics in 2116."

A smartly elaborate series, *The Expanse* tackles timely topics while feeding our space-based fantasies, winning over scientists, critics, and billionaires in the process.

▶ BEST EPISODE Season 3, Episode 13—"Abaddon's Gate." The final episode to air on Syfy paid off three seasons of mystery—*What is the purpose of the protomolocule?*—and unlocked new and exciting adventures for the show's move to streaming.

▶ CHARACTER WE LOVE Even among such a strong ensemble, John Wesley Chatham's Amos—the strong, silent type—stands out. The engineer is a paragon of contradictions: simultaneously reliable and surprising, transparent and opaque, sharp and obtuse. He's the heavy with the heart of gold; the hardened killer who's soft around the edges. All of which makes the character enormously compelling to watch as he engages in his very specific brand of shenanigans.

a nerve. Offering an operatic grab bag of horror tropes, blended through a hypersexualized campy queer sensibility (a subplot involved a ghost in a gimp suit), as well as a deliriously deranged Jessica Lange performance, *AHS*'s success proved that TV horror could work. Moreover, once it was announced that it would be an anthology series, with its own repertory cast, *AHS* all but changed the television landscape, kicking off an anthology boom that continues to this day. Over the years, the franchise has found ways of reinventing itself, eventually stringing together a shared universe across its many iterations—which now includes a spin-off, *American Horror Stories*. Tackling everything from Southern witches (*Coven*) to political cults (*Cult*) and slasher films (*1984*), the long-running drama may sometimes be a mess (*Hotel* anyone?), but it's never boring.

Bates Motel

A&E / 2013–2017
5 SEASONS / 50 EPISODES

 93% 91%

On paper, the prospect of a contemporary TV prequel to Alfred Hitchcock's groundbreaking *Psycho* seems not just misguided but foolish. How could it *not* pale in comparison? Yet the A&E drama, developed by *Lost*'s Carlton Cuse and *Friday Night Lights*'s Kerry Ehrin, set itself on its own path by crafting a truly disturbing (but all too compelling) portrait of the Bates mother-son duo that, while gesturing toward its Hitchcockian origins, felt cut from a different cloth altogether. With the always luminous Vera Farmiga as Norma Louise Bates and the angelic Freddie Highmore as a young Norman, each season of *Bates Motel* got better as the series dove deeper into Norman's frayed mental state, eventually gifting viewers its own spin on Marion Crane (played by none other than Rihanna herself).

Marvel's Agents of S.H.I.E.L.D.

▶ CERTIFIED FRESH STREAK

ABC / 2013-2020
7 SEASONS, 136 EPISODES

 95%   91%

S.H.I.E.L.D. may stand for "Strategic Homeland Intervention, Enforcement, and Logistics Division," but it really means "endurance." The series set out to tell stories about a crack squad of super spies in the Marvel cinematic universe, but that brief only scratched the surface of what it accomplished. Now, in its complete and bingeable form, viewers can see it morph from a scrappy *Avengers*-adjacent show into a legitimate slice of weekly Marvel storytelling. Its strength lies both in its cast—once key members joined in seasons 2 and 3—and its expert use of Marvel Comics ideas too subtle (or crazy) for the feature films, like, say, that demonic book that inspired a scientist to create perfect robot replicas of the team. Holding it all together is the affable charm of Clark Gregg as S.H.I.E.L.D. Agent Phillip J. Coulson, who was first introduced in the Marvel films and whose ability to form bonds with disparate groups of people serves him better here than it ever did on the big screen.

The 100

THE CW / 2014–2020
7 SEASONS / 100 EPISODES

 93%   72%

The CW's soapy apocalypse drama takes place in the far future, when 100 space-dwelling juvenile delinquents land on Earth to see if it's still inhabitable

97 years after a nuclear holocaust. Despite all the radiation, it *is*, and they quickly discover they're not alone. Over the course of seven seasons—on and off Earth—they meet cannibal reapers, underground scientists, doomsday cults, and an apocalypse-predicting artificial intelligence, all usually after the same thing they are: survival, in one form or another. That meant a lot of people simply couldn't survive and no main character was safe, which sometimes led the show into trouble, as when a season 3 death sparked discussion about the harmful "Bury Your Gays" trope. But, for the most part, that constant danger made for a thrilling ride. Impossible, soul-altering decisions lie around every corner, and it's usually Clarke Griffin (Eliza Taylor) who has to make them, sacrificing everything for the survival of her friends, family, and sometimes the entire human race. Everyone makes mistakes (including the show itself), but *The 100* built a vast, loyal, and extremely active fandom that stuck with it through everything.

Outlander

STARZ / 2014–
5 SEASONS / 67 EPISODES

 89% 🗑 **90%**

Based on the best-selling novels by Diana Gabaldon, this prestige time-travel romance from Ronald D. Moore, creator of *Battlestar Galactica*, follows British World War II nurse Claire (Caitriona Balfe) as she accidentally stumbles 200 years into the past by touching a magic set of rocks while on vacation with her husband in Scotland. (Just go with it.) Making the most of her new life, Claire falls in love with a strapping highlander named Jamie (Sam Heughan, object of affection for an extremely rabid online

fan base), and so begins a steamy love story that has defied distance, time, trauma, and near death. Changing genres and time periods nearly every season (with the highest quality in seasons 1, set in 1700s Scotland, and 5, set in pre–Revolutionary War North Carolina), *Outlander* is one of the few romances on TV to center on the female gaze. Still, while love scenes can get ultra-steamy, the fact that there are brutal rapes in every single season—as there are in the source material—makes it a little less liberating to watch.

The Magicians

SYFY / 2015–2020
5 SEASONS / 65 EPISODES

🍅 **91%** 🗑 **80%**

Co-creators Sera Gamble and John McNamara conjure a world of magicians-in-training at a college hidden from the world of nonmagic humans in this adaptation of Lev Grossman's fantasy books. Jason Ralph stars as student Quentin Coldwater, whose love of a fantasy book series fuels his obsession with all things magical. And while Quentin's discovery of magic, along with best friend, Julia (Stella Maeve), forms the early core premise, the story develops to revolve around an attractive group of college-age students, studying under Dean Henry Fogg (Rick Worthy) and the professors of Brakebills University for Magical Pedagogy. This is top-tier fun for the *Harry Potter* generation, though the TV-14 series does tackle some serious issues—the rape of a principal character by a trickster god won't be found in J. K. Rowling's fare. *The Magicians*'s fairies, pixies, vampires, ancient gods, and other magical creatures tend toward mischief and mayhem, driving the series's fantastical story lines over five Fresh seasons.

STAR TREK *STARTER KIT*

Set in a future in which humanity set aside its differences to explore the universe, the Gene Roddenberry–created Star Trek franchise inspired generations to reach for the stars. Across eight distinct television shows (so far), its unique and diverse casts reflect the eras in which they were made and the increasing complexity of its own narrative galaxy: Finding the right Star Trek is as simple as choosing the right Starfleet ship for you.

THE CONSTITUTION CLASS USS *ENTERPRISE* NCC-1701

Star Trek • 🎬 80% 🍿 88% • 1966–1969 • 3 seasons • 79 episodes • NBC

YOUR CAPTAIN
James Tiberius Kirk (William Shatner). Brilliant and daring with a knack for navigating moral dilemmas.

STANDOUT FEATURES
The original series was an exploration of 1960s societal woes, wrapped inside a sci-fi coating. Notable for Leonard Nimoy's performance as Spock, a quick fan favorite.

BOLDEST ADVENTURE
"Balance of Terror"—season 1, episode 14. The *Enterprise* investigates attacks near the Neutral Zone between the Earth-aligned colonies and the Romulan Star Empire.

THE GALAXY CLASS USS *ENTERPRISE* NCC-1701-D

Star Trek: The Next Generation • 🎬 91% 🍿 88%
1987–1994 • 7 seasons • 178 episodes • in Syndication

YOUR CAPTAIN
Jean-Luc Picard (Patrick Stewart). A model of discipline who worked to earn the command of Starfleet's flagship.

STANDOUT FEATURES
With a then-impressive $1.3 million–per–episode budget, the series looked more polished than its predecessor and it explored the notion of a humanist, post-scarcity future.

BOLDEST ADVENTURE
"Yesterday's Enterprise"—season 3, episode 15. The *Enterprise* is plunged into an alternate reality in which the previous ship called *Enterprise* failed to avert a war with the Klingon Empire.

THE DEFIANT CLASS USS *DEFIANT* NX-74205

(Or the Occupied Cardassian Space Station, Designated Deep Space Nine)

Star Trek: Deep Space Nine • 🎬 91% 🍿 87% • 1992–1999 • 7 seasons • 176 episodes • in Syndication

YOUR CAPTAIN
Benjamin Sisko (Avery Brooks). A fiercely passionate man dedicated to his mission—and raising his son Jake (Cirroc Lofton).

STANDOUT FEATURES
The first *Star Trek* show without Roddenberry's input, *DS9* reintroduced interpersonal conflicts and introduced overarching story arcs. Seasons 4 through 7 chronicle tensions (and eventual war) between the Federation and the Dominion, an authoritarian regime from far space.

BOLDEST ADVENTURE
"In the Pale Moonlight"—season 6, episode 19. With the Dominion getting an upper hand in the war, Sisko realizes that he must entice the Romulan Empire to join the conflict.

THE INTREPID CLASS USS *VOYAGER* NCC-74656

Star Trek: Voyager • 🎬 77% 🍿 76% • 1995–2001 • 7 seasons • 172 episodes • UPN

YOUR CAPTAIN
Kathryn Janeway (Kate Mulgrew). A seasoned officer and scientist with the mental fortitude to unite a ship of recruits and deserters after they wind up lost 75 years from Federation space.

STANDOUT FEATURES
The first *Star Trek* to be headlined by a woman often played with time travel and examined the nature of command. *Voyager* also returned to the more episodic nature of the original series.

BOLDEST ADVENTURE
"Year of Hell"—season 4, episodes 8 and 9. When the *Voyager* is overpowered by an alien race using a time weapon to guarantee success, Janeway stays aboard to fix the ship while others become "guests" of the alien commander.

PICK YOUR STARFLEET SHIP

THE NX CLASS *ENTERPRISE* NX-01

Star Trek: Enterprise • ✳ 57% 🍿 79% • 2001–2005 • 4 seasons • 98 episodes • UPN

YOUR CAPTAIN
Jonathan Archer (Scott Bakula). Son of a space pioneer, Archer is eager to get into space, but bristles at Vulcan interference in Earth's interstellar destiny.

STANDOUT FEATURES
The first *Trek* show of the 21st century introduced more sex appeal—see the infamous decontamination scenes—and, eventually, a 9/11 metaphor into its tales of an *Enterprise* before the original *Star Trek*.

BOLDEST ADVENTURE
"In a Mirror, Darkly"—season 4, episodes 18 and 19. Told entirely from the point of view of a fascistic Archer in the "Mirror Universe," the episode sees the *Enterprise* encounter a Constitution-class starship from our reality.

THE CROSSFIELD CLASS USS *DISCOVERY* NCC-1031

Star Trek: Discovery • 🍅 84% 🍿 42% • 2017– • 3 seasons • 42 episodes • CBS All Access

YOUR CAPTAIN
Season 1—Gabriel Lorca (Jason Isaacs), a stern man with the most unlikely of origins. Season 2—Christopher Pike (Anson Mount), a calming presence among the *Discovery* misfits and a rare man of faith in the generally agnostic Starfleet.

STANDOUT FEATURES
Looking like a feature film each week, *Discovery* also sets out to test (and sometimes break) every assumption about the franchise. For starters, the captain is not the main character; Sonequa Martin-Green's Burnham is.

BOLDEST ADVENTURE
"If Memory Serves"—season 2, episode 8. Burnham and Spock (Ethan Peck) arrive on Talos IV—the setting of the original *Star Trek* pilot—to plot their next move and, finally, make some sort of peace after years of estrangement.

THE KAPLAN F17 SPEED FREIGHTER *LA SIRENA*

Star Trek: Picard • 🍅 87% 🍿 56% • 2019– • 2 seasons • 20 episodes • CBS All Access

YOUR CAPTAIN
Cristóbal Rios (Santiago Cabrera). A deeply wounded ex-Starfleet officer who crews his ship with holographic reflections of his own personality.

STANDOUT FEATURES
A thoroughly serialized take on the *TNG* galaxy decades after that show's final feature film adventure. Dedicated to asking hard questions about the Federation, it is both a coda to 1990s *Star Trek* and a window into its future.

BOLDEST ADVENTURE
"Stardust City Rag"—season 1, episode 5. Picard attempts to go undercover on a seedy casino planet to rescue Dr. Bruce Maddox, the only man in Federation space with a true understanding of androids. Their actions invite the attention of Seven of Nine, who is none too thrilled to see Picard.

THE CALIFORNIA CLASS USS *CERRITOS* NCC-75567

Star Trek: Lower Decks • 🍅 67% 🍿 44% • 2020– • 1 season • 10 episodes • CBS All Access

YOUR CAPTAIN
Carol Freeman (Dawnn Lewis). Chafing at her mission of "second contact"—maintaining relations with recently discovered civilizations—Freeman is unusually concerned with status.

STANDOUT FEATURES
It is the second animated *Star Trek* series (the first was a continuation of the original series) and the first *Star Trek* to be an out-and-out comedy with in-jokes that play with the franchise's narrative conventions and long history.

BOLDEST ADVENTURE
"Veritas"—season 1, episode 8. When the command staff is seemingly captured by a race of lizard-like creatures, the Lower Deckers are interrogated about their most recent activities and assignments.

The Boys

AMAZON PRIME VIDEO / 2019–
2 SEASONS / 16 EPISODES

 90% 🍿 **85%**

▶ **CRITICS CONSENSUS** Though viewers' mileage may vary, *The Boys*'s violent delights and willingness to engage in heavy, relevant themes are sure to please those looking for a new group of antiheroes to root for. (Season 1)

▶ **WHAT IT'S ABOUT** In a world where superpowered beings are micromanaged celebrity figures, it's up to a ragtag group of misfits, run by a former CIA operative, to take down the global corporation running the hero circuit before its profiteering racket ruins more innocent lives.

Premiering in 2019, *The Boys* entered an oversaturated market. Superheroes were everywhere. Not just on the big screen, where Marvel and DC blockbusters dominated box office rankings year in and year out, but on television, where you could find them in everything from teen dramas and quirky comedies to broadcast procedurals and multiverse franchises.

In order to stand out in such a crowded field, you needed a hell of a hook. Thankfully, anyone who'd read Garth Ennis and Darick Robertson's comic book of the same name knew *The Boys* had one. Dispensing with much of the fanboy awe that usually accompanies stories about superpowered beings, the series began with its inverse proposition: What if those caped heroes were not just flawed, powerful beings, overcoming obstacles to make the world a better place, but craven narcissists, drug users, sexual abusers, and—upping the stakes even more—corporate-backed warmongering figureheads with neo-Nazi ideologies?

Developed for television by *Supernatural* creator Eric Kripke, *The Boys* came blazing from its very first episode as a scathing superhero takedown with a cheeky sense of humor and an R-rated sensibility. In the fictional world it imagines, supes like "Homelander" (Antony Starr, doing his best psychotic take on Clark Kent's alter ego) and "The Deep" (Chase Crawford, a troubled Aquaman-like figure who gets his own #MeToo comeuppance) are controlled by Vought International, a shadowy corporation that manages its heroes as if they were celebrities while flexing their lobbying power to get military contracts with the US government.

Such a bleak vision plays as a mere backdrop to the true narrative of *The Boys,* which refers not to said crusaders but to a makeshift black-ops team, led by the irascible Billy Butcher (a foul-mouthed Karl Urban), a man with a personal grudge against Homelander who won't rest until he brings down Vought and "The Seven," its prized league of heroes.

The Boys kept Ennis and Robertson's penchant for violence intact, with almost every episode featuring torn limbs, exploding heads, gushing blood wounds, and, in one instance, an entire scene set inside an impaled whale. It can be almost unbearably gory at times: In the pilot episode, Jack Quaid's Hughie Campbell watches as his girlfriend is pulverized to gooey bits when a speedster supe crashes into her, leaving him blood-splattered, holding on to her disembodied hands.

Rooted in an all-too-plausible reality where the likes of Homelander are given talking points whenever they go on talk shows or do press junkets for their blockbuster movies, *The Boys* even finds ways of taking timely critiques—Where's the diversity in The Seven? Why are female superheroes constantly sexualized? Aren't supes mere symbols of US imperialism?—as inspirations for its own story lines, all

while offering gripping action sequences, expertly choreographed fight scenes, and throwaway gags that prove it is never above a low-hanging punch line. (Consider the long-dicked supervillain.)

The first season served as a solid world-building endeavor, but its second season proved that Kripke's drama had even more ambitious goals for its long-term future, taking on Nazi eugenics and white nationalist radicalism while introducing a new member of The Seven who proved an all-too-fitting foil for Homelander.

With its relentless violence and topical commentary, *The Boys* aimed to bludgeon the stranglehold superheroes have on the pop-culture landscape, and it did so by channeling a nihilistic vision of 21st-century America that is as compelling as it is terrifying.

▶ **BEST EPISODE** Season 1, Episode 8—"You Found Me." What's a superhero story without a satisfying climax? Bringing its intro arc full circle (and featuring a helluva last-minute reveal), the Kripke-directed, first-season closer is a stunner.

▶ **CHARACTER WE LOVE** Frenchie (Tomer Kapon), the jack-of-all-trades member of The Boys may be impulsive, but his emotional journey alongside new recruit Kimiko (Karen Fukuhara) is a firm reminder of how big-hearted this bloodthirsty adventure can be.

DEEP ▼ ▼DIVE

Stranger Things

NETFLIX / 2016–
3 SEASONS / 25 EPISODES

 93% 🗑 91%

Stranger Things wasn't always a guaranteed hit. Prerelease hype was minimal, outside of the curiosity factor of seeing Winona Ryder back as a star. Netflix was doing well enough with brand names like *Fuller House*, and originals like *House of Cards* hit their adult demographic, but the streamer was still missing a quadrant-smashing, cross-cultural blockbuster. Enter Hawkins, Indiana, a nice place to be an '80s kid: Arcades and malls to bike to, basements aplenty in which to mount *Dungeons & Dragons* campaigns, and whatever grumblings you hear about invading dimensional monsters are confined to the extremely suspicious laboratory in the middle of the woods. That's where a young girl with kinetic powers named Eleven (Millie Bobby Brown in a star-making turn) has escaped from, emerging in town; and that's when the lives of a pack of boys, their families (including fiercely protective single mother Joyce, played by Ryder), and the troubled police chief Jim Hopper (David Harbour) are thrown upside down. The week *Stranger Things* dropped, the term *Spielbergian* had never been typed with more frequency as critics rushed to inform their readers about the new show, and curious early watchers told their friends about the birth of a new franchise. The series summoned the same wonder and terror as early Steven Spielberg movies and productions (*E.T. the Extra-terrestrial*, *Poltergeist*), the attitude of *The Monster Squad*, and the family camaraderie of *The Goonies*. Each season, *Stranger Things* expands its lore and leans into

new and interesting combinations of its cast, like the increasingly closer pairing of Joyce and Jim, and the unlikely duo of nerd Dustin (Gaten Matarazzo) and reformed jerk Steve (Joe Keery), whose redemption from obstacle boyfriend to protector is one of those great antagonist arcs.

The Haunting of Hill House

NETFLIX / 2018
1 SEASON / 10 EPISODES

 93% 🗑 91%

For anyone who ever said TV could never be as scary as the movies, we direct you to episode 8 of Mike Flanagan's *The Haunting of Hill House*—and specifically to *that* jump scare. The now-notorious jolt (which we won't completely spoil here) was the most effective piece of "gotcha!" horror to grace screens of any size in 2018. And it was just one among a slew of unnerving and scream-out-loud moments Flanagan packed into this landmark genre achievement. The whole gambit of this Netflix limited series is bold: Take a sacred literary text—Shirley Jackson's gothic novel of the same name—and blow it to smithereens with a new modern story, new characters, and split time lines. (The follow-up series, *The Haunting of Bly Manor*, takes a similar approach to the work of Henry James.) Squint, though, and you'll see Jackson's essence there in *House*'s patient, slow-building terror and its devastating look at how we deal with ghosts, real and imagined. As in the novel, there is an Eleanor, but here she is one of five siblings grappling in different ways with the trauma of a childhood experience at the haunted Hill House. As in the novel, too, Eleanor—here "Nell"—dies at the house, though for Flanagan this is the story's beginning and not its end. Over 10 meticulously crafted episodes, we get to know the Crain siblings—both as children and struggling adults—and watch as they work through their terrifying shared memories and the recent death of their youngest sister, all as they're drawn back to the place that started it all. Flanagan has made a name for himself as a modern master of horror with stylish works like *Hush*, *Gerald's Game*, and *The Shining* sequel, *Doctor Sleep*. *Haunting* is—at least for now—his crowning achievement.

The Handmaid's Tale

 ▶ CERTIFIED FRESH STREAK

HULU / 2017–
4 SEASONS / 46 EPISODES

 88% 🗑 78%

The Handmaid's Tale is not for the faint of heart— not Margaret Atwood's 1985 dystopian novel and not the 2017 Hulu adaptation that stars Elisabeth Moss as the resilient, titular "Offred" (née June Osborne). Both are about Gilead, a theonomic regime in a fractured postapocalyptic world that turned fertile women into childbearing "handmaidens" for powerful, if barren, families. The much-lauded series offered a bleak vision of what many feel is an all-too-plausible near future where women like June are seemingly powerless in the face of Gilead's leadership. Brutal, at times to a fault, the show's first season was a runaway Emmy-winning success, celebrated for making Atwood's parable about women's freedoms into a nimble, timely drama. If follow-up seasons proved too dour and belabored for viewers and critics to bear, they still demand your attention, if only so you can revel in the powerhouse performances by the likes of Moss, Alexis Bledel, Ann Dowd, Samira Wiley, and Yvonne Strahovski.

The Terror

AMC / 2018–
2 SEASON / 20 EPISODES

 87% 77%

By the mid-2010s, with *American Horror Story* a critical and ratings success, anthology series were all the rage—particularly among networks looking for a horror hit. AMC tapped into the trend by expanding the slow-burning and literary limited series *The Terror* into an anthology property. Created by David Kajganich and Soo Hugh, what's now known as its first season was a period horror tale about a British Royal Navy expedition to find the Northwest Passage, adapted from the 2007 novel of the same name by Dan Simmons, which was itself inspired by a true story. For season 2, new showrunner Alexander Woo moved to mostly US soil, in Japanese internment camps, with its threat coming in the form of spirits known as *yūrei*. Both seasons stand out for their dazzling period detail, authentic performances from the likes of Jared Harris and Tobias Menzies in season 1 and Derek Mio and George Takei in season 2, and, of course, moments of truly chilling *terror*.

The Mandalorian

▶ HIGHLY ADDICTIVE

DISNEY+ / 2019–
2 SEASONS / 16 EPISODES

 93% 🗑 93%

Baby Yoda. It's hard to overstate just how much the success of Disney+'s first live-action *Star Wars* series rested on those two words. True, the baby-faced character (actually named Grogu) featured in

Jon Favreau's Western-inspired *The Mandalorian* is not, in fact, a younger version of that beloved green Jedi. But the series's meme-generating breakout star captures what made this Pedro Pascal–led show a hit, giving fans a return to form for the long-running George Lucas–created space opera. With its focus on practical effects, colorful supporting characters (including a droid voiced by Taika Waititi and a mysterious agent played by Werner Herzog), and self-contained yet serialized episodes, it immediately felt like old-school *Star Wars*. And boasting a narrative that builds on but doesn't merely repackage familiar tropes from that most famous Skywalker saga, this gritty and witty action-packed series about a bounty hunter following the fall of the Empire feels like a new hope for stories told about a galaxy far, far away.

The Witcher

▶ **HIGHLY ADDICTIVE**

NETFLIX / 2019–
1 SEASON / 8 EPISODES

🍅 **67%** 🍿 **92%**

"Toss a coin to your Witcher, o valley of plenty . . ." If you aren't already singing the next line of the song, you soon will be. Netflix's fantasy epic *The Witcher*, based on the novel series by Andrzej Sapkowski, is remarkable in the way it burrows lines, songs, and even grunts into the viewer's brain. Ostensibly, the series is about a monster hunter played by Henry Cavill who roams a magical continent in search of creatures to kill and coin to collect. But it is really about political upheaval and the dissolution of that magic in favor of our all-too-mundane world. It is also three series in one, as it switches points of view from the Witcher Geralt to a sorceress-in-training and a princess running for her life. The first prestige fantasy show to debut after *Game of Thrones*'s conclusion, *The Witcher* was as richly produced but much, *much* sillier—something its huge popularity suggests fans were very ready for after *Thrones*'s self-seriousness.

DISNEY+ / 2021–
1 SEASON / 9 EPISODES

🍅 **91%** 🍿 **81%**

There was something refreshing about the Marvel Cinematic Universe (MCU) arriving on Disney+ armed with references not only to big-screen spectacles or comic book arcs, but also to sitcoms like *Bewitched* and *The Mary Tyler Moore Show*. As domesticated Avengers Wanda and Vision, Elisabeth Olsen and Paul Bettany spent much of the series spoofing age-old TV classics that had viewers and characters alike coming up with new theories week after week. But with instantly iconic lines turned memes ("What is grief if not love persevering?"), Easter eggs galore (no spoilers here!), and a deliciously campy performance by scene-stealing Kathryn Hahn as nosy neighbor Agnes, *WandaVision* emerged as a lucid exploration of loss and trauma bottled in a show about superpowered beings and craven government agencies. Even as its final episodes couldn't shake off the brazen seriality of Marvel's world-building (what is *WandaVision* if not the MCU's multi-film, cross-platform storytelling persevering?) the series proved that appointment television isn't (just) a thing of the past.

Know Your ★ TV Superproducers

WITH MULTIPLE HIT SERIES, SIGNATURE STYLES, AND BIG-FAT DEVELOPMENT DEALS THAT WILL SEE THEM TELLING STORIES FOR YEARS TO COME, THESE ARE SOME OF THE PRODUCERS DEFINING AMERICAN TV RIGHT NOW.

AVA DUVERNAY

> QUEEN SUGAR
> WHEN THEY SEE US
> CHERISH THE DAY

RYAN MURPHY

> GLEE / AMERICAN HORROR STORY
> AMERICAN CRIME STORY
> THE POLITICIAN / HOLLYWOOD

DuVernay started as a publicist before becoming a filmmaker, first with well-received documentaries and later with features that helped showcase Black stories. Though notoriously snubbed by awards bodies in the film world—seriously, no Best Director nod for *Selma*?—she won an Emmy for her doc *13th* (which was also nominated for an Oscar), and her Netflix limited series *When They See Us* was nominated for 11 Emmys.

Style Signature: Socially conscious filmmaking has always been part of DuVernay's M.O., but she broke ground in TV with her trailblazing all-women director roster for the first season of Oprah Winfrey Network drama *Queen Sugar*.

After well-received but maybe-not-quite-smash hits *Popular* and *Nip/Tuck*, mega-producer Murphy broke out big time with the high school musical dramedy *Glee*, followed by the anthology series *American Horror Story* and *American Crime Story*. His success led to a major $300 million deal with Netflix to create series like *Hollywood*, *Ratched*, and more.

Style Signature: Murphy is known for his troupe of regular collaborators—among them Sarah Paulson, Jessica Lange, and Darren Criss—glossy and progressive productions, and—at least in the case of *AHS*—batsh-t craziness.

FRESHEST SERIES

When They See Us
🍅 96%
🪣 91%

DuVernay wrote and directed every episode of this Netflix mini-series about the Exonerated 5, formerly the Central Park 5, the group of Black and Latino teens wrongly accused and convicted of raping a jogger in 1989.

HIDDEN GEM

Cherish the Day
🍅 78%
🪣 100%

This ambitious OWN drama chronicles the evolution of a couple's relationship, with each episode taking place over the course of one day.

FRESHEST SERIES

Pose
🍅 98%
🪣 89%

The largest cast of transgender actors ever—five in the main cast, plus many more guest stars and behind-the-scenes crew members—make this drama about '80s and '90s ballroom culture authentic in addition to groundbreaking.

HIDDEN GEM

Popular
🍅 60%
🪣 – –

The sharp high school satire that would become *Glee*'s trademark was first perfected in this short-lived soap that introduced taboo and progressive topics by showing the dark side of perfection.

COMMERCIAL BREAK

SHONDA RHIMES

GREY'S ANATOMY / SCANDAL
HOW TO GET AWAY WITH MURDER
STATION 19 / BRIDGERTON

Before she had an entire dedicated night of ABC programming (Thank God it's Thursday!), Rhimes was known for writing fun, frothy features like Britney Spears's *Crossroads* and *The Princess Diaries 2*. But she broke out in a big way with the hospital soap *Grey's Anatomy*, which would lead to a full TV empire (and an eventual deal with Netflix).

Style Signature: The formula for a successful Shondaland series: breezy humor, plus frank discussions of race, sex, and topical issues, plus strong women leads. Add in racially diverse casts and fun, pop music–fueled soundtracks, and you have the makings of a TGIT staple.

FRESHEST SERIES

Scandal
🍅 93%
🗑 74%

Crisis fixer Olivia Pope (Kerry Washington) loves lush coats, red wine, popcorn, and the president of the United States—and solves problems for high-powered Beltway insiders and everyday people alike.

HIDDEN GEM

The Catch
🍅 74%
🗑 83%

This two-season show starred Mireille Enos as a private investigator who, after being swindled by her con-man fiancé (Peter Krause), sets her sights on tracking him down in a delightful cat-and-mouse game that ended far too quickly for our tastes.

GREG BERLANTI

THE FLASH / SUPERGIRL
RIVERDALE / EVERWOOD
THE FLIGHT ATTENDANT

Think you're busy? Try being Berlanti, a man so prolific he had a record 20 series on television at one time in 2020: his "Arrowverse" superhero series (*Arrow, The Flash, Supergirl, Legends of Tomorrow, Batwoman*), Archie Comics–goes–noir drama *Riverdale*, serial killer drama *Prodigal Son*, docuseries *Equal*, and many more. There's a reason Warner Bros. signed him to a $400 million deal.

Style Signature: As one would expect from a man who cut his teeth on *Dawson's Creek*, Berlanti's projects—whether about regular people or superheroes—all tap into the wide range of human emotion. That means laughter and tears and a rich, deep, interior life, regardless of genre—superheroes have feelings too!

FRESHEST SERIES

Doom Patrol
🍅 86%
🗑 73%

The weirdest of the superhero shows bearing Berlanti's name, this DC adaptation features the titular group of outcast heroes who have all suffered life-changing accidents, giving them superhuman abilities — but scarring them (physically and emotionally) in the process.

HIDDEN GEM

Jack & Bobby
🍅 87%

After *Dawson's Creek*, Berlanti created this tragically short-lived series about the teen years of a future US president with a cast of then and future all-stars: Matt Long, Logan Lerman, Christine Lahti, and John Slattery.

KENYA BARRIS

BLACK-ISH
GROWN-ISH / MIXED-ISH
#BLACKAF

Sitcom vet Barris worked on classic early 21st-century series *Girlfriends* and *The Game* (and co-created *America's Next Top Model* with childhood pal Tyra Banks) before he shot to household-name status with ABC's *black-ish*. Then came spin-offs *grown-ish*, *mixed-ish*, and *old-ish*—plus Netflix meta-sitcom *#blackAF*, in which he plays a fictionalized version of himself.

Style Signature: Every Barris project has a few shared trademarks: sharp banter; thoughtful rumination on the intersection of pop culture, class, and race; willingness to experiment with format; and, most importantly, inspiration from his own life.

FRESHEST SERIES

black-ish

🍅 92%

🗑 63%

Anthony Anderson stars as an ad exec and Tracee Ellis Ross as his doctor wife, raising a family in LA while dealing with parenting struggles, nightmare in-laws, and other family problems.

HIDDEN GEM

The Astronomy Club

🍅 100%

🗑 86%

Barris didn't create this one-season Netflix sketch comedy show, starring the Upright Citizens Brigade's first Black sketch team, but he did help shepherd it to air.

J. J. ABRAMS

LOST / FELICITY
ALIAS / FRINGE
WESTWORLD

While he might be a master of mind-bending genre, Abrams's first series was the 1998 WB soap *Felicity*. But it was the spy drama *Alias*, which turned Jennifer Garner into an A-lister, and then *Lost*, which launched a thousand fan theories, that really cemented his position as a superproducer. (That, and the many blockbusters he began to write and direct, starting with *Mission: Impossible III* and eventually rebooting both the *Star Trek* and *Star Wars* franchises.)

Style Signature: Abrams's characters all share similar traits: curiosity, general relatability, and a love of wholesome, '80s-inspired adventure. It's clear that Steven Spielberg is a major influence, particularly in the universal appeal, clever mysteries, surprising plot twists, and complex world-building present in all his projects.

FRESHEST SERIES

Fringe

🍅 90%

🗑 82%

Abrams followed up *Lost* with this mind-trippy, sci-fi drama, involving alternate realities and co-created with Roberto Orci and Alex Kurtzman, his *Star Trek* collaborators. (Read more on page 111.)

HIDDEN GEM

Castle Rock

🍅 88%

🗑 79%

The first two Certified Fresh seasons of this dark, layered drama, set in the world of Stephen King's horror novels, feature characters from *Shawshank Redemption* and *Misery*, among others.

COMMERCIAL BREAK

JENJI KOHAN

WEEDS / ORANGE IS
THE NEW BLACK
GLOW

Former *Gilmore Girls* and *Sex and the City* writer Kohan first made waves with *Weeds*, the dark Showtime comedy about a suburban widow who starts dealing pot to support her two children. She proved with her subsequent series—Netflix prison drama *Orange Is the New Black* and the '80s women's wrestling drama *GLOW*—that she isn't afraid to show a full spectrum of femininity and tackle systemic societal issues in the process.

Style Signature: Even the stereotypically gorgeous blonde women in Kohan's shows are more sardonic than peppy. All her characters are deeply funny, clever, sharp-tongued and unafraid to speak their minds.

FRESHEST SERIES

GLOW

 92%

🗑 86%

It turns out that women-led ensemble dramedy is an ideal genre for Kohan, who followed *OITNB* with this similarly critically loved series, set in the '80s and based on the real-life Gorgeous Ladies of Wrestling. *GLOW*, too, was centered around a diverse group of women and dealt with issues of race, class, fidelity, friendship, and more.

HIDDEN GEM

Teenage Bounty Hunters

 93%

🗑 96%

Teenage twin sisters accidentally find an after-school job hunting "skips"—aka people who have skipped bail—under the tutelage of a wizened bounty hunter. This canceled-too-soon Netflix series managed to address religion, sexuality, and female friendship (with some killer one-liners) before it was axed.

DICK WOLF

LAW & ORDER AND SPIN-OFFS
CHICAGO FIRE /
CHICAGO P.D. / FBI

Former feature film writer Wolf helped transform the police procedural with 1990's *Law & Order*. That series has spawned seven spin-offs, including television's longest-running drama (*Law & Order: Special Victims Unit*), another related franchise (the *One Chicago* universe), and many more.

Style Signature: *SVU* star Ice T once described *Law & Order*'s signature dun-DUN sound as "Dick Wolf's cash register," but the franchise and its famous audio cue did help set the tone for a stylized, optimistic look at first responders and law enforcement in America.

FRESHEST SERIES

Law & Order: SVU

🍅 78%

🗑 89%

Detective Olivia Benson (Mariska Hargitay) and her fearless advocacy for victims of sex crimes anchors what is now TV's longest-running, live-action, primetime series ever (ahead of the original *Law & Order* and *Gunsmoke* with 20 seasons each).

HIDDEN GEM

Chicago Med

🗑 72%

Much as *Law & Order* follows both police and prosecutors involved in crime cases, the *Chicago* universe—*Fire*, *P.D.*, *Med*, and the one-season *Justice*—follows cases long after first responders arrive. Its least-heralded spin-off is *Med*, which revolves around the staff at a city hospital and the cases they treat (many handed off by characters from the other shows).

AMY SHERMAN-PALLADINO

GILMORE GIRLS / BUNHEADS
THE MARVELOUS MRS. MAISEL

JORDAN PEELE

THE TWILIGHT ZONE
THE LAST O.G. / LOVECRAFT
COUNTRY / HUNTERS

Where she leads, we'll follow . . . Former *Roseanne* writer Sherman-Palladino broke out with her WB dramedy *Gilmore Girls*, about a fast-talking, coffee-swilling, pop culture–loving mother and daughter living in the small fictional New England town of Stars Hollow. For the record, Sherman-Palladino doesn't talk nearly as fast as her characters, but she does carry their trademark wit (and she knows how to rock a statement hat).

Peele had made a name for himself in television, thanks to a stint on *MADtv* and the sketch show he created with scene partner Keegan-Michael Key, *Key & Peele*. But it was his groundbreaking, Oscar-winning horror film *Get Out* that skyrocketed his reputation, giving him the power to produce projects as varied as a Lorena Bobbit docuseries, the Nazi-hunting alternate history *Hunters*, and a rebooted version of *The Twilight Zone*.

Style Signature: Rapid-fire dialogue and obscure pop-culture references are a hallmark of any Sherman-Palladino project—on which husband Daniel Palladino frequently writes, directs, and produces—from the prototypes of *Gilmore Girls* to the ultimate speed-talking champion, Midge Maisel (Rachel Brosnahan) of *The Marvelous Mrs. Maisel*.

Style Signature: Like any good comedy writer, Peele's got a knack for observing the smallest details about the world and how they shape people's lives. But it's the creative lens through which he shows those details that makes his voice unique: It's smart and incisive, occasionally goofy, racially conscious, and, most of all, wildly funny or scary where it needs to be.

FRESHEST SERIES

The Marvelous Mrs. Maisel

 88%

🗑 89%

A Jewish 1950s Upper West Side housewife stumbles into a career in stand-up comedy in this Television Academy favorite.

FRESHEST SERIES

Key & Peele

 97%

🗑 94%

Inventive and eclectic, the titular duo tackled everything from systemic racism and toxic masculinity to couples who fight a lot in their beloved sketch series. *Key & Peele* also featured top-notch impressions of President Obama and a pair of valets who looooove "Liam Neesons" and "Bruce Willy."

HIDDEN GEM

Bunheads

🍅 100%

🗑 96%

Sherman-Palladino's last series before *Maisel* proved that she does small town well: This series starred Broadway vet Sutton Foster as a Las Vegas showgirl who moves to a sleepy beach town with her new husband and becomes the ballet instructor for a group of misfit teenage girls.

HIDDEN GEM

The Last O.G.

🍅 - -

 80%

Best known as Tracy Morgan's post–*30 Rock* comeback, this Peele-produced TBS sitcom about an ex-con reintegrating into his now-gentrified Brooklyn neighborhood, was especially satisfying because it marked Morgan's return to form following a devastating car accident.

❙❙ COMMERCIAL BREAK

Real(ish) Worlds

COMPETITIONS AND DOCUSERIES THAT CAPTURED THE ZEITGEIST (AND, YES, STILL HOLD UP)

If genre TV was once a dirty word, reality TV was downright filthy. And for many viewers and people in the industry, it still is. Cheap. Exploitative. Fake. Take your shot: Reality's heard it all before.

At the peak of the reality TV boom in the early 2000s, when record-breaking numbers tuned in to see Kelly Clarkson crowned the first American Idol and watch Richard Hatch outwit, outplay, and outlast his fellow *Survivor* castaways, some were predicting the end of scripted TV altogether. Who needed expensive things like writers when you could just throw people on an island to starve them for a few weeks, or train a camera on Paris Hilton, and *this* many people would watch? Reality's threat never proved existential, but its impact has been major. (Don't agree? Find us someone who *doesn't* know the names of every principal Kardashian-Jenner.)

Of course, *reality TV* is a broad term, encompassing fly-on-the-wall series like *The Osbournes*, talent competitions like *Top Model* and *Top Chef*, plus makeovers (*Queer Eye*), stunt shows (*Jackass*), and more. We go even broader than that in this chapter, adding ambitious crime and nature docuseries into the mix. So it is that you'll find Ozzy Osbourne, Michael Jordan, and David Attenborough together, at last. *Now, just imagine if they were all living under the same roof . . .*

That was kind of the idea behind Jonathan Murray and Mary-Ellis Bunim's *The Real World*, launched in 1992 and considered by many to be the godfather of reality TV. Here, seven strangers from different walks of life are placed in a house for several months and filmed, their exploits edited into booze-filled episodic nuggets. (You can read about

it, and the 1970s PBS limited series that inspired it, in this chapter.) Bunim-Murray Productions didn't stop there, eventually going on to produce *Keeping Up with the Kardashians*, *Project Runway*, and *The Simple Life*, and inspire other series that have had us gasping around the watercooler for two decades.

That zeitgeist-snatching effect is one of the things many of the shows we feature here have in common, no matter how different they may seem. Consider *Making a Murderer*, Netflix's documentary series following the story of a wrongly convicted Wisconsin man who is released, and then arrested shortly afterward for a new crime; in 2015, his quest for a second exoneration dominated the national conversation for weeks and proved Netflix's ability to produce a new kind of viral "event TV." In 2020, the streamer would prove this power all over again with *Tiger King*, the story of exotic animal owner, presidential candidate, and convicted criminal Joe Exotic.

The other feature our selections share: fascinating personalities. From the drag queens lip-syncing for RuPaul's approval and the 600-plus contestants who've carried their torches to Tribal Council, to *Queer Eye*'s charismatic Fab Five and the legendarily soothing and informative naturalist Sir David Attenborough, characters—as much as antics—are what we can't turn away from when we watch reality TV, guiltily or otherwise. Perhaps scripted and unscripted TV isn't so different after all.

The Real World

> ▶ GAME-CHANGER

MTV, FACEBOOK WATCH, PARAMOUNT+ / 1992–
33 SEASONS + 2 REUNION SEASONS / 600+ EPISODES

🍅 – – 🗑 – –

MTV's quest to show viewers what happens "when people stop being polite and start getting real" began when series creators Mary-Ellis Bunim and Jonathan Murray smashed together two very different inspirations. The first was PBS's groundbreaking 1973 docuseries *An American Family*, which had taken 300 hours of footage of the Loud family of Santa Barbara, shot over seven months, and condensed it to 12 hour-long episodes that chronicled the parents' separation and one child's coming out. The other influence: the early '90s popularity of youth-targeted primetime soaps *Beverly Hills, 90210* and *Melrose Place*.

The Real World made conventions like direct-to-camera confessionals staples of the genre.

That high-low culture mix would become a staple of *The Real World*, which each season thrust a group of young adults together in a big home in a new city—New York, then LA, and eventually as far away as Cancun, the setting of a recent revival on Facebook Watch—and kept the cameras running. Widely considered the launch of modern reality TV as we know it, *The Real World* made conventions like direct-to-camera confessionals staples of the genre, and mixed signature reality guilty pleasures like casual hookups, boozy parties, and drama-filled vacations with story lines and characters

that often captured something about the national conversation. Consider activist Pedro Zamora, whose time on 1994's *Real World: San Francisco* as a gay man with AIDS—and who tragically died hours after his season's premiere—drew global attention to the issue. Then-president Bill Clinton credited Zamora, and the show, with offering America a perspective on life with HIV that had never been seen before.

Survivor

> ▶ GAME-CHANGER

CBS / 2000–
40 SEASONS / 596 EPISODES

 🍅 **71%** 🗑 – –

Those who predicted this one-time ratings monster and granddaddy of competition reality TV would be voted off the airwaves after the novelty wore off didn't see this blindside coming: More than 20 years and 40 seasons later, *Survivor*'s torch is still aflame. And while it's not the phenomenon it once was (more than 50 million people tuned in to watch naked Machiavelli Richard Hatch win season 1), it attracts a loyal fan base that tunes in season after season to watch a new set of castaways—and often some returning favorites—form tribes, build shelters, make fire, establish alliances, and then break them as they try to lie, cheat, and charm their way to day 39. The basics of the show, which creator Charlie Parsons established on Sweden's *Expedition Robinson*, remain intact: Tribes face off in epic physical battles, the losers of which must vote a member out at Tribal Council; eventually, they merge and it's an individual game. But Parsons and his fellow executive producers Mark Burnett and Jeff Probst (still the iconic khakis-wearing host), have introduced smart twists throughout the years to complicate the game, the best of which are *Survivor*'s "hidden immunity idols." *Survivor* may have evolved—today fans talk of "old-school" and "new-school" gameplay—but the essential question that draws us back has not: Starving, exhausted, and isolated from those you love, how far would *you* go for a million dollars?

Jackass

MTV / 2000–2002
3 SEASONS / 25 EPISODES

Almost every boy of a certain age knows what it's like to ignore common sense and do something so monumentally stupid that bodily injury is inevitable. That spirit is what drives *Jackass*, Johnny Knoxville's wildly irresponsible prank and stunt show, which aired only 25 episodes over a brief three-season run, but influenced a generation of children (and man-children). Knoxville magazine editor Jeff Tremaine, and director Spike Jonze assembled a merry crew of willing boneheads and filmed the dumbest, most outlandish, most dangerous ideas they could come up with—navigating a room full of mousetraps, driving a hearse whose cargo repeatedly spills out into the street, jumping a river on a BMX bike—to fill out 20 minutes of airtime, and it became a full-on franchise.

Bam Margera, Steve-O, Chris Pontius, Wee Man, and the rest of the gang went on to make a handful of movies and spin-off series filled with equally over-the-top shenanigans, often with equally hilarious results. But the original *Jackass* was a game-changer that presaged a certain breed of YouTube creator—for better or worse—and it remains an always cringe-inducing, frequently laugh-out-loud chronicle of juvenile mischief.

Jackass was a game-changer that presaged a certain breed of YouTube creator— for better or worse.

American Idol

FOX, ABC / 2002–2016, 2018– (REVIVAL)
19 SEASONS / 640+ EPISODES

 68%* 🗑 – –

*FOX RUN

So great a phenomenon was Fox's *American Idol* in its heyday—the number 1 show in America for eight consecutive TV seasons throughout the 2000s—that it was virtually unavoidable. If you didn't understand the dread of "group round" or feel some hitherto untapped rage when Tamyra was voted out, you couldn't hang. Developed by Simon Fuller from the UK's *Pop Idol* (itself developed from New Zealand's *Popstars*), *Idol* was a big-budget twist on the high school talent show. A trio of judges—music producer Randy Jackson, singer and choreographer Paula Abdul, executive and caddish villain Simon Cowell—scoured the country auditioning young hopefuls for the chance to go to Hollywood, where they would be whittled down to a top 10 (eventually more) to face the public vote in a series of live shows. That basic formula has survived a revolving door of new judges, the series's season 15 cancellation, and its revival at ABC. While knowing who wins, and not being able to vote in real time for your faves, makes *Idol* a less-than-ideal binge in some ways, there's something to be said for plunging down a YouTube rabbit hole of the show's best performances and Simon's nastiest barbs, giant cup of Coca-Cola in hand.

Planet Earth

▶ GAME-CHANGER

▶ HIGHLY ADDICTIVE

BBC / 2006
1 SEASON / 11 EPISODES

🍅 95% 🗑 100%

▶ **CRITICS CONSENSUS** *Planet Earth* weaves together innovative camera techniques and patient observation to give viewers an astounding glimpse of the world's perils and wonders, capturing jaw-dropping scenery and animals on both an epic and intimate scale.

▶ **WHAT IT'S ABOUT** Narrated by nature historian Sir David Attenborough, this docuseries takes viewers to some of the most far-flung locales in the world to witness rare natural phenomena and observe exotic wildlife. Each episode utilizes extraordinary cinematography of pristine settings and dramatic storytelling to highlight a different habitat and offers fascinating behind-the-scenes glimpses of the tireless work done to film it.

When *Planet Earth* first premiered in 2006, it arrived with plenty of fanfare behind it, and for good reason. Touted as the most expensive nature series ever produced by the BBC, at a cost of $2 million per episode, it boasted massive scope, state-of-the-art filming techniques, and plenty of never-before-seen footage of rare animals and natural wonders. It was also the latest collaboration between BBC Natural History Unit producer Alastair Fothergill and Sir David Attenborough, one of the world's most celebrated, respected, and charismatic naturalists.

Together, the pair had previously worked on a number of acclaimed nature series, including 2001's *The Blue Planet*, an extraordinary survey of the world's marine life. After the success of that series, Fothergill suggested applying the same expansive treatment to the entire planet. The BBC got right to work sending photographers to the most remote, most extreme, and most alien landscapes in the world with high-definition cameras—it was the first BBC nature series to be filmed entirely in HD—to bring viewers intimate, unprecedented access to creatures and events only a few others had ever witnessed.

The series's various camera crews traveled to 200 locations across five continents to capture the footage, frequently in severe conditions—diving below a frozen lake, scaling a mountain of guano infested with giant cockroaches, braving winter in Antarctica. The equipment they used also made it possible to film from great distances, allowing them to record long, uninterrupted takes of exciting hunts and dramatic struggles for survival—events that were typically near-impossible to shoot.

But the unsung hero of the series was its storytelling. While the visual splendor understandably claimed much of the glory, there was always compelling narrative behind it, the filmmakers investing the singular imagery with real stakes and, in some cases, giving us a few characters to follow. Viewers sympathized with the plight of the polar bear mother who emerges from hibernation with a pair of new cubs, feared for the monkey in India who falls victim to a tiger in pursuit, and marveled at the fantastic and peculiar mating dances of New Guinea's birds of paradise. These captivating vignettes also subtly served to highlight *Planet Earth*'s underlying message of conservation, as viewers came face-to-face with the dramatic effects of climate change, something further explored in the equally beguiling *Planet Earth II*, released in 2016.

Of course, Attenborough's soothing narration pulled the whole enterprise together, as if the entire world were sitting at the feet of its kindly grandfather and listening as he recalled his most spectacular adventures. And, in some sense, this was the truth; Attenborough had been traveling across the world and revealing its secrets to curious audiences since the 1950s, and he had countless accolades, awards, and honorary titles to show for it. While Sigourney Weaver lent her voice to the US version of the series when it premiered a year later, there was no one better suited to narrate *Planet Earth* than Sir David, who endowed every episode with an elegant, measured tone and an air of authority.

Planet Earth was an immediate sensation, and it eventually aired in 130 countries. It also arrived just as the high-definition format began to overtake DVDs, and it rather deservedly became the highest-grossing HD title of 2007. Again, *a nature docuseries was the best-selling HD title of the year.* Ask anyone who remembers the broadcast, and they'll tell you that *Planet Earth* was legitimate appointment television, and those who snagged the series on Blu-ray were eager to share its glory in repeat viewings with everyone they knew.

Attenborough and Fothergill went on to collaborate on other similarly impressive projects, including the aforementioned "sequel," but the original was their crowning achievement. *Planet Earth* not only changed—and upped—the game for nature documentaries, but it became a global phenomenon unlike any before it, spreading a worthy message and earning its distinction as some of the best television ever produced, period.

▶ **BEST EPISODE** Episode 1—"From Pole to Pole." The first episode of the series serves as a sweeping introduction to all the habitats it would cover, cherry-picking some of the most striking images and intriguing stories to pull viewers in. And boy, did it ever work.

▶ **CHARACTER WE LOVE** A lot of beautiful creatures are on display in *Planet Earth*, but it's Sir David Attenborough who takes us on each of their journeys, adding valuable context when needed and quietly stepping into the background when the footage speaks for itself.

BINGE BATTLE

QUEER EYE (2003) ◀ VS ▶ QUEER EYE (2018)

Queer Eye for the Straight Guy, which would nix the "straight guy" part when it expanded its clientele, was an instant cultural phenom when it landed in the early 2000s. Surely a decade-later reboot of the makeover series was doomed to live in the original's shadow, right? Wrong: Lightning struck twice with Netflix's revival. But, mirror, mirror, there can only be one most fabulous version of them all . . .

Queer Eye (2003)

BRAVO / 2003–2007
5 SEASONS / 100 EPISODES

 77%* – –*

*SEASON 1

▶ **WHAT IT'S ABOUT** Meet the Fab Five: food and drink expert Ted Allen; hairstylist and groomer Kyan Douglas; interior designer Thom Filicia; culture connoisseur Jai Rodriguez; and fashion and style guru—and series breakout—Carson Kressley. In each ep, they take on a new client and completely make over their lives—new haircut, new living room, new perspective—ahead of a big event.

Queer Eye (2018)

NETFLIX / 2018–
5 SEASONS / 47 EPISODES

 93% 88%

▶ **WHAT IT'S ABOUT** Meet the new Fab Five: avocado-loving foodie Antoni Porowski; fashion expert Tan France; culture vulture and general inspiration Karamo Brown; designer Bobby Berk; and hair stylist Jonathan Van Ness. As with the original, it's all about "make-betters," but where the OGs stuck mostly to New York and its surrounds, the new crew began in Atlanta, before venturing around the country and even hitting Japan for a special season.

◀ AWARDS ▶

1 Emmy

(for Outstanding Reality Program)

8 Emmys

(including 3 for Outstanding Structured Reality Program)

◀ BEST MAKE-BETTER ▶

Every episode will have you ugly-crying, but the season 2 opener **"God Bless Gay"** is a next-level tearjerker. The focus is selfless community volunteer Mama Tammye Hicks and her gay son Myles, who's just moved home—to their town of Gay, Georgia (really)—and is worried about how he will fit in. The ep has everything: Dual makeovers, a remodeled church community center, and a finale that will break you in the best ways.

It's Carson's fave, and honey we ain't gonna argue—Season 1, episode 20, **"Queer Eye for the Skate Guy: John Z,"** in which the boys make over an already fiendishly handsome figure skater who's planning a date night with his wife and skating partner. As Cressley told *Entertainment Weekly:* "He was like an Armani model . . . He took his shirt off and I just about fainted."

▶ **OUR PICK**　The original broke ground, but the **revival** really was a *Queer Eye*–style "make-better." The decision to start in the South was ingenious, as was the call not to limit their clients to "straight guys" from the get-go. Most ingenious, though, was the casting: This diverse quintet has the kind of crackling chemistry and charisma most sitcoms would kill for and an absolute star in hair-tossing Van Ness.

RuPaul's Drag Race

LOGO, VH1 / 2009–
13 SEASONS / 175 EPISODES

 83% 83%

RuPaul's Drag Race first aired in 2009, and though much has changed after 19 Emmys, 13-plus seasons, seven international editions, and five companion spin-offs, the fabulous freshness of those early episodes remains in the series's DNA. The show is essentially *America's Next Top Model* meets *American Idol* via *Project Runway*, seasoned with more bravado than a WWE smackdown, with the most famous drag queen in the world presiding over a season-long search to find America's next drag superstar. The key to much of its success is the casting, with each season bringing us an uber-talented cast of often bitchy queens—this is not RuPaul's *Best Friend* Race—hand-picked by "Ru," many of whom have gone on to become household names. They sew costumes, act in skits, write songs, impersonate celebs, and lip-sync for their lives in hopes that they possess the charisma, uniqueness, nerve, and talent to win the crown. Once a cult favorite on the LGBTQ-focused network Logo, *Drag Race* is now a worldwide sensation, thanks to global viewership on Netflix, a move to VH1, and its blissful partnership with internet culture (few shows have launched as many memes). The on-screen drama bleeds out into the real world, too, not just with fan bases fighting over favorites at live screening parties, but in more thoughtful battles taking place in the cultural discourse: *Drag Race* has faced criticism for excluding trans contestants, while the popularity of certain types of contestants has raised questions about racism in the drag community and the fandom. It's a show that will make you shriek *and* think.

The Bachelor and The Bachelorette

ABC / 2002–
41 SEASONS / 431+ EPISODES

 62%* – –*

*THE BACHELORETTE, NO SERIES SCORE FOR THE BACHELOR

So. Many. Roses. ABC's dating-show juggernaut has evolved over two decades into something of a *Star Wars*–like TV universe known as Bachelor Nation, with spin-offs—*Bachelor in Paradise! Bachelor Winter Games!*—a zealous fan base, and no end in sight. It's all fueled by the power of love—and definitely *not* the quest for fame—something the basic premise of the original show expertly tapped into: one eligible bachelor spends time with a group of beautiful young women vying for his love, cutting down the selection week by week until he finds his soul mate. Cue happily ever after, or . . . not. (Part of the fun of the series is the occasional shocking and tear-inducing finale. Less fun? Knowing it took them 25 seasons to cast their first Black Bachelor.) Sometimes it *does* work out, though: The first ever Bachelorette—Trista Rehn, runner-up on *The Bachelor* season 1—found love in the spin-off series's inaugural season, and remains married to Ryan Sutter 17 years later.

Anthony Bourdain: Parts Unknown

CNN / 2013–2018
12 SEASONS / 104 EPISODES

 – – 98%

You've never seen a cooking show like *Anthony Bourdain: Parts Unknown*. More than just a series that travels the globe while diving deep into its plethora of cuisines, the 12-time Emmy-winning docuseries from CNN is a rough-and-tumble meditation on the human condition and the bonds that link us all. It strikes that balance, of course, because of its one-of-a-kind host, Bourdain. Since breaking out 20 years ago with his best-selling book *Kitchen Confidential*, he became a significant, uncensored industry voice; in just a handful of years and with several hosting stints under his belt, he skyrocketed to the top of his field by being himself and getting his hands dirty. Fitting his self-proclaimed mission ("I travel around the world, eat a lot of s—t, and basically do whatever the f—k I want"), *Parts Unknown* is today an especially impactful tribute to its peerless host, who died by suicide while filming in France in 2018.

The Great British Baking Show

 HIGHLY ADDICTIVE

BBC TWO, BBC ONE, CHANNEL 4, NETFLIX / 2010–
11 SEASONS / 143 EPISODES

 90% 🍿 98%

Anyone who's found themselves stuck in a loop of cooking competition shows on the Food Network knows how entertaining it can be to watch chefs battle it out over the stove. Take that formula, throw in two handfuls of British accents, a pair of quirky hosts, and judges Mary Berry (and, later, Prue Leith) and Paul Hollywood, and you've got the sublimely entertaining *The Great British Baking Show* (or "Bake Off," as it's known in the UK). Each season of the BBC series, which ballooned in international popularity after becoming available on Netflix, features about a dozen amateur bakers competing in challenges that prove their abilities. After a

series of three face-offs per episode—a "Signature Challenge," in which bakers show off their own recipes; a second "Technical Challenge" in which contestants must perfect a recipe with limited instructions; and a third "Showstopper Challenge," during which they aim to knock the socks off the judges—some poor flour-dusted chef is eliminated. It's light, easy viewing but also compellingly bingeable: With each episode, contestants reveal more about themselves and their motivations, making it fun to latch onto a baker to root for—and devastating if and when your charge gets the chop.

Nathan for You

COMEDY CENTRAL / 2013–2017
4 SEASONS / 32 EPISODES

 97% 94%

It's easy enough to see the comedic potential in the *Nathan for You* premise: Comedian Nathan Fielder helps struggling small business owners increase profits with outrageous marketing schemes. What that doesn't tell you is how earnest those business owners are, how outrageous Fielder is willing to get, and how far the show expands beyond its premise. Take, for example, an episode about a realtor whose Fielder-inspired gimmick is that her properties are ghost-free. The episode ends with a genuine emotional breakthrough during an exorcism. Or a scheme involving a Hollywood souvenir shop and a fake movie that leads to a surprisingly poignant series finale, a twist-filled pilgrimage to Arkansas to help a low-rent Bill Gates impersonator find his long-lost high school sweetheart. *Nathan for You* is an unprecedented mix of high-concept pranks, cringey humor, social commentary, and deep pathos, and it's unlikely we'll see another show capable of successfully replicating that formula for a long time.

CHOOSE YOUR REALITY TV CREW

Once upon a time, famous people actually did things to become famous: Shot hoops well, developed a vaccine or two—things like that. Today? Not so much. With the right last name, a great look, and a savviness with app filters and "personal brands," fame can flicker to life from seemingly nowhere. Social media and increasingly sophisticated phone cameras may be the driving tech force behind this new brand of celebrity, but on TV our cultural turning point was the fly-on-the-wall reality boom of the 2000s, when the likes of Paris Hilton and Kim Kardashian showed that if you wanted people to watch you, all you needed to do was open your door and let the film crew in. Here are five we couldn't look away from—and our guess at how long we'd last in their well-documented company.

Real Housewives of Everywhere

BRAVO / 2006–

10 US ITERATIONS, INCLUDING ORANGE COUNTY, NEW YORK CITY, ATLANTA

Jersey Shore

MTV / 2009–2012
7 SEASONS / 71 EPISODES

 42% 56%

The Osbournes

MTV / 2002–2005
4 SEASONS / 52 EPISODES

 84%

Keeping Up with the Kardashians

E! / 2007–2021
20 SEASONS / 280+ EPISODES

The Hills

MTV / 2006–2010
6 SEASONS / 102 EPISODES

 52%

The crew: Rich housewives, ex-housewives, and often quite busy working wives living in their series's titular cities who drink together, eat together, and can't seem to stop stabbing each other in the back. Standouts include *Atlanta*'s no-holding-back Nene Leakes, and *Beverly Hills*'s restaurateur Lisa Vanderpump, who spun her own successful reality series off *Housewives*.

The vibe: Like Hitchcock's "bomb under the table" theory, assume if there's a glass of wine—or even, say, a table—on-screen, it's about to be thrown.

We'd last... half a day, but we'd come back for one of Andy Cohen's delicious three-part reunion specials.

The crew: A party-hardy group of Italian American twentysomethings sharing a vacation home, among them Nicole "Snooki" Polizzi, Mike "The Situation" Sorrentino, and DJ Pauly D.

The vibe: *"GTL" baby:* That's "Gym Tanning Laundry" to you, and that was the code—along with a hearty dose of partying-till-you-black-out—for those who lived their summers out in the Jersey Shore house. The drunken hookups and breakups reeled folks in; the X-factor of unvarnished stars-in-the-making like Snooki kept them watching.

We'd last... a whole summer, as long as we remembered to line our stomachs, drink plenty of water, and *never* enter Mike's room.

The crew: Heavy-metal god Ozzy Osbourne, wife and manager Sharon, and their rebellious kids Jack and Kelly.

The vibe: With notoriously slurry but charming Ozzy as patriarch—he's admitted he was stoned while the show was filming—there was an anything-goes, car-crash appeal to time spent with the Osbournes at their garish mansion. Amid all the profanities (censored in the United States) and scatological pranks, there were moments of heart and, well, *reality*, as when we watched Sharon battle cancer.

We'd last... a week. The sleepover-while-the-parents-aren't-home appeal is fun, but there ain't much peace and quiet at Black Sabbath HQ.

The crew: Momager Kris Jenner and the blended Kardashian-Jenner clan of Calabasas, California, including sisters Kim, Kourtney, and Khloé—the focus of the early seasons—and half-sisters Kendall and Kylie.

The vibe: Fabulous wealth, famous connections, great contouring, and family squabbles are the DNA of this Ryan Seacrest–created series, which plays out like *The Brady Bunch* with bling. As the years went by, there was a ripped-from-the-headlines appeal, as the Kardashian fam's marriages and bust-ups broke on Perez Hilton and TMZ before the release of the new season gave us the glossy inside scoop.

We'd last... however long Kris instructed us to stay. Seriously, we ain't crossing the queen.

The crew: Aspiring designer Lauren "LC" Conrad, who'd lived out her high school years in drama and luxury on the reality series *Laguna Beach*, and her LA friends and romantic interests—among them eventual couple and series antagonists Heidi Montag and Spencer Pratt, or "Speidi."

The vibe: A universe in which no conversations can be had without a reservation at an LA hotspot, a lighting crew in tow, and the feeling that this might all be scripted—something to which the meta series finale nodded.

We'd last... until the first ep of season 2. Unlike LC, when offered the chance of a lifetime by a fancy magazine editor—as she was in the second season's opener—we definitely *would* have gone to Paris.

The Jinx

HBO / 2015

1 SEASON / 6 EPISODES

 95% 97%

So many true-crime docuseries avenge or martyr their subjects; *The Jinx* does just the opposite. Subtitled *The Life and Deaths of Robert Durst*, creators Andrew Jarecki, Marc Smerling, and Zac Stuart-Pontier's miniseries looks into the eccentric real estate heir and the people in his orbit who have a habit of disappearing or dying in dramatic fashion. In doing so, they helped legitimize the murder-themed miniseries trend that was previously relegated to Investigation Discovery and other niche cable channels. In perhaps one of the genre's best finales, the filmmakers captured Durst confessing his crimes by muttering "What the hell did I do? Killed them all, of course" into a hot mic while off camera—a moment that ignited debates on ethics and whether the filmmakers were withholding evidence from an active investigation. (Durst was arrested on first-degree murder charges related to one of the alleged victims the day before *The Jinx* finale aired; it was revealed during his April 2019 trial that the filmmakers edited these remarks and aired them out of order.)

Making a Murderer

NETFLIX / 2015–2018

2 SEASONS / 20 EPISODES

 84% 98%

Just as the investigative podcast *Serial* had done the year before, 2015's first season of the docuseries *Making a Murderer* took a decade-old case and made it *the* current topic of national debate. It wasn't just whether you believed in the innocence of Steven Avery, the Wisconsin man convicted of murder in 1988, then freed and exonerated based on DNA evidence in 2003, only to be arrested again and convicted of another murder a few years later. It was also how you felt about the actual form of the documentary that told his story. Was *Murderer*, with its sympathetic portrait of the poor and marginalized Avery clan and its bingeable episode-ending reveals, "journalism," "entertainment," or something else? Wherever you landed, it was hard to deny its impact. A loaded petition hit the White House calling for Avery's pardon that December, and Netflix quickly commissioned a follow-up that would dig deeper into the alleged coerced confession of Avery's nephew and convicted accessory, Brendan Dassey. Meanwhile, breakout "stars," defense attorneys Dean Strang and Jerry Buting, embarked on a national speaking tour. But *Murderer's* largest impact is perhaps the cavalcade of docuseries that followed, some of which we feature here.

Wild Wild Country

NETFLIX / 2018

1 SEASON / 6 EPISODES

 98% 88%

Like the best true crime docuseries, this 2018 six-parter by Maclain and Chapman Way—the brothers behind the moving, enjoyable, and decidedly un-*WWC*-like doc *The Battered Bastards of Baseball*—thoroughly sucked us in, forcing us to ask just about anyone, "Have you seen this? No? You *have* to." And we weren't alone. *Wild Wild Country* is an addicting, detailed dive into the Rajneeshpuram cult, which took over a huge stretch of land in the Oregon countryside in the 1980s, prompting outrage from locals, an FBI investigation, and even an assassination plot. Along the way, the "community based on compassion and sharing," to quote one devotee, devolves as the group's leader, the Bhagwan, and the group's spokesperson, Sheela, butt heads. It's weird and, yes, wild stuff, a stranger-than-fiction story, packed with twists, arresting raw footage, and an excellent soundtrack fueled by indie singer-songwriters like Bill Callahan (whose song "Drover" inspired the series's name), Damien Jurado, and Kevin Morby.

The Last Dance

ESPN / 2020
1 SEASON / 10 EPISODES

🍅 97% 🍿 95%

Imagine trying to distill more than 500 hours of footage of an entire NBA season into a 10-part miniseries. Now imagine that the subject of that miniseries is one of the most celebrated basketball teams of all time, led by arguably the most famous athlete ever to walk this Earth. This was the task that lay before filmmaker Jason Hehir, who had to wrangle and reconstruct a mountain of footage of Michael Jordan's Chicago Bulls during their 1997–1998 season, which many thought was going to be the final season of Jordan's career (it wasn't). In other words, this was stuff *everyone* wanted to see. It understandably took a while to put everything together, and *The Last Dance* was eventually set to premiere in June 2020—before the COVID-19 pandemic changed everything. In the wake of quarantine lockdowns, ESPN chose to fast-track production and debut the series early to offer a salve to desperate sports fans looking for a bit of normalcy in increasingly abnormal times. *The Last Dance* not only hit viewers with a powerful dose of nostalgia, but it also offered them unprecedented

behind-the-scenes access, with never-before-seen footage that helped illuminate the relationships, rivalries, and larger-than-life personalities that made the team so exciting to watch. Surprisingly, the normally reticent Jordan also opened himself up in new interviews, commenting on footage and answering sensitive questions with a rarely seen vulnerability and candor. All this added up to a must-see TV event—an impeccably crafted, artfully presented slice of real-life drama that wasn't just a great documentary, but a unifying force of shared escapism for audiences around the world.

Tiger King

NETFLIX / 2020
1 SEASON / 7 EPISODES

🍅 85% 🍿 83%

Charting the wild rise and fall of famed big cat zookeeper Joe Exotic—who's behind bars for an alleged 2017 murder-for-hire scheme as we go to print—*Tiger King* debuted when we needed it most. Hitting Netflix within days of a national shutdown due to the COVID-19 pandemic, and featuring a magnetic, stranger-than-fiction cast of characters (among them the kooky big cat activist–turned–*Dancing with the Stars* chanteuse Carole Baskin), this eight-episode Rebecca Chaiklin– and Eric Goode–directed docuseries was the talk of the internet through summer 2020. Say what you will of Exotic—and between his presidential bid, his polyamorous same-sex marriage, and (oh yeah!) his alleged plot to kill Baskin, there's plenty to say—but the man and his assortment of animal park colleagues, his big cat-loving contemporaries, and his caged tiger companions all make for some must-watch television. Especially for a nation stuck inside.

ROOTS

🏆 78% 🍿 65%
ABC · 8 episodes

1977

Over eight consecutive nights back in January 1977, *Roots* kept a nation enraptured. The ambitious ABC project was an adaptation of Alex Haley's 1976 novel *Roots: The Saga of an American Family*, which chronicled a multigenerational story that began in West Africa in 1750 and took viewers all the way through the American Civil War. Capturing the horrors of slavery with brutal accuracy, by television's standards, *Roots* was an unprecedented ratings smash. An estimated 100 million viewers caught the finale alone, reshaping what the miniseries could accomplish on American TV. (The History Channel's nine-episode adaptation of *Roots*, released in 2016, wasn't quite the "event" the original was, but is every bit as good.)

SHŌGUN

🏆 75% 🍿 92%
NBC · 5 episodes

Set in 17th-century Japan, *Shōgun* continued the trend of adapting best-selling novels, in this case James Clavell's 1975 hit. Starring Richard Chamberlain as Major John Blackthorne, the NBC event immersed viewers in feudal Japan, offering an exotic history lesson through the eyes of a British sailor who becomes embroiled in the dangerous world of its titular warlords. With one in three television sets said to have tuned in for at least part of the show, *Shōgun* proved how hungry TV audiences were for such thrilling tales.

1980

MINI MILESTONES

The "miniseries"—sometimes called a "serial" in the UK, where the form evolved from radio serials—is distinguished from other series by its limitations. With just a handful of eps, usually between three and six, they tell a self-contained story with a clear end in sight and no planned follow-up seasons. Which explains why so many are adaptations of books, plays, or historical events: The pieces are all laid out. Miniseries are small, sure, but their impact can be huge, as seen in these 10 major titles that became must-see events, introduced new talent, and captured, shook up, and altered the zeitgeist.

1983

V

🏆 70% 🍿 77%
NBC · 2 episodes

There are few television moments that can rival seeing Diana, one of the "Visitors" in this landmark two-night sci-fi event, devouring a guinea pig. The moment signaled to viewers that her alien race was—stay with us here—actually scaly, horned reptilians in human skin suits. Initially developed as an adaptation of the antifascist novel *It Can't Happen Here*, the NBC miniseries was eventually given the sci-fi treatment turning *V* into a Nazi parable that went on to influence an entire generation of genre fans.

1989

Credited with reviving the Western in American pop culture, *Lonesome Dove* was originally conceived as a silver screen vehicle for John Wayne. By the time it arrived on television, this tale, starring Robert Duvall and Tommy Lee Jones as two former Texas Rangers who set out to leave their town and join a cattle drive to Montana, reached more than 25 million homes. The miniseries made novelist Larry McMurtry's original characters household names that went on to inspire various TV sequels and prequels in their wake.

LONESOME DOVE

🏆 -- 🍿 100%
CBS · 4 episodes

BAND OF BROTHERS
2001

🏆 94% 🍿 99%
HBO · 10 episodes

With broadcast TV networks moving away from limited series at the dawn of the millennium, HBO seized on their potential to further burnish its brand. *Band of Brothers*, then the most expensive TV miniseries ever made with a budget of $150 million, was based on historian Stephen E. Ambrose's 1992 nonfiction book about the Easy Company of the US Army 101st Airborne Division, and boasted Tom Hanks and Steven Spielberg as executive producers. The Certified Fresh World War II drama instantly cemented itself as one of the most assured depictions of war ever put on the small screen and made good on the network's tagline: This wasn't TV, it was HBO.

Pride and Prejudice

🏆 88% 🍿 95%
BBC · 6 episodes

1995

There is more to this mid-'90s adaptation of Jane Austen's novel *Pride and Prejudice* than the now iconic sight of Colin Firth (here playing an all too dashing Mr. Darcy opposite Jennifer Ehle's witty Elizabeth Bennet) in just a soaked white shirt. But it's hard to deny that said image went a long way toward making this 19th-century period drama about love and marriage feel decidedly modern, inspiring a whole swath of new Austen fans who'd forever pine away for their own Mr. Darcy.

1994

THE STAND

🍿 70% 🍿 66%
ABC · 4 episodes

A writer as prolific as Stephen King has his fair share of TV adaptations (see also: *It*, *11.22.63*, and *Under the Dome*) but none are quite as memorable as this 1994 miniseries starring Gary Sinise and Molly Ringwald, based on his 1978 supernatural novel about a flu pandemic that doubled as a parable about good versus evil. Written by King himself, the highly touted ABC production cost $26 million and pushed standards and practices on broadcast television to their limits. (In December 2020, as the COVID-19 pandemic was raging around the country and the world, CBS All Access released a new adaptation.)

ANGELS IN AMERICA

🏆 90% 🍿 96%
HBO · 6 episodes

2003

Tony Kushner's *Angels in America* is subtitled "A Gay Fantasia on National Themes." Such lofty goals had made his two-part '90s play a landmark of the American stage. At once a gay melodrama, a history of the AIDS crisis, and a meditation on spirituality at the end of the millennium that featured prophets, ghosts, Roy Cohn, Mormons, and, yeah, angels, Kushner's play sounds unfilmable. But with Mike Nichols at the helm (and a cast that included Al Pacino, Meryl Streep, and Jeffrey Wright), HBO made this unabashedly fabulous miniseries a television event for the ages.

2019
CHERNOBYL

🏆 96% 🍿 98%
HBO · 5 episodes

On paper, *Chernobyl* was hardly a guaranteed hit: a drab-looking procedural about the bureaucratic fallout following the infamous Ukraine nuclear disaster—starring a bunch of Brits making no effort to hide their accents. And yet, HBO delivered a sleeper sensation by ratcheting up the tension to unbearable levels—try to breathe as we follow some brave heroes into the reactor on a mission to cool it—and unfolding a story of incompetent government that felt, well . . . *relevant*. *Chernobyl* also marked the day that TV fans who hadn't already fallen in love with Jared Harris—who plays scientist Valery Legasov, one of the few capable minds in the rooms where it happened—joined the club with the rest of us.

WHEN THEY SEE US

🏆 96% 🍿 90%
Netflix · 4 episodes

2019

This Ava DuVernay miniseries chronicled the stories of the "Exonerated Five," the young boys who'd been falsely accused and convicted of the rape of a white woman in New York's Central Park in 1989. The Emmy winner captured in its title an earnest promise: to refuse to see Korey Wise, Kevin Richardson, Antron McCray, Yusef Salaam, and Raymond Santana as criminals and view them instead as innocent boys wronged by a racist justice system. As a piece of television it was staggering. As restorative justice it was unmissable.

▌▌COMMERCIAL BREAK

Animation that Demands to Be ▶Taken Seriously

The Simpsons family has been with us so long that it's easy to forget how groundbreaking it was when they first squeezed onto their famous sofa and entered our living rooms in December 1989. Matt Groening's cartoon series arrived with what were then almost radical intentions: to not only delight kids of Bart and Lisa's age, but to inspire a knowing chuckle in the Homers and Marges of the world—maybe even the Grandpa Abes—with a sharp satire of American life and American comedy. Animated TV, up to this point, hadn't seen anything like it.

Prior to the arrival of Springfield's finest, television cartoons were largely concerned with capturing the youngest eyeballs for the cheapest possible price. In TV's earliest days, studios mostly did so with animated theatrical shorts—witness *The Wonderful World of Disney*—because producing new animated stories was thought to be cost-prohibitive. Hanna-Barbera became one of the first major animation studios to rise to the challenge of making animated shows just for TV, and, with 1960's *The Flintstones*, created the first half-hour primetime animated series. ("Limited animation" became the term for time- and cost-saving animation techniques like bold lines and big close-ups, a staple of Hanna-Barbera and many that followed.)

Disney joined the "originals" fray in the 1980s, kicking off with *Gummy Bears* and *The Wuzzles*, and later favorites like *Duck Tales*; Warner Brothers would reignite its animation studio, too, and in the 1990s, kid-targeted cable station Nickelodeon began mixing its own original animated series in with its offering of imports. Soon, a thriving animated TV industry emerged, with a big focus on the grand prize of winning the not-tall-enough-to-ride demographic.

Groening had other ideas—and he would inspire others to think differently, too. While this chapter doffs its hat to some of the finest and most stealthily complex offerings to emerge from the battle for weekend and after-school supremacy—*Batman: The Animated Series*, *Daria*, and *SpongeBob SquarePants*, among them—the heavier focus is on the kinds of animated series that aimed to superserve the older teens and grown-ups in the house. Their creators saw the form not as a limitation or reason to soften any edges, but as a possibility—a way to bring new textures and irreverence to dramatic, comedic, and genre stories adults could enjoy.

In these pages you'll find the most starkly nihilistic antihero dramedy of all time (Netflix's *BoJack Horseman*); one of TV's most sophisticated space operas (*Star Wars: The Clone Wars*); and the most consistently funny sketch show on American screens (*Robot Chicken*). You'll also find, arguably, TV's most moving sci-fi drama (*Undone*), funniest school comedy (*Big Mouth*), and, of course, its best sitcom (*The Simpsons* ...or *Family Guy*: Check out the Binge Battle between these toon titans on page 158 and decide for yourself).

You'll also find plenty of reason to clutch your pearls, with the likes of unapologetically offensive *South Park* and *The Boondocks*, both of which weaponize their endearingly lo-fi animation styles for maximum shock value—and insight into American society and our racial divide. You won't believe what their cute-looking kid protagonists say—we've come a long way from "eat my shorts"—but you won't soon forget it.

Daria

MTV / 1997–2002

5 SEASONS / 70 EPISODES

 -- --

Dorothy Parker and *Beavis and Butt-head* are not names you typically associate with each other, but both live in the DNA of Daria Morgendorffer, the deadpan star of this brilliant skewering of late 1990s suburbia. Morgendorffer first appeared as a straight-woman foil to the two giggling heroes of MTV's smash animated series, *Beavis and Butt-head*, and was given a spin-off when the network decided to target a younger female audience. Armed with a Parker-esque wit and forged from the kinds of independent-minded schoolgoers that were defining a new breed of TV teen heroine—Lisa Simpson, *My So-Called Life*'s Angela Chase—Daria hit her target. The teen's wry observations about her family, her school, and her new town—the Morgendorffers moved from *Butt-head*'s fictional Highland to the equally fictional and generic Lawndale—became a kind of Greek chorus for disaffected teens across America, counting the days until graduation. *Daria* wasn't just about its hero's dry observations, though: Her relationship with bestie Jane Lane was richer and more complex than viewers were used to from an MTV cartoon. (Also rare for a cartoon at the time: Their love triangle story line was serialized across multiple seasons, and never fully, neatly resolved.) The image of Daria's expressionless face—those flat eyes, those giant spectacles—has become a symbol for those who gritted out high school as nonconformists, because while she made us laugh by calling out the ridiculousness of social cliques and fashion-obsessed popular kids, she also gave us comfort. "I'm not miserable," she says in one episode. "I'm just not like *them*." *Daria* told us it was OK, even great, to be different.

South Park

▶ GAME-CHANGER

COMEDY CENTRAL / 1997–

23 SEASONS / 307 EPISODES

 80% 87%

Pissing off parents and delighting dorm-room denizens since 1997, this unabashedly controversial, crudely animated, and all-these-years-later *still* very funny cartoon about a quartet of foul-mouthed young kids in the Colorado suburbs has irked too many groups to list here. And, to its credit, to this day and despite its popularity, Trey Parker and Matt Stone's series still manages to push buttons as it mines the United States's political and cultural moments for laughs. For all that smart satire throughout, it's really the big dumb laughs that keep us checking in on the show—many of them involving poor Kenny, who's died in the series more than 100 times—the sensibilities of which have had an impossible-to-underestimate influence on our current golden age of adult animation. (Also, if you haven't seen 1999's Certified Fresh film, *South Park: Bigger, Longer & Uncut*, rectify that mistake immediately—or burn in a very strange kinda hell.)

Futurama

FOX, COMEDY CENTRAL / 1999–2003, 2008–2013

7 SEASONS / 140 EPISODES

 93% 96%

Frozen on New Year's Eve, 1999, dim-witted but earnest pizza delivery boy Fry (Billy West) wakes up 1,000 years in the future where he gets a new job as, well, a delivery boy. *But in space!* As part of the *Planet Express* ship crew, he'll sail to every corner of the galaxy, hauling frequently dangerous cargo and plot MacGuffins. His coworkers include Bender (John DiMaggio), a robot fueled by booze; Professor Farnsworth (West again), the company's genius but senile and unscrupulous founder; Dr. Zoidberg (West yet again!), upright crustacean and medical doctor with zero knowledge of human anatomy; and ship captain, Leela (Katey Sagal), a self-serious cyclops whose evolving relationship with Fry forms the emotional core of the series. It can be said the *Futurama* writers knew how to write a killer ending, which makes sense given how much practice they got. Created by *The Simpsons'* Matt Groening, the show's season renewals were virtually always in flux, forcing the staff to write no less than four series finales in case the show didn't get picked up. These send-off episodes reveal the ambition and scope of its creativity, with plotlines featuring Bender becoming an omniscient deity, fiery musicals with the robot devil, time loops and chrono-jumps, and the *Planet Express* ship and all its occupants hurtling into a wormhole, destination unknown. While these all made for some cracking sci-fi comedy, they were also springboards to explore the tenuous affection between Fry and Leela. *Futurama*: Come for the nerd jokes, stay for the romance and sentimentality, leave to cry when someone mentions Fry's dog.

NICKELODEON / 1999–
13 SEASONS / 260+ EPISODES

 **79%**

This long-running series about an optimistic sea sponge, his best buddy—and starfish—Patrick, and the other colorful underwater residents of Bikini Bottom stands out among the titles in this chapter.

There are no brooding antiheroes in this world, no scathing takedowns of celebrity or consumerism, no undertone of cynicism. In fact, there's no cynicism at all: *SpongeBob SquarePants* might be the most purely joyful show on TV. Which is not to say the series, created by the late animator and marine science educator Stephen Hillenburg after the cancellation of his *Rocko's Modern Life*, is shallow. This is surreal silliness of the Pee-wee Herman variety: layered, thoughtful, precise, always surprising, self-knowingly naïve, and delightful at any age. SpongeBob himself, voiced by Tom Kenny as a high-energy always-on jolt of can-do optimism, was just the kind of happy America and the world needed, it seems: The show has become Nickelodeon's most successful ever and evolved into an entertainment empire with multiple films, theme park rides, and a Tony-nominated Broadway musical.

The Venture Bros.

ADULT SWIM / 2003–2020
7 SEASONS / 81 EPISODES (PLUS PILOT AND SPECIALS)

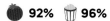 **92%** **96%**

Anyone complaining about having to wait over a year for their favorite show to return should listen for the stifled laughter of any *Venture Bros.* fans nearby, whose everlasting patience was rewarded with seven seasons released over 17 years. That's because the show—about failed super-scientist Dr. "Rusty" Venture (James Urbaniak), living with his two danger-prone teenage sons and the family's bloodthirsty bodyguard, menaced by archrival The Monarch—never got away from its creators. Jackson Publick and Doc Hammer started the series in 2003 on Adult Swim, and between them wrote, directed, and voiced half the characters of each episode, channeling their shared obsessions *(Continued on page 156.)*

Batman: The Animated Series

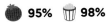

FOX KIDS / 1992–1995
2 SEASONS / 85 EPISODES

🍅 **95%** 🍿 **98%**

▶ **CRITICS CONSENSUS** Stylized animation, dark story lines, and mature character development set *Batman: The Animated Series* apart in the crowded field of Batman adaptations. (Season 1)

▶ **WHAT IT'S ABOUT** With the help of Robin and later on Batgirl, DC's most famous superhero—without actual superpowers—fights crime and solves cases in Gotham City against a formidable rogues' gallery of crooks, thieves, and villains.

The 1989 *Batman* movie made the future possible for the aging DC superhero by capturing the character, Gotham City, and the Joker in a light that felt fresh—and drove audiences to theaters en masse—but director Tim Burton was famously not much of a comic-book reader. It showed in his disinterest in getting into Bruce Wayne's headspace, the deletion of Robin, and his avoidance of anything that would trace the property back to the '60s show or its pulp-pages origin.

But how about living in a world where the two coexisted? The dark fantasy and gravitas, the spandex and dorky sidekick, together at last. But also, make it work as a kids' cartoon, something to air smack-dab in the afternoon.

That was the challenge that lay before Eric Radomski, Bruce Timm, and Paul Dini, between them the principal creators and developers of *Batman: The Animated Series*. The three had worked in different departments on *Tiny Toon Adventures*, so not only did they know a thing or two about modernizing aging properties from the Warner Bros. library, but they came with additional backgrounds in design and animation. It's how they knew to draw *The Animated Series* on black paper, saving time and money, and allowing the dark, noir-inspired light and shadows to shine through each frame.

While the Gotham of the movie was a nightmarish miasma of clashing architectural styles, the show homed in on the Art Deco look to dress the metropolis; it also mixed asynchronous technologies, flooding the streets with 1930s cars and guns while heroes and villains used gadgets and computers from a more advanced time.

The distinct setting is defined from the pilot, "On Leather Wings," featuring Man-Bat as the foe in an episode that climaxes in a dazzling aerial tour of Gotham. Batman grapples with the winged monster, zipping through skyscraper construction sites and caroming off police dirigibles. Credit the creators for pulling Man-Bat out of obscurity and setting him up as the series's maiden villain, which allowed them to create the pilot free from fan expectation and to demonstrate that they were going to be reaching deep.

After all, what's Batman without the bad guys? Though "Leather Wings" was the pilot, Fox Kids debuted *The Animated Series* with a Catwoman episode, capitalizing on the success of *Batman Returns* from the start of summer 1992. Mr. Freeze was reinvented as a tragic figure. Harley Quinn was created for the show, beginning her long, wondrous evolution into DC's most prominent antihero. Which, of course, leads to the Joker, voiced with giddy maniacal aplomb by Mark Hamill. It was a shock back in the day to see *the* Luke Skywalker listed in the credits, but it is one of greatest testaments to the show's quality that neither role now overshadows the other.

He's well matched with Kevin Conroy, as the voice of Batman, who finds all the necessary vocal shadings of this complex character. He's gruff and commanding when suited up, finds the sociable rake when he's wheeling and dealing as Bruce Wayne, paternal when talking to Dick Grayson/Robin or Barbara Gordon/Batgirl, and tortured and vulnerable every time the past catches up with him. More than any other adaptation, *The Animated Series* captures the redemptive spirit of the character: Bruce Wayne's penance for what he sees as a failure to stop his parents' murder isn't just a means to justify beating the snot out of crooks, but a study in hope and optimism during his darkest nights of the soul.

The Animated Series, along with the film *Mask of the Phantasm*—which Radomski, Timm, and Dini breathlessly worked on alongside the show—are the purest distillations of classic Batman. And some would say the best.

▶ **BEST EPISODE** Season 1, Episode 46—"Almost Got 'im." Why pick just a single villain per episode when you can put all of them in a single episode? The Joker, the Penguin, Two-Face, Poison Ivy, and Killer Croc are in a smoky room recounting the closest they ever got to killing Batman in a funny, action-packed 22 minutes with a brilliant finale.

▶ **CHARACTER WE LOVE** Robin. Thought Batman was better off alone? Not only did the creators make the sidekick role fun and vital again, they even gave Robin some of the best episodes, like the two-parter "Robin's Reckoning," which sees him go rogue on an emotional revenge journey.

into an unpredictable and lore-heavy action/dark comedy. It's a world of dense references and re-contextualized public figures: where Klaus Nomi is alive and totally evil, exploding heads with his countertenor voice; where a dying henchman's last wish is to be sung a Technotronic song by his killer; and where a guy with poor marksmanship is derided as someone whose favorite video game is *Riven: The Sequel to MYST*. *The Venture Bros.* was clearly a personal and intimate project for Publick and Hammer, a feeling that was passed on to its fans, who will say this was the only show that ever felt like it was tailored specifically to their tastes. Nothing else shared the same fetishistic celebration of childhood dreams, broken masculinity, hatred and hope, and everything pop culture, from Batman to Bowie. The long gap between seasons that drove away casual viewers and its deep, serialized world building meant that rewatches were practically a requirement, a task happily obliged by enduring fanatics who stuck it out to its shocking—yet not surprising—2020 cancellation.

American Dad!

FOX, TBS / 2005–
17 SEASONS / 300 EPISODES

 -- 🗑 **91%**

Family Guy creator Seth MacFarlane proved the lightning-striking-twice adage wrong with *American Dad!*, another off-the-wall twist on the Norman Lear family sitcoms of yore, this time featuring CIA agent father Stan Smith (MacFarlane), bombshell wife Francine (Wendy Schaal), college-aged hippie daughter Hayley (Rachael MacFarlane, sister to Seth), and bookworm son Steve (Scott Grimes). OK, normal enough family, but let's throw in some

government experiments gone wrong: Klaus, a talking pet goldfish with the brain of an East German athlete, and Roger, a master-of-disguise alien. (The series is at its best when centering on Roger and his increasingly fantastically be-wigged aliases.) Bolstered by its embrace of the cutaway gag, *Dad!* ups *Guy*'s surreal factor by multiples, and, with its high-powered Republican father and left-leaning daughter, delivers sharp political jabs along the way.

Avatar: The Last Airbender

NICKELODEON / 2005–2008
3 SEASONS / 61 EPISODES

🍅 **97%** 🗑 **99%**

Avatar opens to a world in turmoil. Four island nations make up the planet, each associated with an element of nature: the Fire Nation, the Water Nation, and the Earth Nation, and the Air Nation. Gifted people are able to manipulate or "bend" the elements of their home nation in martial arts combat. Keeping the world in balance is the Avatar, a person who can bend all four elements, and whose spirit reincarnates upon death into a newborn of a different nation. When the current Avatar, an 11-year-old Airbender named Aang, vanishes, the islands become vulnerable to the Fire Nation's campaign of total domination. The series begins with Katara and Sokka, brother and sister from a Water Nation tribe, discovering Aang encased in ice 100 years after his disappearance. From that moment, their journey will take them to every nation as the thawed-out Avatar learns to bend all four elements, and discovers the truth behind his vanishing and the motives behind the Fire Nation's aggression. It's a lot of setup for a Nickelodeon cartoon—but the opening narration of each episode nails it, priming the viewer for mystical, comedic, or action-packed 23-minute adventures that explore every side of the battle. This is one of those all-too-rare kids' shows that actually respects children's intelligence and capacity to process complex, mature storytelling. We see Aang's wide-eyed exploration of the world, combined with the heavy weight of his fate, along with Katara and Sokka's evolving roles as his guides, a young girl named Toph who enters as his Earth-bending inspiration, and even complicated characters from the Fire Nation. *Avatar* demonstrates that when a mature kids' show never talks down to its target audience, a whole legion of adult fans will follow. After a movie adaptation that shall not be mentioned, *Avatar* experienced a renewed cultural relevance after landing on Netflix in 2020, along with the equally acclaimed sequel series *The Legend of Korra*, and in 2021 Nickelodeon announced the launch of Avatar Studios, which will develop new series and theatrical films based on the franchise.

Robot Chicken

ADULT SWIM/CARTOON NETWORK / 2005–
10 SEASONS / 200 EPISODES / 10 SPECIALS

 – – 🗑 **91%**

For the last 20 years, some of TV's sharpest sketch comedy has come in animated form, thanks to the stop-motion comedy series *Robot Chicken*. A staple of Adult Swim, Cartoon Network's adult-targeted programming block that kicks off at 9 p.m., the Seth Green– and Matthew Senreich–created show is a perfect bit of bizarreness for anyone who feels *SNL* has lost its edge. Looking to spend time with Bitch Pudding, a Strawberry Shortcake–look-alike with a foul mouth and serious bloodlust? Ever wondered what a half-Santa, half-Frosty monstrosity voiced by Christian Slater would get up to

on Christmas Eve? *Robot Chicken*'s got you. The series is based on *Twisted ToyFare Theatre*, a comic strip in the now-defunct *ToyFare* magazine, which used action figures of famous heroes in its panels. The comic's surreal tone, and frequent placement of major pop culture figures in everyday situations, became *Robot Chicken*'s standout features, too. Looking to ease into the strangeness? Start with 2007's Annie-winning and Emmy-nominated "Robot Chicken: Star Wars," in which every sketch relates to the mega–sci-fi franchise.

Star Wars: The Clone Wars

CARTOON NETWORK, NETFLIX, DISNEY+ /
2008–2020
7 SEASONS / 133 EPISODES

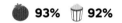 **93%** 🗑 **92%**

Though *The Clone Wars* tells the continuing story of Jedi knights and big-screen *Star Wars* favorites Anakin Skywalker and Obi-Wan Kenobi during the titular conflict, its greatest strength is its cast of original characters you might not know from the feature films. Take Jedi Padawan Ahsoka Tano, who grows from a mouthy kid under Anakin's tutelage to a seasoned warrior, capable of making fateful decisions. Or Captain Rex, the loyal clonetrooper who distinguishes himself as an individual in an army of *literally* uniform soldiers. Some of the characters became so beloved they crossed into other *Star Wars* shows and Disney rides. Long before *The Mandalorian* came along, the series proved that TV was in many ways a stronger medium to tell some *Star Wars* stories and offered more space to ideas just touched on in the films, like the depth of Anakin's emotional turmoil. Though rough in its early going, *Clone Wars* will leave you affected by the time you reach the end and Ahsoka makes her final stand among the clones.

BINGE BATTLE
THE SIMPSONS ◄ VS ► FAMILY GUY

Two prototypical nuclear families go head to head in this battle for animated sit-com supremacy. When they've done fight-fight-fighting, will it be Matt Groening's four-fingered fam or Seth MacFarlane's Quahog clan that comes out on top?

The Simpsons	Family Guy
FOX / 1989–	FOX / 1999–
32 SEASONS / 700+ EPISODES	19 SEASONS / 371 EPISODES

 97%   76%　　　　 – –   62%

▶ **WHAT IT'S ABOUT** The world first got to know Matt Groening's nuclear family in roughly animated sketches on *The Tracey Ullman Show*: boorish patriarch Homer (Dan Castellaneta), housewife Marge (Julie Kavner), hell-raising son Bart (Nancy Cartwright), precocious daughter Lisa (Yeardley Smith), and toddler Maggie. When the family got its own slot on Fox, we also got to know their neighbors, colleagues, drinking buddies, and the wider world of Springfield—state infamously unknown.

▶ **WHAT IT'S ABOUT** Seth MacFarlane's cut-away-loving animated sitcom focuses on self-involved buffoon Peter Griffin (MacFarlane) and his Quahog, Rhode Island family: wife Lois (Alex Borstein), oafish son Chris (Seth Green), brainy and boy-crazy daughter Meg (Mila Kunis), evil newborn Stewie (also MacFarlane), and the sardonic talking family dog, Brian (MacFarlane again).

BINGE BATTLE

Seasons 1–8

◄ PEAK SEASONS ►

Seasons 4–6

The Simpsons never got "bad," as some have claimed, but with great length comes great inconsistency—and it's never matched the sheer episode-by-episode brilliance of its 1990s run. (Though season 14's "How I Spent My Strummer Vacation" is as good a satire of the music industry as you'll find, and a later-seasons high point.) It's in these early years that you'll discover the iconic eps and moments that made the show the most influential and endlessly referenced sitcom ever: Mr. Burns eating a three-eyed fish, the family bursting into song with "You don't win friends with salad," Homer plummeting down the Springfield gorge ("d'oh . . . d'oh"), and more.

What do you do after you've been canceled—*twice*? If you're Seth MacFarlane, you come back stronger than ever. *Family Guy* was briefly canceled after its second season, and officially canceled after its third in 2002; but when Fox saw the success of its reruns on Adult Swim and major DVD sales, the network ordered new episodes that aired from 2005. They kicked off a streak that expanded on some of the funniest running jokes (Ernie the Giant Chicken was back for more epic battles), fully unfettered psycho baby Stewie, and introduced more hilarious side characters.

◄ BEST CHARACTER ►
(NOT IN THE FAM)

We choo-choo choose **Ralph Wiggum,** the son of the police chief with a heart three times the size of his brain and more unknowing one-liners than just about anyone in Springfield.

We cast our vote for **Mayor Adam West**, voiced by . . . the late Adam West until he died in 2017. His harebrained schemes—cementing coffins to prevent zombie uprisings—may not be great governance, but they bring the big LOLs.

34 Annies
(the awards of the International Animated Film Association)

◄ AWARDS ►

3 Annies

► OUR PICK This was always going to be an uphill climb for the Griffins, who only really exist because the Simpsons came before them. And while these days a new episode of *Family Guy* may come loaded with slightly more zingers than a new episode of **The Simpsons**, we pay our respects to the original and give the win to the fivesome from Springfield.

The Boondocks

ADULT SWIM / 2005–2014
4 SEASONS / 55 EPISODES

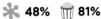 48% 🗑 81%

▶ **CRITICS CONSENSUS** *The Boondocks* succeeds in unsettling viewers, but its controversial humor and biting tone won't sit well with everyone. (Season 1)

▶ **WHAT IT'S ABOUT** Based on Aaron McGruder's popular comic strip, this satirical series centers on the Freemans, a Black family living in a mostly White suburb on the South Side of Chicago. There's a wise 10-year-old with a militant streak, Huey (Regina King); his brash and gangsta culture-obsessed younger brother, Riley (also King); and Grandad (John Witherspoon), their guardian and a former civil rights activist.

When Aaron McGruder adapted his comic strip into a television series, he committed to never *ever* watering down the cutting commentary that made it as controversial as it was beloved. He cemented that commitment in the very first episode, when preteen Huey—named after Black Panther founder Huey P. Newton—tells a group of country club folks: "Jesus was Black, Ronald Reagan was the Devil, and the government is lying to you about 9/11!" Like many Americans who caught this fiery, divisive, and brilliant series, Huey's well-groomed White audience just about lost their collective minds.

For four seasons, *The Boondocks* litigated the Black American culture clash—Malcolm versus Martin, thug life versus Howard—challenging the idea of a Black monolith and groupthink while delivering hilarious and thought-provoking television.

Take season 3's premiere episode, "It's a Black President, Huey Freeman," in which reactions to the election of President Barack Obama are nuanced and distinct among the three leads: Huey, the cynical and radical progressive is apathetic; Grandad is blindly optimistic; and Riley is defiant in his support—despite not knowing anything about Obama's policies. Or the Peabody-winning "Return of the King." In this season 1 lightning rod, an alternate time line shows a fresh-from-a-coma Martin Luther King Jr. consuming contemporary Black culture and being disgusted by it. Looking out at a rowdy crowd, gathered for another "I Have a Dream" speech, the animated MLK demands attention by shouting, "Will you ignorant n—as *please* shut the hell up?!" (The series's free use of the "n" word was one of its most contentious features.)

So, yes, no subject or figure was safe from McGruder and cowriter Rodney Barnes's fearless pen: Not Tyler Perry, Condoleezza Rice, not even Oprah. *The Boondocks* enlisted the help of some of the biggest names in Black Hollywood to its take-no-prisoners cause, as well as some the most venerated actors of our generation—none more so than four-time Emmy and Oscar winner Regina King, who voiced Huey and Riley. MTV host Sway Calloway, Quincy Jones, Wu-Tang rapper Ghostface Killah, and (strangely) director Werner Herzog all made appearances voicing themselves, too, while Snoop Dogg, comedian Katt Williams, Mos Def, and Busta Rhymes voiced fictional characters . . . definitely *based* on themselves.

When you're throwing that many punches, and throwing them this hard, you're going to have a few swings and misses. Episodes were pulled from the air, references to Rosa Parks were removed from an early episode following her death, and many of the series's dizzyingly sharp highs are countered by lows, like the much-derided "The Story of Jimmy Rebel," in which self-loathing side character Uncle Ruckus befriends a racist country singer.

But if we were to pinpoint *The Boondocks*'s original sin—at least in the eyes of its critics—it would be that its creators took the quietly muffled grumbles of marginalized people and brazenly amplified them before many were ready to even acknowledge that they existed. Through the mouths of babes, literally, accompanied by outlandish characters of every stripe and creed, *The Boondocks* said out loud what many were thinking, and still are, but few dared to speak aloud.

▶ **BEST EPISODE** Season 1, Episode 2—"The Trial of Robert Kelly." Fifteen years before the Lifetime docuseries *Surviving R. Kelly* laid out charges of child abuse and sexual assault against R&B superstar R. Kelly, *The Boondocks* tapped into the OJ-like rift that accusations against Kelly caused within the Black community. McGruder called out the #FreeRKelly movement with Huey—always the series's moral center—asking supporters outside a courthouse: "What the hell is wrong with you people? Every famous n—a that gets arrested is not Nelson Mandela . . . You wanna help R. Kelly? Then get some counseling for R. Kelly . . . But don't pretend the man is a hero."

▶ **CHARACTER WE LOVE** Huey may be the heart of the series, but Riley *is* the series: Littered with contradictions—boorish and self-destructive, charming and stunningly gifted—he is the best and the worst of *The Boondocks*.

Archer

FX, FXX / 2009–
11 SEASONS / 118 EPISODES

 90% 85%

One benefit of animation as a storytelling medium is that it allows for maximum creativity with minimal production costs, and nowhere is that more evident than in the evolution of FX's *Archer* over the course of its 11 seasons. What began ostensibly as an absurd send-up of James Bond–style espionage thrillers, centering on a egomaniacal spy named Sterling Archer (H. Jon Benjamin) and his dysfunctional agency, eventually took a hard left into anthology territory, even setting entire seasons in Archer's twisted mind. This gave the show's writers the freedom to reimagine the cast as 1980s drug runners, or the motley crew of a futuristic spaceship. Creator Adam Reed has admitted that some of this experimentation was born of boredom, but *Archer's* distinct art and animation style, brutal wit, and top-notch cast—as well as Reed's willingness to do things just for the hell of it—have helped it outlast scores of other adult-skewing animated series, many of which it inspired.

Adventure Time

CARTOON NETWORK / 2010–2018
10 SEASONS / 283 EPISODES

 100% 93%

There's a reason that older audiences have flocked to this bubbly cartoon. Originally developed as a stand-alone short film, creator Pendleton Ward's surreal comedy harbors a subversive streak. It follows a boy named Finn, the long-limbed last surviving human after a nuclear catastrophe, and his best friend, a talking dog named Jake, who together navigate a post-apocalyptic world populated by ice wizards, vampires, sentient confections, and other whimsical creatures. It plays like the most wholesome acid trip ever. But the show is bolder and more clever than its kiddie fantasy trappings: It's peppered with sly references to *Dungeons & Dragons*, Finn actually ages with each season—take that, *Simpsons*!—and Jake's girlfriend is a rainbow unicorn who only speaks Korean. These are the kinds of small details that have attracted the grown-ups, compelled HBO Max to commission four specials it aired in 2020, and inspired the kind of countless fan theories normally reserved for sophisticated science-fiction. Then again, maybe that's exactly what *Adventure Time* really is.

Bob's Burgers

FOX / 2011–
11 SEASONS / 211 EPISODES

 91% 88%

Meet the Belchers. There's Bob (H. Jon Benjamin), proprietor of a struggling All-American eatery, his wife Linda (John Roberts), and their three kids: The derriere-obsessed Tina (Dan Mintz), the musically inclined Gene (Eugene Mirman), and their youngest, sweet schemer Louise (Kristen Schaal). *Bob's Burgers's* restaurant setup allows quirky characters to come and go as needed, like fan-favorite handyman regular Teddy (Larry Murphy) or Bob's professional rival Jimmy Pesto (Jay Johnston), but the show's flexible enough to veer into murder mysteries, musicals, and even some mildly frightening holiday episodes. Silly and scatologically obsessed, but sweet to its core, the series survived an iffy first season or two on the strength of the different

Belcher personalities, the pitch-perfect voice acting, and the fact that, as far as animated sitcom families go, this is a pretty functional unit. It's reminiscent of creator Loren Bouchard's previous show, the cult favorite *Home Movies* (also featuring H. Jon Benjamin, in his breakout role), which also boasted carefully fashioned parents-and-kids dynamics.

Big Mouth

▶ PERFECT CERTIFIED FRESH STREAK

NETFLIX / 2017–
4 SEASONS / 41 EPISODES

 99% 🗑 77%

The middle schoolers of this crude and ingenious series—voiced by John Mulaney, co-creator Nick Kroll, and others—are shadowed by "hormone monsters" from the moment they hit puberty. These horned, hairy, and wizened creatures are there to guide our heroes through the most awkward times of their lives—but do not always offer the most clear-headed advice. And therein lie the LOLs. In fact, you'll laugh so hard at the antics of central hormone monsters Maurice and Connie (the latter voiced by Maya Rudolph at the peak of her powers), you may not even notice the seriousness of the topics *Big Mouth* covers, such as a devastating divorce or parental neglect, and the sensitivity with which it covers them. And then there are the bodily fluids. The kind of story lines that would cause a good deal of pearl-clutching in the Standards and Practices departments of most networks are par for the course here: the art of female masturbation, heavy flows (at the worst of times), and the importance of safe sex. Season 2's much-lauded "The Planned Parenthood Show" treats the search for the perfect form of birth control like an episode of *The Bachelorette*. (The diaphragm does *not* get the rose.)

BoJack Horseman

▶ CERTIFIED FRESH STREAK

NETFLIX / 2014–2020
6 SEASONS / 77 EPISODES

 93% 🗑 95%

There is something rather absurd about describing *BoJack Horseman.* It's a truly spectacular treatise on depression and addiction that stars Will Arnett as a past-his-prime actor (and horse) who'd made a name for himself on the fictional family sitcom *Horsin' Around*. Yet the mix of puns and ridiculous imagery—Amy Sedaris voices a pink-haired feline talent agent called Princess Carolyn, for example—are what allowed this Netflix animated comedy to go into ever darker territory. During its six seasons, *BoJack* told stories about suicide, the #MeToo movement, grief, and asexuality with the same ease as it crafted hilarious visual gags like Cindy Crawfish, Parrotmount Studios, and *Krill & Grace*. This Raphael Bob-Waksberg–created and Lisa Hanawalt–designed show is at once an homage to, and a powerful rebuke of, Peak TV's anti-hero dramas, a self-aware tragic farce examining why 21st-century audiences were so drawn to broken, narcissistic, alcoholic male figures.

Tuca and Bertie

NETFLIX, ADULT SWIM / 2011–
2 SEASONS / 20 EPISODES

 98% 🗑 67%

Few shows debut to the kind of dizzying acclaim and thoughtful discourse with which the first season of Lisa Hanawalt's *Tuca and Bertie* was greeted. Especially the kind of shows populated by fast-talking birds, vaping plants, lakes made of Jell-O, and end credits that might include oddities like "Awkwafina as Bertie's breast." But *Tuca and Bertie*, Hanawalt's adaptation of her *Tuca the Toucan* web comic, really was that mind-blowingly good from its first moments. The poppy look of the series will be familiar to anyone who has seen *BoJack Horseman*—Hanawalt was production designer on that series—with its world of humanoid animals, and blink-and-you'll-miss-them sight gags and puns (Bertie works at publisher Condé *Nest*). And *Tuca* shares with *BoJack* a determination to use its animal cast to delve into the darkest corners of human nature. But its primary concerns are different. Where BoJack was classic TV antihero material—self-destructive, selfish, and, crucially, a man—Tuca, the vivacious toucan voiced by Tiffany Haddish, and Bertie, the anxiety-riddled songbird voiced by Ali Wong, are just two thirtysomething friends trying to get by in life.

> *Tuca shares with BoJack a determination to use its animal cast to delve into the darkest corners of human nature.*

Will Tuca end up just like her lonely, alcoholic auntie if she doesn't change her ways? Can Bertie really make it as a pastry chef? How will Tuca get rid of the sex bugs she just caught? (The sex bugs grow to human-size and wreak havoc in a supermarket.) Most importantly: Can these two women be there for each other through it all? When the series does swerve into very dark territory—as in the award-winning "The Jelly Lakes," a singularly affecting look at the impact of sexual assault—it does so through a distinctly female lens. That lens is unique in the world of adult animation, which was part of why fans were so angry

with Netflix's decision to cancel the show after just one season. Commentators filled pop culture sites, lamenting the loss of not just a hilarious and heartfelt animated series with a female point of view, but one whose cast was headlined by two women of color. Like most *Tuca* episodes, though—even the dark ones—the ending here is happy: Adult Swim stepped in to give the series a new home, starting in 2021.

Undone

AMAZON PRIME VIDEO / 2019–
2 SEASONS / 16 EPISODES

 98%　 93%

What do you do when you've just upended the world's assumptions about what's possible in animated television with the aggressively dark and complex *BoJack Horseman*? If you're Raphael Bob-Waksberg and Kate Purdy, you outdo yourself with *Undone*. The co-creators' second collaboration is about a young San Antonio woman Alma (Rosa Salazar) who—following a near-fatal car crash—suddenly finds herself able to shift through time and space. When her newfound abilities reconnect her with her long-dead father (Bob Odenkirk), the duo teams up to solve his murder. Style-wise, Amazon Prime Video's first animated series is singularly ambitious, combining traditional animation, hand-painted backgrounds, performance capture (an actor's movements are filmed and then used as basis of animation), and rotoscoping (you may recall the technique from Richard Linklater's *A Scanner Darkly*), but it's the equally ambitious, non-linear storytelling that distinguishes *Undone*. Purdy, who has talked openly about her own nervous breakdown and family history of schizophrenia, deftly and movingly explores what it's like to lose control of one's center—walls and skies crack and crumble around Alma at points. This is something she also did in the acclaimed *BoJack* episode "Time's Arrow," which plunged viewers into the dementia-addled mind of the hero's mother and for which Purdy won a Writers Guild Award.

Rick & Morty

ADULT SWIM / 2013–
5 SEASONS / 51 EPISODES

 94%   93%

When Morty's grandpa, scientific inventor Rick Sanchez, moves into the family house and sets up their garage as his base of experimental operations, it's like Morty's nerd dreams for adventure have come true. Accompanying Rick with his portal gun and intergalactic car, Morty's life is all about travelling the stars, encountering aliens, "smuggling" space seeds, tearing apart time and reality, and burying your alternate dimensional self in the backyard. All in a boy's life. Created by Dan Harmon and Justin Roiland (who also voices the two characters), the show quickly gained traction for its intricate storytelling and the nihilistic and frequently cruel comedic twists on sci-fi tropes, with the insanity spilling into Rick's daughter's family life. Rick himself has emerged as a post-modern icon, an alcoholic fourth-wall–breaking vulgarian whose accumulation of the universe's knowledge leaves him on the edge of suicidal oblivion. At its best, when mixing the sitcom with its unhinged sci-fi takes, the show can pack a surprising emotional wallop.

FROM PLAYING CARDS TO ▶ #HASHTAGS

The Evolution of TV Fandom

BOOKS

For bookworms, novelizations, tie-ins, and dense series guides were a chance to look for TV fandom at the local bookstore.

The first: Back in 1960, beloved author Beverly Cleary wrote a *Leave it to Beaver* tie-in novel (and two others thereafter!).

The essential: Fictional mystery writer "Richard Castle" (of *Castle* fame) released a real-life *New York Times* best seller.

PLAYING CARDS

With both simple tie-in cards and elaborate collectible games, fans have long enjoyed the chance to play along with their TV obsessions.

The first: eBay holds plenty of vintage 1960s Topps playing cards featuring artwork from shows like *The Flintstones* and *The Addams Family*.

The essential: No show's success is as intertwined with its collectible card game as *Pokémon*. Gotta catch 'em all!

WIKIS

The collaborative nature of wikis made sharing the wealth of aggregate fan knowledge on any given show simpler than ever before.

The first: The encyclopedia in the *Stargate-SG1* fan site Gateworld (founded in 1999) was arguably a precursor to many contemporary TV wikis.

The essential: Lostpedia, now hosted by wiki-hosting service Fandom, was a go-to spot for *Lost* fans eager for answers.

RECAPS

The ability to record and rewatch television made it easier to offer granular, episodic analysis on sites like *Television Without Pity*.

The first: Recapper extraordinaire Alan Sepinwall credits Tim Lynch's rundowns of *Star Trek* spin-offs with inspiring his own takes on *NYPD Blue*.

The essential: Tom & Lorenzo's "Mad Style" recaps of *Mad Men* focused on the show's fashion.

PODCASTS

As podcasts took off, fans, critics, and later creators and even networks realized their potential for hosting engaging TV deep dives—sometimes episode by episode.

The first: *The Signal* (2005–2014) gave "Browncoats" (*Firefly* fans) a chance to revisit the cult hit show.

The essential: HBO's *Lovecraft Country Radio* showed how a podcast can broaden a show's already ambitious goals.

LIVE TWEET -ALONGS

Viewers revamped appointment television in the digital era by turning Twitter into an online watercooler.

The first: Fox's action-drama *Drive* lasted just four episodes, but @foxdrive broke ground when, in April 2007, it hosted the first coordinated live-tweet event on the nascent platform.

The essential: With hashtags like #AliTellsAll, *Pretty Little Liars* (aka @PLLTVSeries) enthralled fans.

Sometimes what's on-screen just isn't enough for the truly ravenous fan. Since almost the dawn of TV, audiences have sought ways to engage with their favorite characters and stories beyond a show itself—eating up universe-expanding books, taking control of the action with games, and using new technologies to mobilize when the thing they love comes under threat. Here's how fans have been breaking TV out of the box from the '60s to today.

SAVE THE SHOW CAMPAIGNS

Coordinated campaigns in support of canceled shows have made networks listen. Sometimes.
The first: The OG *Star Trek* benefited from two letter-writing campaigns that bolstered early season renewals.
The essential: When Netflix's *One Day at a Time* reboot was canceled, fans of the Latinx sitcom rallied around the #SaveODAAT hashtag: Pop TV saved the show... for 1 season.

FANFIC

With "fan fiction," audiences have been able to reimagine their fave TV shows in their own words and find like-minded fellow readers.
The first: 1967 *Star Trek* fanzine *Spockanalia* was an early platform for many stories featuring the Enterprise crew.
The essential: *Buffy* fanfic-ers made a cottage industry out of Sunnydale tales and turned portmanteaus like "Spuffy" into genres of their own.

ONLINE FORUMS

As they began "surfing the Net," fans turned to forums and message boards (and later blogs and subreddits) to talk up the latest WTF TV twists.
The first: Spaces like the alt.tv.xfiles news group and the Idealists Haven spurred early online *X-Files* fandom.
The essential: Reddit subthreads rule now and Westeros fans reign supreme in /r/gameofthrones and /r/freefolk.

MAGAZINES

Glossier than their zine brethren, fan-aimed mags boast interviews, set photos, and features on niche TV fare.
The first: Launched in 1973, *Doctor Who Magazine* is the longest-running TV tie-in magazine.
The essential: From *Alias* to *Xena: Warrior Princess*, publisher Titan Magazines' enviable roster of titles at the turn of the century was a haven for TV geeks.

AFTER-SHOWS

Taking a cue from radio and late night, studios began offering fans in-depth roundtable shows immediately following buzzy series.
The first: Thank MTV Canada's *The After Show* (cohosted by a pre–*Schitt's Creek* Dan Levy!) for pioneering the genre, with talk shows following *The Hills* and *Laguna Beach*.
The essential: *The Walking Dead's* aftershow, *Talking Dead*, is the template to follow.

POP-UPS

Immersive experiences have turned fictional spaces like *Friends*'s Central Perk and *Gilmore Girls*' Luke's Diner into Instagram-ready sensations.
The first: The 2016 "Saved by the Max" cafe experience let Chicago visitors relive their '90s *Saved by the Bell* fantasy before it moved to LA.
The essential: Re-creating *Fleabag*'s Guinea Pig Cafe, aka Hillary's cafe, in LA was a stroke of whimsical genius.

COMMERCIAL BREAK

Mysteries and Mind-f—cks

THE WEIRD, WONDERFUL, AND TOTALLY PERPLEXING

Are you a "second-screener"— someone who can't put their phone or tablet down while bingeing a show? Then you might want to skip this chapter altogether: The series herein demand your undivided attention with intricate plotting and a labyrinth's worth of WTF twists.

Not the kind of person who can handle a sudden alien appearance in the final moments of your small-town crime series? You might want to move along, too. Sh-t's about to get weird.

That's the thing about the relative creative freedom offered in an era of competitive streaming services, cable channels, and networks throwing money at big ideas they hope will stick: Creative people are going take that freedom and *run with it*. Run all the way to, say, a story of eight interconnected strangers on different parts of the planet who discover they're somehow emotionally and physically connected, as *Matrix* filmmakers Lana and Lily Wachowski did with *Sense8*. (Cue the orgies—*really*.) Or to parallel Earths, one ravaged by a suspect virus, as in the criminally underrated and relentlessly mind-bending *Counterpart*. Or to a town like Twin Peaks.

David Lynch's hugely influential series about the murder of homecoming queen Laura Palmer may have come decades before Peak TV experimentation was the norm, but it is the spiritual ancestor to many of the titles featured in this chapter: mysterious, bizarre, blackly comic, and determined to be unlike anything else on TV.

Like Lynch, some of the other big-name creatives in these pages—J. J. Abrams, Damon Lindelof, Sam Esmail, Phoebe Waller-Bridge—sought to fully stretch the form of TV and defy our expectations of genre with these titles. Sometimes they achieved that through an element of strangeness (cue the orgies!), but even more often through adding surprising characterizations to traditional formulas. Britain's *Happy Valley*, for instance, gives us a pair of solid, if familiar mysteries, elevated by one of the most complex and distinctive detectives to ever work a TV case in Sarah Lancashire's Catherine Cawood.

Innovation doesn't always connect with audiences. For every hit, like Abrams's ABC phenomenon *Lost*, or BBC America's eccentric and queer spy thriller *Killing Eve*, there are gone-too-soon underperformers like *The OA* and, well, *Twin Peaks*, which saw a massive ratings decline in season 2 once its nation-captivating mystery was resolved and most of what was left was just the Lynchian weirdness. (Which we love here.) Innovation can also lead to inconsistency: great seasons followed by head-shakingly rough seasons that creators perhaps never prepared for (*True Detective*, *Broadchurch*), and series that crash-landed in their final episodes, struggling to figure out how to tie up their complicated threads (*Lost* again).

But that's a symptom of ambition, the nature of risk, and it's little surprise that each series here has tapped into a diehard fan base of varying size, grateful for what that ambition generated. If you're feeling brave, put the phone down and see what they're obsessing over.

Twin Peaks

 GAME-CHANGER

ABC, SHOWTIME / 1990–1991, 2017 REVIVAL

3 SEASONS / 48 EPISODES

 82% 🍿 89%

Even 30-plus years after its debut, there's still nothing like *Twin Peaks*, arguably the most culty "cult TV show" of all time. It's surreal, campy, absurd, disturbing, and a bunch of other adjectives that make it pretty amazing that it was presented to ABC's massive mainstream audience in the spring of 1990. (To put it in perspective, the top shows on the network that year were *Roseanne*, *America's Funniest Home Videos*, *Full House*, and *Family Matters*.) At its most basic, Mark Frost and David Lynch's mystery is about FBI Special Agent Dale Cooper (Kyle MacLachlan) investigating the murder of homecoming queen Laura Palmer in a small town filled with quirky locals. But it's not just an excuse to veer into dreamy, WTF territory, although there is plenty of that. It's also absorbing and has some serious narrative legs, unfolding over that original two-season run, a prequel film (1992's *Twin Peaks: Fire Walk with Me*), and 2017's masterfully cinematic revival of the series on Showtime.

Lost

▶ **GAME-CHANGER**
▶ **HIGHLY ADDICTIVE**

ABC / 2004–2010

6 SEASONS / 121 EPISODES

🍅 85% 🍿 91%

There was a point in the mid-aughts when, noticing some sleep-deprived, bleary-eyed coworker,

we'd ask what they were up to last night. Did they close out a bar? Or just have a kid? The answer, invariably, was that they were getting into *Lost*—and were addicted, realizing that, as soon as an episode ended with its signature sonic beat and title, *not* playing the next one on the DVD, even past 2 a.m., was a fool's errand. Sixteen years after its debut on ABC, the sprawling drama-mystery still packs that "We *have* to see what happens next" punch. Do some of the jokes and dialogue ring a bit cheesier than we recall? Sure. Does the gulf between some actors' talents and others' seem a little wider these days? Yeah. But does the *meat* of it—Michael Giacchino's emotive score, the labyrinthine plot and exciting reveals—remain pretty revolutionary (and generally great)? Absolutely.

> *Let's not lose sight of* Lost's *achievement in inspiring the next generation of left-turning TV.*

This tale, about a group of disparate flight survivors carrying (excuse the pun) emotional baggage while surviving on an island, beautifully builds a weird world, throwing out philosophical references and plot clues (but what do those numbers really *mean*, man?) while still maintaining a narrative arc. That's no easy feat. And while more than a few fans were disappointed with the finale's revelation, let's not lose sight of *Lost*'s achievement in providing hours and hours of excellent WTF-inducing entertainment and inspiring the next generation of left-turning TV. That *Lost* co-creators Damon Lindelof and J. J. Abrams went on to have their hands in *Watchmen* and *Lovecraft Country*, respectively, seems hardly coincidental.

Broadchurch

  PERFECT CERTIFIED FRESH STREAK

ITV / 2013–2017
3 SEASONS / 24 EPISODES

🍅 92% 🗑 92%

There is a relative glut of shows like *Broadchurch*— UK crime series set in an idyllic small town, in which colorful locals are suspected of killing, often, a child. But what puts this bit of slickly shot British prestige television in a different league largely comes down to the casting of its leads. You simply don't see gripping whodunits from across the pond that are heightened by stars like Olivia Colman, a future Best Actress Oscar winner, and David Tennant. In the first and best season of the show, Colman plays a cheery detective working alongside her new, crotchety boss (Tennant), and it's the entertaining interplay of lightness and darkness between the two characters, perhaps even just as much as finding out who murdered an 11-year-old boy in a coastal village, that urges you to watch *just one more* episode well past your bedtime.

Top of the Lake

BBC UKTV, BBC TWO, SUNDANCE TV /
2013–2017
2 SEASONS / 13 EPISODES

 83%   71%

By the time *Top of the Lake*'s season 2 (subtitled *China Girl*) opened with the tired "dead girl" trope that has driven the bulk of procedural dramas for the last several decades, few people worried that the BBC Two, BBC UKTV, and Sundance Channel (now SundanceTV) co-production was going to do anything conventional with the well-worn storytelling hook. Its first season, which introduced Detective Robin Griffin (a post-*Mad Men* Elisabeth Moss) as she investigated the disappearance of a pregnant teen in New Zealand, had already announced the Jane Campion and Gerard Lee creation as a welcome feminist riff on dramas about sexual assault and violence against women. With a tone that teetered between the ethereal and the earthy—with enough off-kilter comedy, courtesy of Holly Hunter's bewigged, androgynous, Swiss spiritual leader—*Top of the Lake* was an immediate revelation, firmly cementing itself as a new classic of the genre.

A welcome feminist riff on dramas about sexual assault and violence against women

---

Fargo

  PERFECT CERTIFIED FRESH STREAK

FX / 2014–
4 SEASONS / 41 EPISODES

🍅 93% 🗑 84%

How do you possibly spin a TV series off Joel and Ethan Coen's seminal film *Fargo* and not only *not* screw it up, but deliver something special in its own right? The answer: big courage, big quirk, and smart writing about (sometimes) dumb criminals. The first season of creator Noah Hawley's FX anthology series stars Allison Tolman as a dogged small-town cop and Martin Freeman as a meek insurance salesman turned criminal in mid-2000s Minnesota and has the strongest ties to the beloved 1996 movie, but subsequent seasons play looser with the source *(Continued on page 174.)*

The Leftovers

▶ **PERFECT CERTIFIED FRESH STREAK**

HBO / 2014–2017
3 SEASONS / 28 EPISODES

 91%   🗑 90%

▶ **CRITICS CONSENSUS** Its dour tone and self-seriousness may make for somber viewing, but *The Leftovers* is an artfully crafted, thought-provoking drama that aims high and often hits its mark. (Season 1)

▶ **WHAT IT'S ABOUT** It has been three years since 2% of the Earth's population disappeared without a trace. As the townsfolk of Mapleton, New York, grapple with their loss, turning to cults and self-described saviors alike, they find there may never be a satisfying sense of closure for those who have been left behind.

The premise of Tom Perrotta's novel *The Leftovers,* which tracks the aftermath of the world's "Sudden Departure," is decidedly bleak. As is its HBO adaptation. For three glorious and, to its feverish evangelizers, all-too-underrated seasons, the Damon Lindelof–developed drama managed not only to successfully adapt Perrotta's novel but to expand and improve upon it.

Crafting what, in its first season, felt like a family melodrama weighted with big ideas around grief and faith, *Lost* co-creator Lindelof immediately proved he could capture the spirit of Perrotta's language. The novelist's sparse and incisive sentences are crisp revelations, rooted in a mundanity that quickly opens up to a philosophical abyss with discomfiting clarity—"Laurie Garvey hadn't been raised to believe in the Rapture. She hadn't been raised to believe in much of anything, except the foolishness of belief itself," he writes in the opening of that 2011 book. They set the tone for the collaboration between Lindelof, who cowrote almost every single one of the show's 28 episodes, and the best-selling writer, who served as an executive producer.

Which is not to say this was wholly a faithful adaptation. Neither writer was precious about killing their darlings. (Literally: Don't get too attached to any one character.) The duo exhausted their source material in season 1, which introduced the Garveys, including Justin Theroux's police chief Kevin (who struggles to keep the peace in Mapleton) and Amy Brenneman's Laurie (his estranged wife who's joined a chain-smoking nihilistic cult called the Guilty Remnant). They then moved the story away from Perrotta's quaint portrait of a small town and more fully embraced a magical-realist sensibility that felt very much in tune with Max Richter's melancholy score.

As they did, *The Leftovers* actually got better.

If the first season could be described as a downer, its subsequent seasons, which moved from New York state to Texas and later still to Australia, were buoyed by a welcome sense of humor that was still rooted in telling an increasingly intricate story that was also, almost literally, biblical. Case in point: Its second season opener, titled "Axis Mundi," begins with a flashback to prehistoric times and features an earthquake that leaves a town's lake waterless, an inauspicious omen of things to come.

That kind of ambitious storytelling was polarizing. Modest ratings and a cold shoulder from the Emmys—the show only ever earned a single nomination, for Ann Dowd's masterful performance as the Guilty Remnant's Patti Levin—meant

The Leftovers remained an obsession for a small but fervent few who were just as entranced by Theroux's instantly iconic gray sweatpants and the drama's near-perfect needle drops (look out for the Wu Tang Clan's "Protect Ya Neck [The Jump Off]") as they were by the show's ability to pull off setting an entire episode on a boat full of lion-obsessed sex cult members.

Sandwiched between Lindelof's two heavily awarded TV hits, *Lost* and *Watchmen*, *The Leftovers* can seem like minor work. But this miracle of a drama may well be his crowning achievement. By the time he re-teamed with Regina King (a standout in seasons 2 and 3 here) to reimagine Alan Moore and Dave Gibbons's seminal graphic novel *Watchmen,* those who'd seen how he'd turned Perrotta's meditation on grief into a full-blown mythological examination of our modern belief systems knew that such an ambitious goal was an inevitable next step for one of the most inventive literary adaptors in contemporary American television.

▶ **BEST EPISODE** Season 2, Episode 8—"International Assassin." An intentionally befuddling trip to the world of the undead that showcases *The Leftovers* at its boldest, this Craig Zobel–directed hour of television is grandiose and surreal in the best kind of way.

▶ **CHARACTER WE LOVE** Nora Durst (Carrie Coon), as complex a grief-stricken character as television has ever delivered (neither hysterical nor numb, though with hints of both throughout), who emerged as the show's blessed centrifugal force.

DEEP ▼ ▼ DIVE

material. There's flashing between the present and the past—and to other parts of the country—to fill out stories we only partly know, as when season 4 jumps to 1950s Kansas City to spend time with Chris Rock as the head of a crime family briefly touched on in previous episodes. And then there's the bizarre stuff: Witness season 2 episode "The Castle," in which Kirsten Dunst's dim beautician Peggy Blumquist is completely unfazed by a UFO sighting after a massive shoot-out. Does all this dark humor come with its share of Easter eggs and good-old Midwestern charm? You betcha.

Happy Valley

▶ HIGHLY ADDICTIVE

BBC ONE / 2014–
2 SEASONS / 12 EPISODES

🍅 98% 🍿 96%

Writer Sally Wainwright is responsible for some of the best British TV of the past two decades: her beloved 2000s comedy *At Home with the Braithwaites*; Certified Fresh period series *Gentleman Jack*; and *Last Tango In Halifax*, the popular tale of two childhood sweethearts who come together in their sixties after their spouses die. But her masterwork—so far, at least—is the cop thriller *Happy Valley*, which might just be the most ironically named TV show of all time. West Yorkshire's Calder Valley, where the series is both set and shot, may look idyllic from a distance, but Wainwright zooms in for a hard close-up, thrusting into focus the domestic violence, disaffection, and drug abuse that lie beneath its picturesque surface, and never letting us look away. It's a bracing inversion of every quaint and bloodless village murder mystery to come before. Series hero, Sergeant Catherine Cawood (Sarah Lancashire), is a similar

middle finger to our expectations: She's a woman in a man's world—her own local cop shop *and* the TV world of small-town lead detectives—and damaged seemingly beyond repair as she begins investigating the kidnapping that forms the spine of the first season.

Happy Valley might just be the most ironically named TV show of all time.

In season 2, Cawood herself comes under suspicion as she looks into a human trafficking case, but it's her personal mission—an obsession with bringing to justice the man who raped her daughter eight years ago, leading to her daughter's suicide—that makes *Happy Valley* such an edge-of-your-seat and gut-wrenching ride. Lancashire, something of a national TV treasure in the UK, is astonishingly good as the weary and doggedly focused Cawood, and pairs perfectly with *Downton Abbey*'s Siobhan Finneran as her sister and recovering addict Clare. Their frank talks and occasional laughs, over tea or a cigarette, give *Happy Valley* a welcome dash of warmth amid the gloom.

True Detective

HBO / 2014–2019
3 SEASONS / 24 EPISODES

 78%   75%

Let's get this out of the way: The second season of Nic Pizzolatto's anthology crime series wasn't so hot, even with that engrossing lead performance by Colin Farrell. The third one, starring Mahershala Ali, was better, with traces of what made the original so inspired, but hardly enough to live up to it. Which is all to say: That first season really was something, an uncompromising marriage of visions—every episode was written by Pizzolatto and directed by Cary Joji Fukunaga (who would go on to direct the Bond film *No Time to Die*)—about two detectives, played by Matthew McConaughey (never better) and Woody Harrelson, trying to solve the cultish murder of a prostitute in the backwoods of Louisiana. Jumping between the initial investigation in 1995 and a revelatory follow-up 12 years later, it's a noirish, disturbing, philosophically loaded affair, complete, in its fourth episode, with one of the all-time-great tracking shots.

Mr. Robot

▶ **PERFECT CERTIFIED FRESH STREAK**

▶ **HIGHLY ADDICTIVE**

USA NETWORK / 2015–2019
4 SEASONS / 45 EPISODES

 94% 94%

What's a hacker to do when a mysterious man who goes by "Mr. Robot" (Christian Slater)—who may or may not be real—asks him to use his skills for the greater good? If you're Elliot Alderson (Rami Malek in his breakout role), a paranoid young man struggling with social anxiety, dissociative identity disorder, and clinical depression, you opt in, becoming the unreliable narrator in Sam Esmail's dizzyingly timely techno-thriller. *Mr. Robot*'s later seasons could never match its near-flawless debut, every episode of which scored 100% on our Tomatometer. But as an auteurist piece of television that feverishly played with cinematographic gimmicks, designed to be painstakingly dissected ad nauseum by audiences asking WTF was happening (watch out for the Alf cameo!), Esmail's show proved in its final season that it could still pack a punch (see it's nearly dialogue-free Christmas Day episode from 2019).

Sense8

NETFLIX / 2015–2018
2 SEASONS / 24 EPISODES

 86% 91%

The premise of Netflix's globe-trotting sci-fi show *Sense8* is, understandably, a hard pill to swallow. Created by *The Matrix*'s Lana and Lilly Wachowski, along with J. Michael Straczynski, the drama follows the eight titular "sensates" (humans who have an emotional and psychic connection with one another) as they try to figure out why they're so linked and why they're hunted by a shadowy organization intent on neutralizing their powers. But once you embrace the show's bizarre setup (and its steamy sex scenes), *Sense8* emerges as an ambitious and deeply queer examination of identity in the 21st century. With an avid fan base that rallied to make sure its season 2 cliff-hanger ending wouldn't be the last viewers saw of the sensates—a wrap-up film was released in 2018—*Sense8* spoke to a community famished for multilingual stories about global connection that prized empathy across and despite cultural differences.

Happy!

SYFY / 2016–2019
2 SEASONS / 18 EPISODES

 84% 89%

There's never quite been a show like *Happy!* The series initially centers on a former cop turned hitman who starts to see a little girl's imaginary friend, Happy; together, they roam New York during the Christmas holiday to save the girl and uncover a child-smuggling ring, perpetrated by a popular children's entertainer. Despite that harrowing description, *Happy!* managed to be wildly funny in all its darkness. The love child of comic-book genius Grant Morrison and *Crank* codirector Brian Taylor, the series also shines thanks to its incredible leads: Christopher Meloni as unwashed ne'er-do-well Nick Sax and Patton Oswalt as the voice of Happy, a sickly adorable phantom resembling a blue stuffed Pegasus. Inverting his *Law & Order: Special Victims Unit* cop persona, Meloni is a gleeful thrill seeker while Oswalt offers Happy the right sort of saccharine innocence. The pair lead viewers on a tour of comical depravity that should be disgusting, but manages to find its way back to heartwarming.

The OA

▶ GONE TOO SOON

NETFLIX / 2016–2019
2 SEASONS / 16 EPISODES

🍅 **84%** 🍿 **84%**

Netflix ostensibly canceled this sci-fi series after two seasons—or so we're led to believe. But anything is possible in the world of *The OA*, including parallel dimensions, interpretive dance opening portals to other worlds, and a telepathic octopus who is also the angel of death. Actress and writer Brit Marling, who co-created the series with frequent collaborator Zal Batmanglij, stars as Prairie Johnson, a blind woman who mysteriously returns to her hometown, sight restored, seven years after going missing. Calling herself "The OA" ("Original Angel"), Prairie enlists a group of followers to perform a series of movements that open a door to another dimension. Sound bats—t? Season 2 gets even more mind-trippy and indescribably meta. Suffice it to say that it needs to be seen to be believed, but, once you're on board, you'll be practicing your movements in no time.

The Sinner

▶ HIGHLY ADDICTIVE

USA NETWORK / 2017–
3 SEASONS / 24 EPISODES

🍅 **90%** 🍿 **72%**

USA's super-bingeable anthology crime series looks at the ways an immersion into fanatical beliefs can influence a person's perception of right and wrong—usually causing murderous results. Season 1, which is based on Petra Hammesfahr's 1999 novel, stars Jessica Biel as a wife and mother who suddenly, and seemingly inexplicably, kills a man on the beach; season 2, which stars Carrie Coon, focuses on a cult; and season 3, which stars Matt Bomer, looks at Friedrich Nietzsche's concept of the Übermensch (or superior human). The main connector in all these stories is Bill Pullman's Harry Ambrose, a police investigator with a knack for looking into ulterior motives and who has his own familiar demons with which to reckon. The series is often cited as an example of how basic cable channel USA shifted its brand in the latter half of that decade from quick-witted (but frequently underestimated) programming like *Psych* to grittier series with a social message, like *Mr. Robot*.

Counterpart

▶ GONE TOO SOON

STARZ / 2017–2019
2 SEASONS / 20 EPISODES

🍅 **100%** 🍿 **90%**

Creator Justin Marks's espionage thriller *Counterpart* lassos you in with a gimmick and holds you in place with a singularly complicated and engrossing story—one that has zero time for any second-screen viewing, so pay attention! J. K. Simmons stars as Howard Silk, a mild-mannered cog in the bureaucratic wheel at the Office of Interchange, who exchanges coded messages he doesn't have the privilege of understanding with others like himself and is a devoted husband to the currently comatose Emily (Olivia Williams). Simmons also plays *another* Howard, this one a more aggressive version of the first who exists in a—ahem—*counterpart* realm of the world he knows. This Howard has more clearance and comes with the news that there's a mole in the operation and assassins are afoot.

Holds you in place with a singularly complicated and engrossing story

---

The show's effective use of clone-related fakeouts and flashes to alternate worlds and times keeps Howard, and viewers, at attention. But the way *Counterpart* hides these clues and half-truths among the supporting players, building them up with standout episodes of their own, may be its most lasting mark on the genre. The first season's "The Sincerest Form of Flattery," takes on the human casualties of war by concentrating on Nazanin Boniadi's underestimated housewife Clare and the life she didn't have the chance to live before she was given orders to wed the ignoramus Peter Quayle (Harry Lloyd). The second season's "Twin Cities" flashes back in time to show how these characters got into this mess in the first place by tracing younger versions of James Cromwell's mysterious Yanek (played by Samuel Roukin). *Counterpart*'s original airing on niche premium cable channel Starz didn't do it any favors when it came to finding a large audience, but the series's star power, coupled with a fresh take on the espionage drama, has drawn an adventurous audience on streaming.

Killing Eve

▶ PERFECT CERTIFIED FRESH STREAK

BBC AMERICA / 2018–
3 SEASONS / 24 EPISODES

 89%  **86%**

Killing Eve, creator Phoebe Waller-Bridge's adaptation of author Luke Jennings's novels, doesn't just work because of the tangy sweet sardonicism underlying every moment of this cat-and-mouse game between two women who are each way too good at their jobs. Nor does this tale of Sandra Oh's British intelligence officer Eve Polastri and her conquest, Jodie Comer's Villanelle—an ace assassin who spends nearly every moment when she's not elaborately murdering someone pouting like a petulant child—entice simply because of its eroticism. (And while Villanelle's sartorial choices are a draw—including a now-iconic, gauzy pink party dress—they're not the main one.) What makes *Killing Eve* so addicting is that it truly seems to understand what it means to be a woman in the 21st century. There is a large amount of undermining and double-crossing at their respective jobs, for starters: Eve's boss, Fiona Shaw's Carolyn Martens, is not the mentor Eve thought she'd be; Villanelle's handler, Kim Bodnia's Konstantin Vasiliev, can only handle someone who behaves. But the show also revels in the sometimes Sapphic, sometimes antagonistic social construct of female relationships. Each woman is drawn to the other out of a kinship in feeling like her counter is the only one who really understands. But they've also each been taught not to trust the other, and jealousy and obsession can feed off this. This is still a game, after all, and playing by someone else's rules is liable to get you stabbed in the gut or shot in the back.

Mindhunter

NETFLIX / 2017–
2 SEASONS / 19 EPISODES

 97%   95%

▶ **CRITICS CONSENSUS** *Mindhunter* distinguishes itself in a crowded genre with ambitiously cinematic visuals and meticulous attention to character development. (Season 1)

▶ **WHAT IT'S ABOUT** Starting in the late 1970s, FBI agents Holden Ford (Jonathan Groff) and Bill Tench (Holt McCallany), as well as psychologist Wendy Carr (Anna Torv), interview notorious serial killers to see what made them tick and to investigate fresh cases.

Was there anyone better suited to breathe new life into the well-worn territory of television murder investigations than David Fincher? The *Se7en* director's fingerprints—the dim lighting, the bleak atmospherics, the eerily calm killers, the endless paper trail for weary detectives in bad suits drinking bad coffee—are all over *Mindhunter*. It's like his acclaimed film, *Zodiac*, writ large. Where other shows often build toward a big reveal, *Mindhunter* focuses on the *process,* not the payoff, so that understanding what would make someone do the unthinkable or running into another case cul-de-sac is just as thrilling as finding out that *the killer was the father the whole time.*

This Netflix show, created by British playwright Joe Penhall and based on the book *Mindhunter: Inside the FBI's Elite Serial Crime Unit* by former FBI agent John E. Douglas and co-author Mark

Olshaker, opens with a literal bang (Spoiler alert: A nude dude blows his head off during a hostage negotiation), only to slow down considerably to a simmer, following the grind of two FBI agents—Jonathan Groff's newbie and Holt McCallany's vet—hopping from police station to police station to tell officers what they've gleaned at the bureau.

But what about those thrills, you ask? Just wait until the arrival of Ed Kemper (Cameron Britton, who deservedly garnered an Emmy nom for Outstanding Guest Actor in a Drama Series) in the first of the agents' many interviews with serial killers. Dubbed the "Co-Ed Killer," the hulking, bespectacled Kemp coolly, soberly, intelligently, and almost genially details his thinking about the rapes, murder, and necrophilic acts for which he was convicted. It's utterly disturbing and chilling TV—made all the more so knowing it was based on interviews with the real-life Kemper—and, even though it's merely a conversation, far scarier than any cutaway shot to a bloody scene that a lesser show would throw at you.

Mindhunter bounces between jails across the country and conversations with famous killers (Richard Speck, "Son of Sam" David Berkowitz, Jerry Brudos—a great Happy Anderson, all grins and deflection—and Charles Manson) as the FBI team fine-tunes its psychological findings in hopes of solving current cases. About those: There are a bunch, but the standouts involve the eerie, episode-opening drop-ins on the BTK Killer, as well as the arc on the Atlanta child murders, which unfolds over much of the second season.

But what keeps us invested in *Mindhunter*, and what ties these disparate crimes and conversations together, are the people on the outside, not the criminals behind bars. The interplay between the agents played by Groff (Boy Scout–like, sharp, yet socially and professionally aloof) and McCallany (chain-smoking, rougher around the edges in a dad-means-well kind of way) provide some much-needed comic levity. And Anna Torv, as their removed, closeted psych professor turned colleague, is thankfully put into the spotlight in season 2.

Toss in some great period details and a soundtrack of choice AM-radio cuts by the likes of Talking Heads ("Psycho Killer," naturally), Led Zeppelin, Roxy Music, and the Pretenders, and we're in for many more seasons—though the series's future is in question—even if they keep us up at night.

BEST EPISODE ▶ Season 1, Episode 2—"Episode Two." Expertly directed by Fincher, this one boasts the tough-to-shake first meeting with a chatty, candid Ed Kemper.

CHARACTER WE LOVE ▶ Bill Tench (Holt McCallany), whom we'd pay good money to have too many beers with at a dive and, as a few of his neighbors do during a cookout, get him to dish on what these psychopaths confided.

The Outsider

HBO / 2020
1 SEASON / 10 EPISODES

 91% 🗑 83%

In 2020, was the world really asking for another screen adaptation of a Stephen King book? Given that there'd been, you know, a trillion of them since the mid-1970s, our guess is maybe not. Which makes how strongly this HBO miniseries—developed (and mainly written) by Richard Price, the novelist who penned top-shelf fare for the network like *The Wire* and *The Night Of*—grabbed us that much more impressive. A mashup of genres (a sort of police procedural turned thriller turned supernatural horror, capped off with some killer action sequences), the slow-burning show follows the investigation of the murder of an 11-year-old boy in rural Georgia, which winds its way to discovering that (spoiler alert) there's an evil entity consuming people in the town. As the chief detective, Ben Mendelsohn is captivating, as usual, worn down and whispery yet inquisitive, but it's Cynthia Erivo as Holly Gibney, the alert PI with, let's say, unusual insights, who lights up the screen.

Russian Doll

NETFLIX / 2019–
1 SEASON / 8 EPISODES

 97% 87%

Raspy-voiced comic actress Natasha Lyonne followed up to her seven-year run on *Orange Is the New Black* with this dark time-loop comedy that provided the perfect bit of wish fulfillment for disaffected thirtysomethings and those who think back

to that time in their lives with longing, and maybe a bit of regret. Lyonne, who also co-created and wrote on the show, stars as Nadia, a chain-smoking, unmotivated New York game developer who, while attending her 36th birthday party, suddenly realizes that she is doomed to live the night on repeat forever—despite all the elaborate ways she tries to end it and her life. Co-created by Lyonne, Amy Poehler, and Leslye Headland, the show sets things up cleanly, and has fun with the *Groundhog Day*–style repetition—the use of Harry Nilsson's upbeat song "Gotta Get Up" is employed with sweet irony, and friend Maxine's daily greeting of "Sweet birthday baby!" was an instant novelty tee favorite. But it's *Doll*'s deviations from the time-loop formula and subversions of our expectations—bringing in another looper (a wonderfully dorky Charlie Barnett) and weaving an intricate mystery with existential consequences—that make this a puzzle worth bingeing. Over and over.

Homecoming

AMAZON PRIME VIDEO / 2018–2020
2 SEASONS / 17 EPISODES

 78% 🗑 67%

If there was one person well-equipped to adapt a popular podcast into a visually dazzling and twist-filled drama, it was Sam Esmail. The *Mr. Robot* creator's love of using form—varying aspect ratios and robust soundscapes—to evoke mood and telegraph temporal shifts in narrative came in handy in telling the story of Heidi Bergman (Julia Roberts), whom we meet as a waitress in the present day but whose past work, at a government-contracted agency helping vets, drives much of the plot of this thriller. Structured as a mystery around what exactly happened at the "Homecoming" site, the first season of the acclaimed drama—winner of our Golden Tomato award for mystery series in 2018—was a study in carefully calibrated paranoia. Without Roberts and Esmail, its second season had a decidedly different tone. Starring Janelle Monáe alongside returning cast members Hong Chau and Stephan James, Eli Horowitz and Micah Bloomberg broadened the scope of their original podcast to deliver a timely, queer, and critically more polarizing look at the US military–industrial complex.

THOUGHTS ON THE FUTURE OF TV
(FROM THOSE WHO MAKE IT)

ROBERT AND MICHELLE KING

Creators of *The Good Wife*, *The Good Fight*, *Evil*

Our hope is that so-called "mini-rooms"—which is a way to pay writers less for their scripts, and then exclude them from the production process—disappear. We hope that TV even more closely resembles the artistic achievements of 1970s filmmaking, and not the blockbuster mentality of post-1980s features. We hope that TV creators explore the form more—break more rules, stop thinking of TV as primarily dialogue-driven. And finally, we hope that serialized TV stops thinking of itself as eight-hour movies (who wants to ever watch an eight-hour movie?), and instead looks toward the great long-form literary works for their inspiration. Actually, one more hope: We hope we're still making TV in 20–30 years.

KATE PURDY

Creator of *Undone*, writer/producer *BoJack Horseman*

Looking to the future, I want TV that downloads directly into my brain. There's so much amazing TV, but I don't have time to watch it. *Can someone please make a device that allows me to have seen everything without actually having to watch anything?* I've tried just lying to friends and saying I've seen stuff, but that never works out past the first question. Also, I hope we keep making wonderfully specific TV that tells stories about people whose lives and experiences have traditionally been less represented. I want to quantum-brain-download more of that!

RONALD D. MOORE

Creator of *Battlestar Galactica*, *Outlander*, *For All Mankind*

I think streaming will become a completely seamless experience where a viewer's entire library will be available across all platforms without the need to log in to any particular service. There will be a single gateway that will invisibly handle the purchase of content from multiple sources and present the viewer with the results, not the process. This will get rid of the multiple apps and payments, making the experience smoother and still allowing the owners of content to be paid different rates in the background. In short, we'll start just watching TV again instead of differentiating between all the various services, which will be aggregated for us.

MIKE FLANAGAN

Creator of *The Haunting of Hill House* and *The Haunting of Bly Manor*

Streaming allows for an intimate, uninterrupted relationship between the storyteller and the viewer. Working with Netflix, I've seen firsthand how it removes so many of the middlemen and allows long-form stories to be crafted based on what's best for the *story*. I hope that over the next few decades we see more stories designed for that kind of transmission, unspoiled by advertiser influence and tailor-made for its audience. If it works, we could see a kind of creative renaissance on par with Hollywood in the 1970s, and it could allow for some of the most vital, enduring storytelling of our time.

ERIC KRIPKE

Creator of *Supernatural*, co-creator of *The Boys*

As I look ahead at the future of television, one thing seems obvious and inevitable: The TVs will become our robot overlords. We'll toil in the Netflix data mines and serve as unwilling concubines to Baron Von Pornhub. If anyone dares defy this streaming supremacy, they and their children will be slaughtered by Disney+, and Mickey Mouse will wade knee-deep in their blood. Also, there will still be *Friends* reruns.

ROBIN THEDE

Showrunner and performer, *Black Lady Sketch Show*

I hope that more people of color dominate TV spaces in front of and behind the camera so that our stories are told through authentic lenses and voices. I hope that adding diversity to a cast and crew isn't a trend, but a thoughtful foundation for any show. I hope that women run as many shows as men and that writers of color are paid and promoted equally as much as their white counterparts. I hope that stereotypes are no longer funny and, instead, authentic and relatable experiences become the bedrock of situational comedy. I hope that dramas focus less on trauma and more on healing. I hope that sketch comedy is seen as a home for all types of people, not just a privileged few. I hope that late-night TV looks more like a reflection of the American population. And, perhaps most importantly, my hope for the next 20 to 30 years of TV is that I will still be making it!

ANNA KONKLE

Co-creator and star, *PEN15*

Growing up, television was the biggest source of entertainment in my home. Dad and I had a handful of favorite shows and we channel-surfed between them, dodging commercials with ambidextrous acuity. Today, TV is plentiful and endless, DVR-ed, binged and consumed on demand. I have a greater number of favorite shows now and I've guaranteed the extinction of commercials by purchasing streaming packages. I watch when I want to. I'm in control—but I'm not sure I like it.

I do love witnessing the scope of show bosses expanding beyond white guys: who is allowed creator status continues to change and stretch and it's obviously imperative this continues—for art's sake and society's. With that said, I'd like to watch our improved-upon programming within the old construct of television that we grew up on. Unable to record it, we made it a priority of the week. I miss the rhythm, the ritual of tuning in at a certain time; we were on TV's schedule, not the other way around, and I think I had more reverence for it that way.

So here's a request: I'd like to consume it all on just one platform and on a schedule, like the old times. Built to feel like old-school TV. Maybe this will be some app someone will build. If so, I'm buying.

BARAN BO ODAR AND JANTJE FRIESE

Creators, *Dark*

We hope that the era of innovation and bold ideas in TV doesn't come to an end too soon. The past few years have proven that quality counts and that a niche show from a local market can actually reach a broad global audience. Seeing stories from all around the world is something we should cherish and will hopefully lead to more diverse narratives. Plus: we're just as keen as anyone to find out how social interaction or gaming will transform TV shows in the future.

▌▌COMMERCIAL BREAK

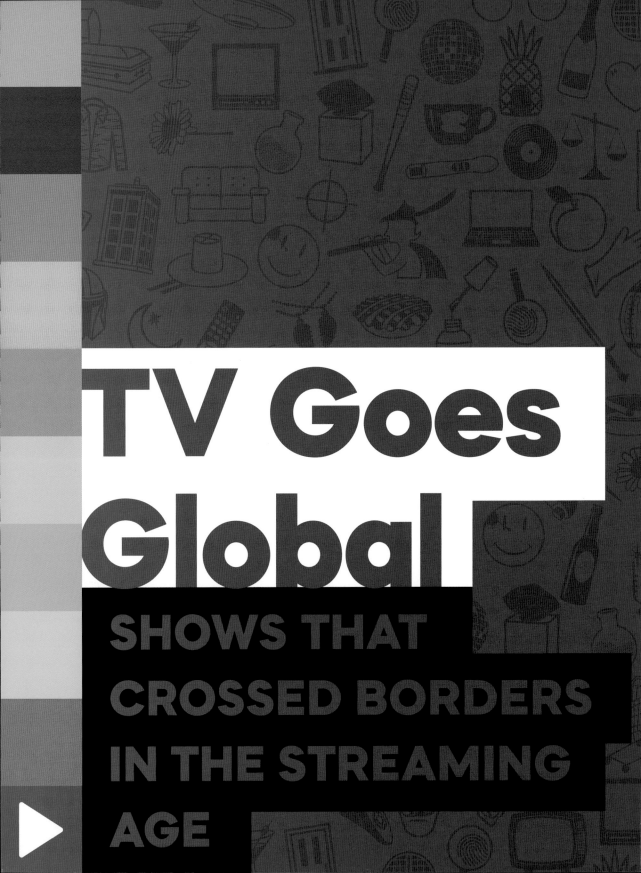

TV Goes Global

SHOWS THAT CROSSED BORDERS IN THE STREAMING AGE

That Netflix's *Money Heist* was the most talked-about show in America when its fourth "part" dropped in April 2020—as well as the most "in demand" series on the planet that same month, according to the data firm Parrot Analytics—does not seem so surprising on the surface. The series about an epic bank robbery gone wrong is, after all, a compulsively watchable and Fresh crime thriller with lovable characters and suspense to spare. But it is also a Spanish production, titled *La casa de papel* (the house of paper) in its native language; its phenomenal popularity signaled something of a sea change in America's viewing habits.

It used to be that foreign TV series took a little effort to find. Pre-streaming, if you were in the know—the kind of viewer who also sought out foreign films at arthouse theaters, say—you probably heard about the acclaimed French horror series, *The Returned*, on Sundance TV, or Germany's Cold War thriller, *Deutschland 83*, on the same channel. You might have tracked down the Danish political drama *Borgen*, on DVD, to keep up with a know-it-all colleague. In the streaming era, though, borders have been blasted away. Now, series like *Money Heist*, the Italian crime drama *Gomorrah*, and the Korean epic *Kingdom* are not just available for curious in-the-know viewers to seek out at the tap of a button, they're being served directly to us via "the algorithm." (Love *Riverdale*? Then you will *love* Spain's high school thriller, *Elite*. Promise.)

For the likes of Netflix, which are seeking inroads in overseas markets—and are often required to satisfy local content requirements to operate in those markets—buying up foreign series and producing new foreign shows is smart business. For TV lovers, it's been great news for your queue. In this chapter, we're globe-trotting through some of the best foreign-language series out there. There's the aforementioned *The Returned* and *Borgen*, but also the Scandinavian murder mysteries *The Killing* and *The Bridge*. There's Netflix's *Dark*, Germany's mind-bending answer to *Stranger Things*, along with the Spanish soap phenomenon, *Gran Hotel*, which, like several shows on this list, spawned an inferior American remake.

It's not just the major streaming platforms bringing the world closer together: HBO gives us a grittier glimpse of Naples than we might be used to in its Italian co-production, *My Brilliant Friend*, while smaller streaming apps, like the Asian-focused Viki, have opened up Japanese, Chinese, and Korean series to the world. (Want to get a K-drama fix? Check out page 196.)

Cultural nuances abound in the following pages, and enrich the viewing experience of each recommendation, but what stands out as you read—and, hopefully, then watch—is the universality of the themes that emerge. These series tackle everything from the weight of grief (*The Returned*) and the cost of power (*Borgen*) to the divide between rich and poor (*Elite*) and the comfort of companionship and a good meal (*Midnight Diner: Tokyo*).

Streaming has made the world a smaller place—we highly recommend turning the subtitles on and exploring.

The Killing

DENMARK

▶ **HIGHLY ADDICTIVE**

DR1 / 2007–2012

3 SEASONS / 40 EPISODES

What's in the water in Scandinavia that makes its police procedurals just that much richer? Is it the landscapes covered in snow, the worn-down detectives, the grisly murders, or the tense atmospherics? We're . . . not sure. But *The Killing* (*Forbrydelsen* in Danish) was a phenomenon for good reason, influencing not only the many murder-investigation series that would follow in the subregion (most notably *The Bridge*, see page 188) but far beyond it, including a solid American remake. Over the course of five years, its three seasons—the first solving the rape and murder of a teenager, the second focusing on a military cover-up, and the third a child kidnapping—set a high bar for how to unfold knottily plotted conspiracy dramas. Also, let's give special shout-outs to star Sofie Gråbøl, who expertly portrays the closed-off workaholic detective Sarah Lund, and the tough-to-resist way the show ends each episode with a dialogue-free montage of the suspects and major players. Just try not to play the next ep after viewing one of those. We dare ya.

Midnight Diner: Tokyo Stories

JAPAN

MBS, NETFLIX / 2009–2019

5 SEASONS / 50 EPISODES

🍅 **100%** 🗑 **94%**

You don't have to choose between dubbing or subtitles to understand the message at the heart of this Japanese series: Food is universal. Based on the best-selling manga "*Shinya Shokudo*," *Tokyo* is imminently bingeable thanks to its short running time (each episode is 24 minutes long) and stand-alone nature. All episodes take place in the titular diner, a teeny restaurant hidden down a back alley in the bustling district of Shinjuku. The Midnight Diner is only open from midnight to 7 a.m., and is typically populated by a motley group of strangers, sharing in the sacred ritual of late-night comfort food. The mysterious proprietor, the Master (Kaoru Kobayashi), will cook anything for his customers if they provide the ingredients, and the series explores universal themes (of family, of loneliness, of lost loves) through each signature dish. It's a poignant and joyful exploration of what it means to be human, which is what both food and television are all about.

Borgen

DENMARK

▶ **GAME-CHANGER**

▶ **HIGHLY ADDICTIVE**

DR1, NETFLIX / 2010–2013

3 SEASONS / 30 EPISODES

 **100%** 🗑 **99%**

Within the early 2010s' wave of Danish dramas that found a foothold with US audiences, *Borgen* (or "The Castle") may well be the best of the lot. Preempting the real-world election of Denmark's first female prime minister, creator Adam Price's *Borgen* charts the unlikely political journey of Birgitte Nyborg Christensen (Sidse Babett Knudsen), who at the top of the series is elected to her nation's highest office. Hailed upon its premiere by the *Sunday Express* as "*The Killing* meets *The West Wing*," this political drama masterfully blends character-driven developments with timely, subject-based storytelling, plunging audiences smack-dab in the day-to-day political proceedings of elected office and the ethically gray waters therein. More than just the story of a woman's unexpected rise, *Borgen* deals with the ways in which politicians maintain power once elected and explores how even the best-intentioned men and women negotiate, compromise, and at times lose sight of the ideals that brought them there in the first place. That's not to mention dramas of a more personal nature on the home front. (Hint: Birgitte undergoes a name change in a time jump between the first and second seasons.) Better still, you don't need even a cursory knowledge of Danish politics to appreciate what goes down in this hour-long drama; prevalent in all systems of power, the themes of *Borgen* know no borders. And now that it's surging in popularity years after its premiere, thanks to Netflix, you'd better binge soon: DR1 and the streamer have announced that new episodes are on the way.

Gran Hotel
SPAIN
ANTENA 3 / 2011–2013
3 SEASONS / 39 EPISODES

 🍅 – – 🗑 – –

The year is 1906. The setting is the sumptuous, family-owned, aptly titled Grand Hotel near the town of Cantaloa, in Spain. There, a dashing young man takes a job as a bellboy, hoping this gives him enough cover to find out what happened to his sister, a maid whose mysterious absence has been met with chilly indifference. As he uncovers the many secrets lurking underneath the hotel's highly polished exterior, he falls for the daughter of the hotel's owner, who becomes an unlikely ally in his quest for the truth. Their star-crossed-lovers story line, paired with the whodunnit feel of this grandiose period piece (one key clue is a *golden* knife!), made this Spanish production a hit at home and abroad—it's the kind of soapy goodness Aaron Spelling and Darren Star used to deliver. Produced by newcomer Bambú Producciones, the series has since been broadcast in over a dozen international networks and spawned remakes in France, Egypt, Mexico, Italy, and even in the United States via ABC's short-lived 2019 drama *Grand Hotel.*

Gomorrah
ITALY
▶ **GAME-CHANGER**

SKY ATLANTIC , SUNDANCE TV, HBO MAX / 2014–
4 SEASONS / 48 EPISODES

 🍅 **87%** 🗑 **92%**

When journalist Roberto Saviano released his first book, *Gomorrah: A Personal Journey into the Violent International Empire of Naples' Organized Crime System*, in 2006, he surely knew his life was going to be forever changed. You don't infiltrate and expose the inner workings of the Camorra—the Mafia-like organization that originated in Campania (the region is home to Naples)—and not expect repercussions. So it is that Saviano and several family members have been living under police protection for 15 years. What he may *not* have expected was for the best-selling exposé to lead him to the world of entertainment, first with the Certified Fresh 2008 film based on his book, and then with this phenomenally successful drama series, which he himself created. The show's plot will be familiar to anyone who knows the difference between a don and a consigliere: A power vacuum opens up when the head of Naples's Savastrano clan is arrested; ambitious middleman Ciro (Marco D'Amore) must make moves as factions go to war. Critics have dubbed it "Italy's answer to *Breaking Bad*," a "darker, grown-up version of *The Sopranos*," and "the *Wire* of Italy." All true. But with Saviano at the helm, there's a richness and downbeat reality to *Gomorrah*'s characters and violence that stands out, and made this propulsive, brutally entertaining series a smash for UK pay TV station Sky Atlantic.

The Bridge
SWEDEN / DENMARK
SVT1/DR1 / 2011–2018
2 SEASONS / 20 EPISODES

 -- 🗑 93%

In Nordic noir's crowded field of standouts—Denmark's game-changing phenom *The Killing*, featured in this chapter, and Iceland's literally and figuratively wintry *Trapped*, to name just two—which one is the cream of the crop? If imitation really is the sincerest form of flattery, it has to be *The Bridge* (*Bron/Broen* in Swedish/Danish), Hans Rosenfeldt's ridiculously addicting police procedural. Need proof? *The Bridge* has been adapted a whopping five times throughout the globe. (See the sidebar on this page for a breakdown of each.) And it's not hard to understand why: The concept—a body being discovered on the border of two countries, with detectives from either side having to piece together the case—is pretty irresistible. In the first season of the OG, that corpse is, yes, on a bridge, cut in half between Sweden and Denmark. But *The Bridge*'s strengths aren't just its novel setup, or how it unfolds its twists and red herrings. It's all grounded by Saga Norén (the great Sofia Helin), a truly original character, laser-focused yet lacking any awareness of social cues, and, in the first two seasons, the yin to her yang, a warmer, across-the-water detective counterpart (an excellent Kim Bodnia, who would go on to shine in *Killing Eve*).

PICK YOUR BORDER

Swedish-Danish series *The Bridge* inspired a slew of remakes. Which one's right for you? Check them out below.

▶ UK / FRANCE
The Tunnel
SKY ATLANTIC, CANAL+ / 2013–2018
3 SEASONS / 24 EPISODES

🍅 91% 🗑 73%

It's not a bridge this time but—you guessed it—a tunnel that sets the scene for this three-seasoner, which opens with the discovery of half of the body of a French politician and half of one of a Brit prostitute on their respective sides of the "Chunnel."

▶ USA / MEXICO
The Bridge
FX / 2013–2014
2 SEASONS / 26 EPISODES

🍅 88% 🗑 85%

Diane Kruger (*Inglourious Basterds*) and Demián Bichir (*A Better Life*) lead the cast of this FX adaptation as investigators—the former from the United States, the latter from Mexico—solving the murder of a judge on the bridge connecting El Paso and Juárez. Season 1 was Certified Fresh at 91% on the Tomatometer, while the finale of a follow-up reached a still-impressive 86%.

▶ ESTONIA / RUSSIA

The Bridge

NTV / 2018–
2 SEASONS / 20 EPISODES

Corpses are discovered over the Narva River (on what's called the Friendship Bridge, no less)—or, that is, *halves* of corpses, one part an Estonian politician and the other a Russian student. The two countries band together to find the killer.

▶ MALAYSIA / SINGAPORE

The Bridge

NTV7, HBO ASIA, VIU / 2018–
2 SEASONS / 20 EPISODES

Two detectives (Malaysia's Bront Palarae and Singapore's Rebecca Lim) butt heads while delving into a crime scene on the Malaysia-Singapore Second Link, a bridge connecting the two nations. The show's second season expands geographically, throwing Indonesia into the mix.

▶ GERMANY / AUSTRIA

Pagan Peak

SKY DEUTSCHLAND / 2019–
1 SEASON / 8 EPISODES

The most recent foray into *Bridge*dom kicks off with a grisly discovery not on a bridge or in a tunnel but atop a country-connecting mountain pass. (It's also been picked up for a second season.)

Money Heist

SPAIN

▶ HIGHLY ADDICTIVE

ANTENA 3, NETFLIX / 2017–
2 SEASONS (IN 4 PARTS) / 31 EPISODES

 93%   80%

With character names like Tokyo, Lisbon, Berlin, and Nairobi, it's perhaps not a surprise that *La casa de papel* became an international phenomenon. Created for Antena 3, a Spanish commercial television network, the thriller had a killer hook: a masked group of criminals storm the Royal Mint of Spain with the goal of printing and absconding with €2.4 billion. Structured around the heist itself, the show used flashbacks to flesh out the weeks-long planning that brought these code-named strangers together under the tutelage of a mysterious man known to all as "The Professor." The drama's "eat the rich" anarchist spirit, best summed up by its now ubiquitous iconography (the team's red jumpsuits and Dalí masks), gave the twist-stuffed series an urgent political message that, while rooted in Spanish culture, resonated across the world. Originally aired as a 15-episode limited series, told in two parts, the show barely held on to its viewership over its 2017 run. When Netflix acquired exclusive streaming rights and recut Álex Pina's creation into 22 shorter episodes (primetime dramas in Spain run for 70 minutes), the newly retitled *Money Heist* became a word-of-mouth hit as well as the most-watched non–English language series on the streamer in 2018. The announcement of a Netflix-backed continuation was inevitable. Armed with a bigger budget and a bold marketing team, *Money Heist* went bigger and bolder for its third and fourth globe-trotting parts, which introduced new characters while reuniting the surviving OG team for, you guessed it, one last heist.

The Returned

FRANCE

**CANAL+, SUNDANCETV,
AMAZON PRIME VIDEO / 2012–2015**
2 SEASONS / 16 EPISODES

 97% 🍿 94%

▶ **CRITICS CONSENSUS** A pleasant change from typically gory zombie shows, *The Returned* is a must-see oddity that's both smart and sure to disturb. (Season 1)

▶ **WHAT IT'S ABOUT** A small town in the French Alps is shaken to its core when loved ones who have been dead for years inexplicably return from the grave. Their miraculous reappearance is met with both celebrated reunions and rageful confusion, and an irreparable schism slowly divides residents in unpredictable but devastating ways.

The Returned is a take on the living dead you've never seen before. It's available to stream now, but this hit French series from creator Fabrice Gobert—and based on the 2004 film *They Came Back (Les Revenants)*—found an international audience even before the height of streaming and the explosion in availability of foreign series. It won a Peabody Award and an International Emmy for Best Drama Series prior to getting picked up by the UK via More4 and the United States via SundanceTV.

The series earned those accolades by being much more than just *The Walking Dead* with subtitles. While its logline suggests a horror series, *The Returned* is most impactful when tugging at your heart, rather than raising your blood pressure. It is a horror story as allegory for grief, kinship, and the ties that bind in life and death; there are bursts of violence and darkness aplenty over its 16 episodes, but most compelling are the season-long dramas among its lineup of unforgettable characters.

That's in no small part thanks to its impressive ensemble, particularly the central Séguret family. Yara Pilartz has emotional depth beyond her years as Camille, a 15-year-old who returns four years after dying in a tragic school bus accident to find her parents, Claire (Anne Consigny) and Jérôme (Frédéric Pierrot), separated and her twin sister, Léna (Jenna Thiam), now four years her senior. The relief, confusion, grief, and rage sewn into the moment of their reunion is an emotional gut punch. Consigny, a famed French actress best known in the States for *The Diving Bell and the Butterfly*, is particularly shattering as a grieving mother, refusing to part ways with her daughter a second time.

It's through Claire and the rest of the town's bereaved—Clotilde Hesme as Adèle Werther, a soon-to-be-remarried widow faced with the return of her lover, Simon, is also excellent—that *The Returned* asks a question that lingers long after its final credits: What would you do if given the opportunity to commune with the dead? That question ultimately divides the town as the deceased continue to return in greater numbers, a child belonging to both worlds is conceived, and a powerful but mysterious young boy named Victor (Swann Nambotin) suggests that there's more to what's happening than meets the eye. Upon learning of the growing resurrections, some locals commit suicide at the prospect of seeing their own children again; others use the opportunity to harness power within the township and rise as leaders for, or against, the dead.

Through it all, audiences, too, are forced to pick sides, and—when the living are faced with a devastating choice in season 1's climactic standoff—compelled to reflect on those we've loved, lost, and wish could come back. With even meatier plots and mysteries—a "returned" serial killer seeking revenge, a secret murder-suicide cult, unexplained mass deaths of livestock and other animals, and the curious depletion of water levels behind the town's dam—there's plenty to keep viewers of all kinds on the edge of their seats.

Whether you're looking for melancholic introspection, knockout performances, transporting atmospheres, or—sure—zombies, *The Returned* is guaranteed to provide it all in spades.

▶ **BEST EPISODE** Season 1, Episode 1—"Camille." *The Returned* has plenty of mystery to come after this 2012 pilot, but "Camille" is a pitch-perfect introduction to its tone and aesthetic.

▶ **CHARACTER WE LOVE** While *The Returned* is a truly ensemble effort, no one can walk away not feeling for Claire Séguret (Anne Consigny). Her first scenes with her resurrected Camille will make you want to call your own mom.

DEEP DIVE

Dark

NETHERLANDS

NETFLIX / 2017–2020
3 SEASONS / 26 EPISODES

 95% 95%

▶ **CRITICS CONSENSUS** *Dark*'s central mystery unfolds slowly, both tense and terrifying, culminating in a creepy, cinematic triumph of sci-fi noir. (Season 1)

▶ **WHAT IT'S ABOUT** When two young boys go missing in a small German town, four unknowingly connected families are put into varied states of emotional turmoil, and one ambitious teen attempts to harness the powers of time travel to set things right.

Dark should come with a warning for first-time viewers: "If you watch this series, you won't be able to get it out of your head." So awesomely addictive and emotionally consuming are its knotty plotlines, it's little wonder that it developed a fervent online fan base of family tree–mappers and amateur time-travel theorists. (A fan base that frequently lets us at RT know *this* is streaming's best sci-fi teen drama, and not that *Stranger Things* business.)

From creators Baran bo Odar and Jantje Friese, Netflix's first German-language original series leapt to the top of our queue upon its 2017 premiere for its enticing promise of small-town conspiracy laced with family drama. We stuck around after its perfectly paced unveiling as not just a missing-children mystery, but an ambitious time-traveling sci-fi saga.

The action picks up with our hero Jonas Kahnwald (Louis Hofmann), who, after spending time in a psychiatric hospital following his father's unexplained death by suicide, returns to high school and a town changed by the disappearance of two young boys: Erik Obdendorf (Paul Radom) and, soon after, Mikkel Nielson (Daan Lennard Liebrenz). Revisiting the caves where Mikkel was last seen, Jonas finds a wormhole that throws him 33 years back in time. (The first season will also jump to other time periods 33 years apart.) With this new discovery, he makes it his mission—with continuously spectacular if not always successful results—to fix the time line and set things right for the missing. Toss in a looming apocalypse, caused by Winden's nuclear power plant, an opposing effort from a secret society of Travellers, visitors from the future coaxing him to act this way and that, and his unending desire to be with the love of his life, Martha Nielson (Lisa Vicari)—all of it riding on Jonas's shoulders.

Then, of course, the series manages to reinvent and fold in on itself countless times over to reveal just how Jonas is related to Mikkel and the other bonds within this knot of time that keep them and the rest of our ensemble together.

Dark doesn't shy away from dabbling in more high-concept philosophies of time, fate, and the meaning of reality as we know it. It becomes evident through the series's three seasons that each character is a pawn on the chessboard of their own journey, acting and reacting in largely predetermined ways by the infinite loops of action preceding them. While their experienced reality mirrors free will, *Dark* reveals that notion for what it is: an illusion. The characters' slow realization of that truth adds even more emotional heft to this already beguiling series.

Don't expect to get all the answers as questions arise. Audiences learn the complexities of *Dark*'s secrets right along with its characters, which is what makes its puzzle-box structure such a rewarding viewing experience. But the biggest twist of all? *Dark* does eventually snap everything into place

and beautifully crystallizes the power of a well-told, one-of-a-kind story in the process.

▶ **BEST EPISODE** Season 3, Episode 8—"The Paradise." A series finale is a tough ask for any creator to pull off, especially when your series is as ambitiously complex as *Dark*. But, astoundingly, this emotional capper hits all the right notes and ties up all the right threads.

▶ **CHARACTER WE LOVE** Katharina Nielsen (Jördis Triebel) is heartbreakingly left with a missing son, a missing husband, and a mounting world of grief and uncertainty—but she's also one of the primary reasons that you hope it all works out in the end. Give the girl a break, already!

Deutschland 83
Deutschland 86
Deutschland 89

GERMANY

RTL, SUNDANCE TV, AMAZON PRIME /
2015–2020

3 SEASONS / 26 EPISODES

 91% 84%

Created by American writer Anna Winger (show-runner of Netflix's Emmy-winning limited series *Unorthodox*) and her German husband Joerg Winger, this gorgeous period spy thriller follows twentysomething East German patrol guard Martin (Jonas Nay), sent to West Germany as an undercover agent for the Stasi, the East German secret police. Set in 1983 (its subsequent seasons take place in '86 and '89, respectively), the Peabody Award–winning drama examines the Cold War from the East German perspective and through the eyes of Martin, who begins to question what he's actually fighting for. Though a flop in Deutschland itself, the series was a critical darling abroad, thanks to the charming Nay, tense spy sequences, and its '80s-tastic soundtrack—the title sequence is set to Peter Schilling's "Major Tom (Coming Home)."

Babylon Berlin

GERMANY

▶ HIGHLY ADDICTIVE

SKY 1, DAS ERSTE, NETFLIX / 2017–

3 SEASONS / 28 EPISODES

 –– 96%

This splashy international Netflix import is reportedly Germany's most expensive TV drama ever—and it shows. *Babylon Berlin* is a slightly surreal, entirely immersive police drama, set at the height of the Weimar Republic in 1929, with massive Art Deco sets and lush '20s costuming. The story follows Cologne detective Gereon Rath (Volker Bruch) as he heads to Berlin on assignment to take down an extortion ring, and the rebellious flapper police clerk Charlotte Ritter (Liv Lisa Fries), whom he takes under his wing after realizing her potential as an investigator. Adding an extra layer of tension is the clash between Berlin's communists and the growing Nazi party as Hitler rises to power. The series's period elements and almost Lynchian tone make this much more than a standard-issue cop drama. Charlotte's climb up the career ladder—and her introduction as a defiant, modern woman—is just as relatable 100 years later, even though the show lives in an era when women characters could easily be subjugated in service of "history."

Elite

SPAIN

▶ HIGHLY ADDICTIVE

NETFLIX / 2018–

3 SEASONS (IN 4 PARTS) / 24 EPISODES

 97% 86%

It's *Gossip Girl* meets *Big Little Lies* with a telenovela twist in *Elite*, Netflix's second Spanish series after its successful *Cable Girls*. When a construction accident at a public high school in Madrid destroys the building, the company responsible funds a trio of underprivileged kids to attend the ritzy Las Encincas private school. Upon arrival, they shake up the status quo among the filthy-rich and sexed-up student body—standouts among them Miguel Bernardeau as posh bad boy Guzmán and Mina El Hammani as Nadia, the Muslim scholarship kid who's looking to rebel. Things only get shakier when murder rocks the campus. In similar fashion to HBO's rich-folks-murder mystery series *Big Little Lies*, *Elite* plays fast and loose with time, only slowly revealing the prime suspects, and even the victim's identity, making each season a who-dunnit *and* who-was-it-done-to. *Elite* has a little more on its mind than just murder and sex, though; each new coupling or betrayal allows showrunners Carlos Monte and Cario Madrona to explore issues driving debate in Spain today, primarily class discrimination, Islamophobia, the politics of sex, and the wide gulf between the rich and poor. Of course, it's not a show you have to think about too hard, if that's more your speed: There's *mucho* steaminess and twists, and jaw-droppingly luxurious clothes and property distract and delight.

My Brilliant Friend

ITALY / USA

TIMVISION, RAI 1, HBO / 2018–
2 SEASONS / 16 EPISODES

 96%

It would be disingenuous to describe this Italian American series—a co-production with HBO and the European broadcasters TIMVision and Rai 1 and based on Elena Ferrante's Neapolitan novels—as a tale of female friendship (though that's what the official description says). Like the best-selling books on which it is based, it's really about the devastating power of those friendships—the euphoric highs and brutal lows. It's told through the eyes of our narrator, Elena, a woman reflecting on her lifelong relationship with a girl she meets in elementary school in 1950s Naples. This is not a sunny, idyllic portrait of Italian life; it's a realistic look at the cycles of violence and anger that permeate the duo's impoverished upbringing, and as Lenù and Lila grow up, how their relationship shifts over time. Each season is a

faithful adaptation of one of Ferrante's books, which covers a specific period of Lenù and Lila's lives and means the lead actresses, played by Elisa Del Genio and Ludovica Nasti as young girls in season 1 and as young women by Margherita Mazzucco and Gaia Girace in season 2, change each season as well.

Giri / Haji

JAPAN / UK

▶ GONE TOO SOON

BBC, NETFLIX / 2019
1 SEASON / 8 EPISODES

🍅 100% 🍿 88%

One of the most exciting aspects of streaming's border-smashing approach to programming and production is that it has revealed audiences as more adventurous than networks perhaps gave them credit for. The success of *Borgen*, *Fauda*, and countless Scandi thrillers showed decision makers that English speakers were more than willing to scale the "one-inch-tall barrier of subtitles," as Korean director Bong Joon-ho described it, and embrace foreign series. As long as they're awesome, that is. Which presumably gave the BBC some confidence, and comfort, when it green-lit and, with Netflix, co-produced this bilingual and *definitely awesome* crime drama from writer Joe Barton. It follows Japanese detective Kenzo Mori's (Takehiro Hira) journey from Tokyo to London to find his brother, a former gangster, or *yakuza*, who's become embroiled in a UK gang war. It's not a foreign series per se, but is instead caught thrillingly between two cultures, just like its protagonist, who finds himself seduced by life and love away from Tokyo as he gumshoes his way toward his target. Violent, stylish, and tense from its first episode—the first half of which is spoken fully in Japanese—*Giri/Haji* has the genre's staple gunplay and gangsters but is elevated by a killer ensemble whose story lines are all equally rich and complex. Look out for Will Sharpe in a BAFTA-winning turn as charismatic and damaged rent boy Rodney, who becomes entangled in Kenzo's mission and family to devastating and ultimately moving ends.

Kingdom
SOUTH KOREA

▶ HIGHLY ADDICTIVE

NETFLIX / 2019–
2 SEASONS / 12 EPISODES

 96% 96%

How do you breathe new life into a genre that's been done to death? (*Un*death?) For Netflix, the answer lay in lavish period costumes, fiendish political intrigue, and a change in setting. *Kingdom*, the Korean zombie series set in the early 1600s, is based on the web comic *Kingdom of the Gods* and plays like *House of Cards* meets *The Walking Dead*—with big swords and fabulous hats. For the first two epic seasons, we follow Crown Prince Lee Chang (Ju Ji-hoon), an incorruptible king-to-be on the political outs who finds himself protecting the people of a plague-ridden region; physician Seo-Bi (Bae Doo-na), who works to understand—and hopefully cure—the terrifying disease; the evil chief state councilor, Lord Cho Haj-ju (Ryu Seung-ryong); and a crew of nobles, peasants, and politicians, variously jockeying for power and survival. The series is Netflix's first South Korean production, and no expense was spared—it looks as epic as *Game of Thrones* or *The Witcher*. But *Kingdom* soared to the status of global phenomenon on the back of character work and a social message about haves and have-nots that's sharp enough—and timely enough—not to get lost in translation.

WANT MORE K-DRAMA?

K-드라마

Over the last five years, a Korean TV wave has swept up audiences outside of Asia who are watching "K-Dramas" in huge and growing numbers, thanks to streaming services like Netflix, Viki, Amazon, Hulu, YouTube, and more. If you want to get lost in *Hallyu*—a Chinese term for the mammoth popularity of Korean music, film, and TV— here are three great shows to start with. (Bonus: If you love K-Pop, most of the series have soundtracks by some of the hottest Korean artists.)

Guardian: The Lonely and Great God

(2017)
STREAM IT ON: VIKI
GENRES: DRAMA, FANTASY

쓸쓸하고 찬란하신

What It's About: *Train to Busan*'s Gong Yoo plays a general in Korea's Goryeo era (918-1392), cursed to become a 900-year-old goblin. He cannot find peace until he meets his goblin bride, who turns out to be a young student in modern-day Korea who can see ghosts—plus he will need the help of a Grim Reaper with whom he forms an adorable bromance. (It's complicated.) Themes of life and death blend effortlessly in this comedy hybrid with plenty of action, romance, and laughs.

Watch It If You Like: *iZombie*, *Once Upon a Time*, *Supernatural*, *The Vampire Diaries*, *Being Human*

Sky Castle

(2019)
STREAM IT ON: VIKI
GENRES: DRAMA, SUSPENSE

SKY 캐슬

What It's About: Four wealthy women living in a private community are obsessed with making sure their children get accepted into a prestigious university—at any cost. But this is not your average rich-housewives drama: The parents are ruthless and dangerous, and the children sometimes suffer the consequences, but at other times the series digs into the hypocrisy of the system. Yes, an American remake is in the works.

Watch It If You Like: *Succession*, *Empire*, *Dynasty*, *Gossip Girl*, *Beverly Hills, 90210*

Crash Landing on You

(2019–2020)
STREAM IT ON: NETFLIX
GENRES: DRAMA, ROMANTIC COMEDY

사랑의 불시착

What It's About: A rich heiress is paragliding when she is suddenly blown into North Korea by freak weather; she literally "crashes into" a North Korean soldier, who decides to help her escape back to the south. Along the way—surprise!—they fall in love. Two popular K-Drama actors, Hyun Bin and Son Ye-jin, star alongside a strong supporting cast, including actors from Bong Joon-ho's Oscar winner, *Parasite*.

Watch It If You Like: *Always Be My Maybe*, *New Girl*, *Catastrophe*

Glossary

Tomatometer Score: This is the number next to the red tomato or green splat—it represents the percentage of professional critic reviews that are positive (or "Fresh," in our terms) for a film or TV show. For TV and streaming series, we feature scores for individual episodes (where there are enough reviews), individual seasons, and for whole series; those whole series scores are the average of the season scores.

> **Fresh Tomatometer Score:** When at least 60% of reviews for a show are positive, you'll see a red tomato to indicate its Fresh status.

> **Rotten Tomatometer Score:** When less than 60% of reviews for a show are positive, you'll see a green splat to indicate its Rotten status.

Certified Fresh: What's Fresher than Fresh? At Rotten Tomatoes, it's "Certified Fresh," a special distinction awarded to the best-reviewed TV shows. In order to earn the Certified Fresh badge—it's the one with the golden halo and green ribbon—a TV season must have a Tomatometer Score above 75% and a minimum of 20 reviews, five of which must come from our "Top Critics." Note that in TV and streaming, only seasons can be Certified Fresh, and the majority of scores you see in this book are *series*-level scores.

Certified Fresh Streak / Perfect Certified Fresh Streak: A term tagged to certain entries in this book, a Certified Fresh Streak is denoted for titles that have three or more seasons in a row achieve Certified Fresh status; we call it a "Perfect" Certified Fresh Streak when a show with three or more seasons has achieved Certified Fresh status for *all* of its seasons.

Audience Score: Denoted by a popcorn bucket, this is the percentage of users—as opposed to pro critics—who have rated the show positively. When at least 60% have given the show a rating of 3.5 stars or higher, a full popcorn bucket is displayed to indicate its Fresh status; a tipped-over green popcorn bucket represents Rotten shows that didn't hit that benchmark.

Critics Consensus: This blurb summarizes what Tomatomer-approved critics had to say about a season or episode of a show; it highlights common themes our curation team finds in the pool of reviews.

Primetime: A term you'll see often in our early chapters—and one which has lost some prevalence in recent streaming-dominated years—"primetime" is simply the regularly occurring time when the TV audience is expected to be the greatest: i.e., between 8 p.m. and 11 p.m. every night, kicking off a little earlier on Sundays. The biggest and broadest-appealing shows get the primetime slots on network and cable TV.

Peak TV: The term "Peak TV" has changed over time. Coined originally by FX's John Landgraf to describe something of a potential problem—an era of *too much* good TV—it has come to refer to both the extraordinary volume of TV and streaming options, but also to the idea that we are living at the time of the best TV ever . . . the, well, *peak.*

Showrunner: This is the person who has overall creative control and authority, and management responsibility, for a series. They're the last word. They are usually the lead producer—credited as an executive producer—and oftentimes the writer who created the series. Creative control *can* change, of course, with changes in showrunners along the way, as we've seen on shows like *The Walking Dead.*

Streaming Wars: Business loves a good battle metaphor, and that's exactly what this is: a catch-all term for the rise in new streaming services—among them Disney+, Apple TV+, Peacock, HBO Max, and so on—competing with the likes of Netflix, Hulu, and Amazon Prime, who all entered the space first. This "war" is marked by big spending on big talent to create marquee shows and build up subscriber bases, and has so far only had a few true victims (Vale, Quibi).

Acknowledgments

In a book about the best and most bingeable TV ever made, it seems only right to start by thanking the geniuses responsible for making all the great TV featured in these pages. To every showrunner, writer, castmember, and crewmember who contributed to these series—and the thousands of other shows that keep the dent in our couches so damn deep—we thank you.

We are especially appreciative of the creators and showrunners who shared with us their hopes and predictions for the future of TV and streaming on pages 182–183: Mike Flanagan, Jantje Friese, Anna Konkle, Michelle and Robert King, Eric Kripke, Ronald D. Moore, Baron Bo Odar, Kate Purdy, and Robin Thede. Thanks for making us laugh, cry, and (sometimes) scream; for entertaining and challenging us; and for giving us so much to think, talk, and, yes, *write* about.

Speaking of writing: This book has been a labor of love for the Rotten Tomatoes Editorial team, which spent many months narrowing down the featured titles, and whose insightful and engaging words tell the story of TV's evolution across our ten chapters. The core team—Jacqueline Coley, Debbie Day, Ryan Fujitani, Joel Meares, and Alex Vo—was assisted by a battery of talented contributors, many of them Tomatometer-approved critics, including Erik Amaya, Tre'vell Anderson, Jean Bentley, Manuel Betancourt, Robert Daniels, Whitney Friedlander, Benjamin Lindsay, Tim Lowery, and Kimberly Potts.

Special thanks, too, to Rotten Tomatoes' Senior Art Director, Courtney Kawata, and Senior Designer, Yerania Sanchez, who designed our cover and many of the book's special features, as well as to our head of production, Eileen Rivera, for contributing her knowledge of K-drama. Contributor Yasmin Tayag earns an extra loud shoutout for her delightful comic strip about what happens inside of us when we binge.

Nearly every department at Rotten Tomatoes touched our *Ultimate Binge Guide* in some way, from our PR and marketing team to our legal department and social media leads; particularly crucial were the contributions of Haña Lucero-Colin and Robert Fowler, from our Curation team, who tirelessly scoured the world for reviews to ensure the Tomatometer Scores for every series featured herein were as up-to-date as possible as we headed to press.

We also want to acknowledge our colleagues at Fandango, our parent company, who share our love and enthusiasm for entertainment. The support and leadership of Chief Creative Officer Sandro Corsaro and Fandango President Paul Yanover has been especially invaluable.

In our second book together, Running Press proved once again to be a fantastic publishing partner at every turn. We are grateful for the thoughtful guidance of our editor there, Jess Riordan, and the talents—and patience!—of Alex Camlin, the peerless designer who made this thing look so great . . . and who probably never wants to see a note from us again. We also want to acknowledge the extended Running Press team: Kristin Kiser, Frances Soo Ping Chow, Jessica Schmidt, Kara Thornton, Alina O'Donnell, Amy Cianfrone, and Leah Cohen.

Finally, we want to thank TV critics and journalists everywhere. Their sharp analysis not only lies behind every Tomatometer score and Critics Consensus you see in this book, but their work has helped us better understand, appreciate, and engage with this incredible medium that has been shaping our culture for 70-plus years. As we continue to climb the steep pathways of this thing called Peak TV—with new players, storytellers, and technologies emerging around every bend—we're grateful to have them by our side.

Contributors

Rotten Tomatoes team:

Jacqueline Coley (Deep Dives: *Insecure, The Boondocks*)

Debbie Day (Deep Dives: *Justified, The Expanse*)

Ryan Fujitani (Deep Dive: *Planet Earth*)

Courtney Kawata (Design and illustration for interstitials: *Choosing the Right Arrowverse Show for You, Star Trek Starter Kit: Pick Your Starfleet Ship, Mini Milestones*)

Joel Meares (Deep Dives: *The Golden Girls, The Good Wife/The Good Fight, The Americans, Buffy the Vampire Slayer*)

Eileen Rivera (*Want More K-Drama?*)

Yerania Sanchez (Design and illustration for interstitials: *Bingeing Before the Binge, Back to School: The Best in Class for TV's Teen Dramas, From Playing Cards to Hashtags*)

Alex Vo (Deep Dives: *Police Squad!, It's Always Sunny In Philadelphia, Batman: The Animated Series*)

Contributors:

Erik Amaya (*Choosing the Right Arrowverse Show For You, Star Trek Starter Kit*)

Tre'vell Anderson (Deep Dive: *Pose*)

Jean Bentley (*Five Ways HBO Changed TV Forever, Know Your Very Special Episodes, Five Ways Netflix Changed TV Forever, Know Your TV Superproducers*)

Manuel Betancourt (*Mini Milestones, From Playing Cards to Hashtags*, Deep Dives: *The Boys, The Leftovers*)

Robert Daniels (Deep Dive: *Watchmen*)

Whitney Friedlander (*Those Were the Days: The Groundbreaking 1970s Comedy of Norman Lear*, Deep Dive: *Ramy*)

Benjamin Lindsay (*The Law & Order Case Files*, Deep Dives: *The Returned, Dark*)

Tim Lowery (Deep Dive: *Mindhunter*)

Kimberly Potts (*Back to School: The Best In Class for TV's Teen Dramas*)

Yasmin Tayag (*The Science of Binge Watching*)

Index